MW01709574

first steps®

First Steps in Mathematics

Number

- **Understand Operations**
- **Calculate**
- **Reason About Number Patterns**

Improving the mathematics outcomes of students

Government of Western Australia
Department of Education and Training

Rigby
Harcourt Education

First Steps in Mathematics: Number
Understand Operations, Calculate and *Reason About Number Patterns*

Rigby
Harcourt Education
22 Salmon Street, Port Melbourne, Victoria 3207
World Wide Web http://www.rigby.com.au
Email info@hi.com.au

Offices in Sydney, Brisbane, Perth and Adelaide. Associated companies, branches and representatives throughout the world.

© Reed International Books Australia Pty Ltd 2004
First published 2004

2008 2007 2006 2005 2004
10 9 8 7 6 5 4 3 2 1

Reproduction and communication for educational purposes
The Australian *Copyright Act 1968*, (the Act) allows a maximum of one chapter or 10% of the pages of this book, whichever is the greater, to be reproduced and/or communicated by any educational institution for its educational purposes provided that the educational institution (or the body that administers it) has given remuneration notices to Copyright Agency Limited (CAL) under the Act.

For details of the CAL licence for educational institutions contact:
Copyright Agency Limited, Level 19, 157 Liverpool Street, Sydney NSW 2000, tel (02) 9394 7600, fax (02) 9394 7601, email info@copyright.com.au

Reproduction and communication for other purposes
Except as permitted under the Act (for example, any fair dealing for the purposes of study, research, criticism or review) no part of this book may be reproduced, stored in a retrieval system, communicated or transmitted in any form or by any means without the prior written permission. All enquiries should be made to the publisher at the address above. This book is not to be treated as a blackline master; that is, any photocopying beyond fair dealing requires prior written permission.

Text by Sue Willis with Wendy Devlin, Lorraine Jacob, Beth Powell, Dianne Tomazos and Kaye Treacy
Edited by Anne Mckenna
Text and cover design by Jennifer Johnston
Illustrations by Ian Forss, pp. 1, 2-3; all other illustrations by Neil Curtis

Printed by Shannon Books

National Library of Australia
Cataloguing-in-Publication data:
First steps in mathematics : understand operations,
calculate, reason about number patterns.

Bibliography.
ISBN 0 7312 3970 9.

1. Mathematics - Study and teaching (Primary). 2. Mathematics - Problems, exercises etc. I. Willis, Sue, 1948- . (Series : First step in mathematics).

372.7044

ISBN 0 7312 3970 9

Contents

Foreword

The ***First Steps in Mathematics*** Resource Books and professional development program are designed to help teachers to plan, implement and evaluate the mathematics curriculum they provide for their students. The series describes the key mathematical ideas students need to understand in order to achieve the mathematics outcomes described in the Western Australian *Curriculum Framework* (1998).

Each Resource Book is based on five years of research by a team of teachers from the Department of Education and Training, and tertiary consultants led by Professor Sue Willis at Murdoch University. The ***First Steps in Mathematics*** project team conducted an extensive review of national and international research literature, which revealed gaps in the field of knowledge about students' learning in mathematics.

Using tasks designed to replicate those in the research literature, team members interviewed students in diverse locations. Analysis of the data obtained from these interviews identified characteristic phases in the development of students' thinking about major mathematical concepts. The Diagnostic Maps—which appear in the Resource Books for Number, Measurement, Space, and Chance and Data—describe these phases of development.

It has never been more important to teach mathematics well. Globalisation and the increasing use of technology have created changing demands for the application of mathematics in all aspects of our lives. Teaching mathematics well to all students requires a high level of understanding of teaching and learning in mathematics and of mathematics itself. The ***First Steps in Mathematics*** series and professional development program will enhance teachers' capacity to decide how best to help all of their students achieve the mathematics outcomes.

The commitment and persistence of many teachers and officers of the Department of Education and Training, who contributed to the research and development of ***First Steps in Mathematics***, is acknowledged and appreciated. Their efforts have resulted in an outstanding resource for teachers. I commend this series to you.

Paul Albert
Director General
Department of Education and Training
Western Australia

CHAPTER 1

What Are the Features of this Resource Book?

The ***First Steps in Mathematics: Number*** Resource Books will help teachers to diagnose, plan, implement and judge the effectiveness of the teaching and learning experiences they provide for their students. ***First Steps in Mathematics: Number*** has two Resource Books. The first book examines the outcomes relating to Understand Whole and Decimal Numbers and Understand Fractional Numbers. The second book includes Understand Operations, Calculate and Reason About Number Patterns.

This Resource Book includes the following elements.

- Diagnostic Map
- Mathematics Outcomes
- Levels of Achievement
- Pointers
- Key Understandings
- Sample Learning Activities
- Sample Lessons
- 'Did You Know?' sections
- Background Notes

Diagnostic Maps

The purpose of the Diagnostic Maps is to help teachers:

- understand why students seem to be able to do some things and not others
- realise why some students may be experiencing difficulty while others are not
- indicate the challenges students need to move their thinking forward, to refine their preconceptions, overcome any misconceptions, and so achieve the outcomes
- interpret their students' responses to activities.

Each map includes key indications and consequences of students' understanding and growth. This information is crucial for teachers making judgments about their students' level of understanding of mathematics. It enhances teachers' judgments about what to teach, to whom and when to teach it.

Using the Diagnostic Maps

The Diagnostic Maps are intended to assist teachers as they plan their mathematics curriculum. The Diagnostic Maps describe the characteristic phases in the development of students' thinking about the major concepts in each set of outcomes. The descriptions of the phases help teachers make judgments about students' understandings of the mathematical concepts.

The text in the shaded sections of each map describes students' major preoccupations, or focus, during that phase of thinking about the mathematics strand.

The 'By the end' section of each phase provides examples of what students typically think and are able to do as a result of having worked through the phase.

The achievements in the 'by the end' section should be read in conjunction with the 'As students move from' section. The 'As students move from' section includes the preconceptions, partial conceptions and misconceptions that students may have developed along the way. These provide the learning challenges for the next phase.

Together, the 'By the end' and 'As students move from' sections illustrate that while students might have developed a range of important understandings as they passed through the phase, they might also have developed some unconventional or unhelpful ideas at the same time. Both of these sections of the Diagnostic Map are intended as a useful guide only.

Mathematics Outcomes

The mathematics outcomes indicate what students are expected to know, understand and be able to do as a result of their learning experiences. The outcomes provide a framework for developing a mathematics curriculum that is taught to particular students in particular contexts. The outcomes for Number are located at the beginning of each section of the two Resource Books.

Levels of Achievement

There are eight Levels of Achievement for each mathematics outcome. The ***First Steps in Mathematics*** Resource Books address Levels 1 to 5 of these statements because they cover the typical range of achievement in primary school.

The Levels of Achievement describe markers of progress towards full achievement of the outcomes. Each student's achievement in mathematics can be monitored and success judged against the Levels of Achievement.

As the phases of the Diagnostic Maps are developmental, and not age specific, the Levels of Achievement will provide teachers with descriptions of the expected progress that students will make every 18 to 20 months when given access to an appropriate curriculum.

Pointers

Each Level of Achievement has a series of Pointers. They provide examples of what students might typically do if they have achieved a level. The Pointers help clarify the meaning of the mathematics outcome and the differences between the Levels of Achievement.

Key Understandings

The Key Understandings are the cornerstone of the ***First Steps in Mathematics*** series. The Key Understandings:

- describe the mathematical ideas, or concepts, which students need to know in order to achieve the outcome
- explain how these mathematical ideas relate to the levels of achievement for the mathematics outcomes
- suggest what experiences teachers should plan for students so they achieve the outcome
- provide a basis for the recognition and assessment of what students already know and still need to know in order to progress
- indicate the emphasis of the curriculum at particular stages
- provide content and pedagogic advice to assist with planning the curriculum at the classroom and whole-school levels.

The number of Key Understandings for each mathematics outcome varies according to the number of 'big mathematical ideas' students need to achieve the outcome.

Sample Learning Activities

For each Key Understanding, there are Sample Learning Activities that teachers could use to develop the mathematical ideas of the Key Understanding. The activities are organised into three broad groups.

- Beginning activities are suitable for Kindergarten to Year 3 students.
- Middle activities cater for Year 3 to Year 5 students.
- Later activities are designed for Year 5 to Year 7 students.

If students in the later years have not had enough prior experience, then teachers may need to select and adapt activities from earlier groups.

Sample Lessons

The Sample Lessons illustrate some of the ways in which students have responded to Learning Activities for the Beginning, Middle and Later groups. The emphasis is on how teachers can focus students' attention on the mathematics during the learning activity.

'Did You Know?' Sections

For some of the Key Understandings, there are 'Did You Know?' sections. These sections highlight common understandings and misunderstandings that students have. Some 'Did You Know?' sections also suggest diagnostic activities that teachers may wish to try with their students.

Background Notes

The Background Notes supplement the information provided in the Key Understandings. These notes are designed to help teachers develop a more in-depth knowledge of what is required as students achieve the mathematics outcomes.

The Background Notes are based on extensive research and are more detailed than the descriptions of the mathematical ideas in the Key Understandings. The content of the Background Notes varies. Sometimes, they describe how students learn specific mathematical ideas. Other notes explain the mathematics of some outcomes that may be new or unfamiliar to teachers; for example, Understand Operations.

CHAPTER 2

The Number Outcomes

The Number strand focuses on numbers and operations—what they mean, how we represent them, and how and why we use them in our everyday lives. As a result of their learning, students will develop a good sense of numbers and operations and the relationships between them. Students will develop confidence in their ability to deal with numerical situations with flexibility, ease and efficiency.

To achieve this, students require a sound grasp of the meanings of numbers and how we write them. They also need to develop an understanding of the meaning and use of basic operations, a working and flexible repertoire of computational skills, and the capacity to identify and work with number patterns and relationships. A wide range of learning experiences will enable students to understand numbers, understand operations, and to calculate and reason about number patterns and relationships.

As a result of their learning experiences, students at all levels should be able to achieve the following outcomes.

Understand Whole and Decimal Numbers

Read, write and understand the meaning, order and relative magnitudes of whole and decimal numbers, moving flexibly between equivalent forms.

Understand Fractional Numbers

Read, write and understand the meaning, order and relative magnitudes of fractional numbers, moving flexibly between equivalent forms.

Understand Operations

Understand the meaning, use and connections between addition, multiplication, subtraction and division.

Calculate

Choose and use a repertoire of mental, paper and calculator computational strategies for each operation, meeting needed degrees of accuracy and judging the reasonableness of results.

Reason About Number Patterns

Investigate, generalise and reason about patterns in numbers, explaining and justifying the conclusions reached.

Integrating the Outcomes

Each mathematics outcome in Number is explored in a separate chapter. This is to emphasise both the importance of each outcome and the differences between them. For example, students need to learn about the meaning, properties and use of addition (Understand Operations) as well as being able to add numbers (Calculate). By paying separate and special attention to each outcome, teachers can make sure that both areas receive sufficient attention, and that the important ideas about each are drawn out of the learning experiences they provide.

This does not mean, however, that the ideas and skills underpinning each of the outcomes should be taught separately, or that they will be learned separately. The outcomes are inextricably linked. Consequently, many of the activities will provide opportunities for students to develop their ideas about more than one of the outcomes. This will help teachers to ensure that the significant mathematical ideas are drawn from the learning activities, so that their students achieve each of the mathematics outcomes for Number.

A Snapshot of the Levels of Achievement in Number

Students should not always be expected to be at the same level of achievement for each of the outcomes in Number. Students vary, so some may progress more rapidly with several aspects of Number than others. Teaching and learning programs also vary and may, at times, inadvertently or deliberately emphasise some aspects of Number more than others.

Nevertheless, while the outcomes for Number are dealt with separately in these materials, they should be developing together and supporting each other, leading to an integrated set of concepts within students' heads.

The levels for each mathematics outcome indicate the typical things students are expected to do at the same time. Generally, students who have access to a curriculum that deals appropriately and thoroughly with each of the outcomes reach a particular level at roughly the same time for each outcome in Number.

> *A student has achieved a level of a* ***particular outcome*** *when he or she is able to do all the things described at that level consistently and autonomously over the range of common contexts or experiences.*
>
> *A student has achieved a level of a* ***set of outcomes*** *when he or she consistently and autonomously produces work of the standard described over the full range of outcomes at that level.*

Judgment will be needed to decide whether a student has achieved a particular level. When mapping and reporting a student's long-term progress, a teacher has to find the specific outcome level or the level for the set of outcomes that best fits the student, in the knowledge that no description is likely to fit perfectly.

The Level Statements for Number are on pages 156 to 168 of *Number* Book 1.

CHAPTER 3

Understand Operations

This chapter will support teachers in developing curricula that relate to this outcome in Number:

Understand the meaning, use and connections between addition, multiplication, subtraction and division.

Overall Description

Students understand the meaning of addition, subtraction, multiplication and division, as distinct from how to carry out the calculations associated with them. They decide which operation is needed, including in contexts where no obvious verbal cues indicate which operation is expected. For example, they can see 'take away' and 'comparison' situations as each involving subtraction and can write the appropriate subtraction.

Students recognise the need to multiply and divide in situations involving repeated addition, arrays, rates and conversions, areas, and enlargements and reductions. They also know that multiplication does not always 'make bigger' and can say under what circumstances it does and does not. They also recognise and can deal with both familiar and unfamiliar situations involving ratio and proportion.

Students understand key relationships within and between the four basic operations. They use these to construct equivalent expressions, to find unknown quantities and to assist computation. For example, they think of nine as composed of four and five so that $9 = 4 + 5$, but also $9 - 4 = 5$ and $9 - 5 = 4$. Understanding such relationships enables students readily to solve problems such as $\square - 7 = 11$ or even $\square - 348 = 434$.

Levels of Achievement	**Pointers** Progress will be evident when students:
Students have achieved Level 1 when they visualise self-generated or orally presented number stories and partitions of small numbers, representing them in materials, drawings, on a calculator or by role-playing.	• visualise small numbers as groupings of other numbers, e.g. see seven as :: :. and as :.: : and as ::: . • combine and separate collections to represent small numbers in different ways, e.g. *I took eight blocks from the bag. I had three red ones and five blue ones; I had four thick ones and four thin ones.* • can think of number questions about stories read to them, e.g. *How many students were in the family? Who was the oldest?* • use objects to represent a number story and manipulate the objects to find a solution, e.g. when told a story about black pups and brown pups, they represent the pups with two colours of buttons • 'act out' or draw a picture to represent a story involving a small number of things, e.g. they pretend to be pups and act out the story
Students have achieved Level 2 when they understand the meaning and connections between counting, number partitions, and addition and subtraction, using them to represent situations involving all four basic operations.	• select addition for situations that involve combining collections, e.g. they add 27 cats and 29 dogs to find out how many pets • use materials and diagrams to represent 'take-away' situations (e.g. *I had 25 cards and I gave away 11 of them. What have I left?*) and the comparison of two groups (e.g. *The table is 27 hands long and 13 hands wide. What is the difference?'* and *'The book costs $24 and I have $17. How much more do I need?'*) and select subtraction to solve them • use addition/subtraction relationships and number partitions to write sets of related number statements, e.g. 4 + 5 = 9 so 4 = 9 – 5 and 5 = 9 – 4 • use their understanding of number partitions to rewrite 'hidden number' questions, such as 17 + □ = 36, so they can work them out on a calculator • use materials and diagrams to represent multiplication stories that can be thought of as repeated addition, and division stories that can be thought of either as repeated subtraction or 'sharing out'
Students have achieved Level 3 when they understand the meaning, use and connections between the four operations on whole numbers, choosing appropriate operations to construct and complete simple equivalent statements.	• understand that multiplication can be used for repeated addition situations, e.g. enter 4 x 15 on their calculator to find the cost of four items that each cost 15 cents • use materials and/or diagrams to represent cross-product situations involving small numbers (e.g. four types of sneakers and three colours of laces) and hence explain that multiplication can solve them • select an appropriate division to deal with whole number sharing and grouping (including measurement) situations • restate multiplication and division problems in symbols, e.g. say *Each side of the banner is 1.35m so to find the distance around it I need to find 4 x 1.35* • write both sharing and grouping stories that relate to a symbolic number sentence involving multiplication or division of whole numbers, e.g. write both sharing and grouping stories leading to 30 ÷ 5 = □ • relate alternative everyday language expressions to one arithmetic expression, e.g. 45 ÷ 5 = □ may be read 'What is 45 divided by five?' or 'How many lots of five in 45?'
Students have achieved Level 4 when they understand the meaning, use and connections between the four operations on whole and decimal numbers, choosing appropriate operations (whole multipliers and divisors) to construct and complete equivalent statements.	• select appropriate operations to deal with situations involving decimal fractions (whole number multipliers and divisors), e.g. given *'I have three lengths of ribbon, each 4.5 m long, to be cut into nine pieces of equal length'*, write 4.5 ÷ 3 or (3 x 4.5) ÷ 9 • decide what needs to be calculated and therefore what information needs to be obtained for a practical task, e.g. black edging costs $5.40 per metre; work out the cost of replacing the edging on your desk • complete numerical statements involving brackets, e.g. (19 + 6) x □ = 50 or (19 + □) x 2 = 50 • use number relationships to complete and justify statements without resorting to computation, e.g. use =, < or > in these sentences, 263 x 5 ... 120 x 10; 27 x 80 ... 54 x 40 • solve simple missing number problems, i.e. equations, that are expressed in words, e.g. solve *I thought of a number, doubled it and added one and the answer was 17; what was the number?* by working back from 17 or by 'guessing, checking and improving'
Students have achieved Level 5 when they understand the meaning, use and connections between the four operations on whole, decimal and fractional numbers, choosing appropriate operations including where fractional and decimal multipliers and divisors are required.	• use multiplication in calculating amounts from simple familiar rates such as price and for areas and cross products, e.g. multiply as a shortcut to estimate the area of a rectangular playing field that is about 105 (metre) strides by 220 (metre) strides • recognise the need to multiply where the multiplier is a decimal greater than one (e.g. find about how much time it will take to run 2.75 km if you can run a kilometre in about 4.5 minutes, or less than one (e.g. *How much is 0.2 kg of cherries if 1 kg costs $12.95?*) • recognise the need to divide where the divisor is a decimal greater than one or less than one, e.g. how many 1.75 L containers can be filled from a 40 L container, or how many pieces 0.4 m long can be cut from 10 m of fabric? • use division in dealing with situations that involve dividing a smaller number by a larger number, e.g. find how long each piece of tape would be if we cut a 5 m length into eight equal pieces • understand the effect of multiplying and dividing by fractional and decimal numbers less than one

Key Understandings

Teachers will need to plan learning experiences that include and develop the following Key Understandings (KU). These Key Understandings underpin achievement of the outcome. The learning experiences should connect to students' current knowledge and understandings rather than to their year level.

Key Understanding	Stage of Primary Schooling—Major Emphasis	KU Description	Sample Learning Activities
KU1 Adding and subtracting numbers are useful when we: • change a quantity by adding more or taking some away • think of a quantity as combined of parts • equalise or compare two quantities	Beginning ✔✔✔ Middle ✔✔✔ Later ✔	page 12	Beginning, page 14 Middle, page 16 Later, page 18
KU2 Partitioning numbers into part-part-whole helps us relate addition and subtraction and understand their properties.	Beginning ✔✔✔ Middle ✔✔✔ Later ✔✔	page 20	Beginning, page 22 Middle, page 24 Later, page 26
KU3 Multiplying numbers is useful when we: • repeat equal quantities • use rates • make ratio comparisons or changes, e.g. scales • make arrays and combinations • need products of measures.	Beginning ✔✔ Middle ✔✔✔ Later ✔✔✔	page 28	Beginning, page 30 Middle, page 32 Later, page 34
KU4 Dividing numbers is useful when we: • share or group a quantity into a given number of portions • share or group a quantity into portions of a given size • need the inverse of multiplication.	Beginning ✔✔ Middle ✔✔✔ Later ✔✔✔	page 40	Beginning, page 42 Middle, page 44 Later, page 46
KU5 Repeating equal quantities and partitioning a quantity into equal parts helps us relate multiplication and division and understand their properties.	Beginning ✔✔ Middle ✔✔✔ Later ✔✔✔	page 52	Beginning, page 54 Middle, page 56 Later, page 58
KU6 The same operation can be said and written in different ways.	Beginning ✔✔ Middle ✔✔ Later ✔✔	page 62	Beginning, page 63 Middle, page 64 Later, page 65
KU7 Properties of operations and relationships between them can help us to decide whether number sentences are true.	Beginning ✔ Middle ✔✔ Later ✔✔✔	page 66	Beginning, page 68 Middle, page 69 Later, page 71
KU8 Thinking of a problem as a number sentence often helps us to solve it. Sometimes we need to rewrite the number sentence in a different but equivalent way.	Beginning ✔ Middle ✔✔ Later ✔✔✔	page 74	Beginning, page 76 Middle, page 77 Later, page 79
KU9 We make assumptions when using operations. We should check that the assumptions make sense for the problem.	Beginning ✔ Middle ✔✔ Later ✔✔	page 82	Beginning, page 84 Middle, page 85 Later, page 86

Key

✔✔✔ The development of this Key Understanding is a major focus of planned activities.

✔✔ The development of this Key Understanding is an important focus of planned activities.

✔ Some activities may be planned to introduce this Key Understanding, to consolidate it, or to extend its application. The idea may also arise incidentally in conversations and routines that occur in the classroom.

KEY UNDERSTANDING 1

Adding and subtracting numbers are useful when we:

- ***change a quantity by adding more or taking some away***
- ***think of a quantity as combined of parts***
- ***equalise or compare two quantities.***

This Key Understanding is about the meaning of the addition and subtraction operations and when to use them, rather than how to carry out calculations. Students should learn to recognise a wide range of problem types to which addition and subtraction apply. These should include change situations (add some or take some away), combine situations, and compare and equalise situations. Examples of each of these problem types are provided in the Background Notes on page 87. Students should be helped to see how these types of problems can all be thought of in terms of part-part-whole, and can be solved using the same operations.

Students will gain full command of some problem types earlier than others. However, this does not mean that they should only deal with one type at a time. A wide range of addition and subtraction problems should be posed from the early school years, although the numbers involved may be quite small to begin with. Initially, students should solve problems by acting them out, modelling them with materials and diagrams, and imagining them in their 'mind's eye'. Students who have achieved Level 1 can do this for self-generated or orally presented stories involving small, easily visualised numbers.

Many students have always come to school recognising and naming numbers, even if they do not fully understand them. Nowadays they will often meet the operation symbols simply by playing with calculators. They should be provided with a calculator from the earliest primary years and encouraged to explore its functions. When they do so, they will want to name various operation keys. Rather than meeting the concepts and attaching the symbols to the concepts later, they are more likely to meet the symbols and, over time, develop and enrich the meanings they attach to them.

The goal is for students to build connections between dramatic, physical, diagrammatic and verbal forms of problems and the symbolic representations of them. Students who have achieved Level 2 represent problems involving whole numbers in a variety of ways. They can link various problem situations to the addition and subtraction operations and the symbols. They link the various addition situations to the part-part-whole notion, so they understand *why* the addition symbol works in each case. Similarly, they link various subtraction situations to part-part-whole and to the subtraction symbol. They write suitable number sentences.

At Level 3, students deal with all the problem types in contexts involving large whole numbers. At Level 4, they also do this in situations where there are no obvious verbal cues to suggest which operation is required, where intuition about the size of the answer may not help choose an operation, and where measured quantities including decimals and fractions are involved.

SAMPLE LEARNING ACTIVITIES

Beginning ✔✔✔

Role Play

Have students act out the characters in a story. Each time people come or go, a child records the number and the operation/action or sign on a board, e.g. + 2, – 1. At the end of the story, ask: Which part of the story was the '+ 2' for? Could it have been when the wolf ran away? Why? Which part of the story could '3 + 1' be about?'

Plus or Minus

Retell a favourite story to students and have them hold up a card showing either '+' or '–' each time a character joins or leaves the scene. Ask students to compare and explain their choice. Have them write a number sentence for a part of the story.

Equal Groups

Ask students to suggest ways to make equal groups in everyday tasks, e.g. as they pack equipment away or distribute materials, ask: What could you do if there should be six glue sticks but there are only two? What could you do if there are eight felt pens but there should be six?

Messages

Organise students into pairs. Each student has an identical group of objects, e.g. Unifix cubes, on each side of a barrier. Ask one partner to combine or separate their group of objects and show what they did by a drawing or by writing numbers and signs on a message.

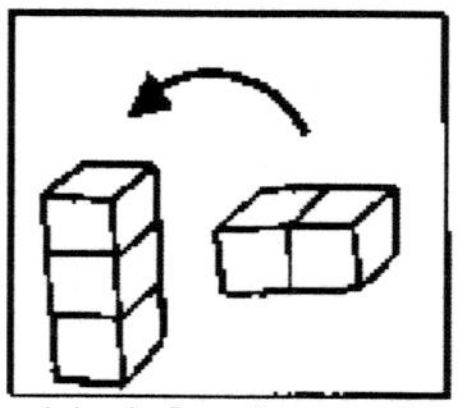

I added 2 cubes on to my stack of 3 cubes.

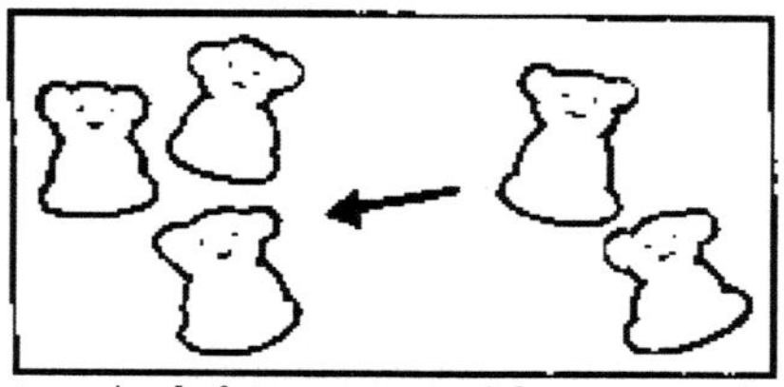

I pushed 2 bears and 3 bears together.

They pass the message over the barrier for their partner, who uses it to replicate the action. The first student checks to see if it is correct. After several turns, with students swapping the tasks, have them sort and display the messages in 'combine' and 'separate' groups. Introduce the '+' and '–' signs, or use messages that show numbers and signs as a way to represent the materials and actions. Draw out that different situations can be shown as 2 + 3: I pushed two bears and three bears together; I added two cubes on to my stack of three cubes. (See Sample Lesson 1, page 36.)

Think Board

Encourage students to show they have made the connections between symbols and real-life situations using a simplified think board. Ask them to tell a story that is represented by symbols such as 4 + 9 or 13 – 6, and show how this is represented by materials or a diagram.

Separating Objects

Ask students to describe the different ways a group of objects can be separated. Use toy animals, counters or play dough to represent a story such as: Five birds in a tree. Three flew away. How many birds left in the tree? Using familiar stories such as *Five Little Monkeys* (Hanzl and Gardner, 1998), focus on the use of terms such as 'went away', 'left' and 'two from five'. Ask: Which key on our calculator takes away?

Matching Collections

Following the previous activity, ask students what they did to match the actual objects to the number of birds in the story. They might say: *I put out five counters to show the birds. Then I took away two counters to show the birds that flew away.* Ask: So what is the difference between the five birds that were in the tree and the birds that are there now? Use terms such as 'how many more' and 'the difference'. Record their explanation on the board as they retell it. Focus on their decisions to 'add more' or 'take away some'.

Number Line

Have students use a number line to compare two different-sized groups and say how many more are in one group. Focus on the smaller number and ask: What would you do to the smaller number to make it the same as the bigger number? What would you do to the larger number to make it the same as the smaller number? Which movement shows joining, and which shows separating?

Early Bird

Ask students to describe how they show or think about the amounts for comparison problems. Use a picture of 13 birds and seven worms and ask: Suppose the birds all try to get a worm. Will every bird get one? How many birds won't get a worm? How do you know? How else could we work it out? Ask students to draw the solution and say what they did. Help them write a number sentence for their drawing.

Word Problems

Write different types of change situation word problems based on the same story idea. For example: A farmer had 11 chickens, he bought seven more and then he had 18 altogether; or, the farmer had 18 chickens, seven escaped and then he had 11 left. Present the problems with start, change and result unknown. Have students describe, draw and write number sequences to show how they joined and separated the groups to find the solutions. (See Background Notes on page 87 for further examples of change problems.)

SAMPLE LEARNING ACTIVITIES

Middle ✓✓✓

Think Board

Draw up a think board (see Background Notes, page 87). Put an example in one of the sections and ask students in groups to represent the problem in the other sections. For example, start with a story such as: Jonathan has collected 12 toys. Eight are cars. The rest are trucks. How many are trucks? Have students show it in materials, as a picture, as a number sentence, and write the answer. Ask: Which sign did you choose, and why? What was it about the story that told you it was an addition/subtraction?

Story Problems

Give students two story problems using the same numbers and operation: one showing a change situation and the other a combine situation. For example, a change situation: There are eight galahs in a tree. Some more birds came. Now there are 25 birds in the tree. How many birds came? Or, a combine situation: There are 25 birds in a tree. Eight are galahs and the rest are cockatoos. How many are cockatoos? Ask: If the numbers are the same, what is the difference in these problems? What made you think of them both as addition/subtraction?

Classroom Problems

Have students mentally solve change problems that arise in the classroom, e.g. 14 students went to lunch; how many are left? They then work out a number sentence to represent what they did. Ask: What made you think it should be an addition/subtraction sentence?

Comparing in the Classroom

Broaden the previous activity to include combine, and then compare and equalise situations. For example:

- In October and November, 96 mm of rain fell in Kununurra. If 26 mm fell in October, how much rain fell in November? (Combine)
- Simon's corn plant measured 117 mm and Sharn's measured 145 mm. How much taller is Sharn's plant? (Compare)
- There are 114 children going to the sausage sizzle, and each child needs to have a paper plate. I already have 75 paper plates. How many more plates do I need to buy? (Equalise)

Analysing Word Problems

Have students work out which numbers in a word problem show the whole and which show the parts. They then say whether it is a part or the whole that is not known. For example:

- If two penguins ate 32 fish between them and one penguin ate 19, how many fish did the other penguin eat? If 32 is the whole and 19 is the part, what do we do to find the other part?

Number Lines

Extend the approach in the previous activity. Ask students to solve change, combine, compare and equalise, and addition and subtraction problems using a number line to represent the parts and the whole. For example: A new computer game costs $76. Jo has saved $44. How much more does she have to save?

Writing Problems

Ask students to write problems for others to solve while studying, say, Society and Environment. For example: If McCormick invented the harvester 154 years ago, what year was it invented? Students need to say which operation is required and why, then decide on the number sentence to use to solve the problem. Ask: How did you know what order to put the numbers in? Why did you decide to put 154 second (i.e. after the current year)?

Classifying Problems

Ask students to classify word problems according to whether they could be solved using addition or subtraction. Start with sets of problems involving change situations all using the same pair of numbers. Some should include extra numbers. For example: Anna had some cards. Her nine-year-old brother gave her three more. Now she has ten cards. How many did she have to start with? Students will discover they need a third group—problems that can be solved either with addition or subtraction. Discuss the groups. Ask: What do all of the problems in the addition group have in common? What makes them all addition? Note that the 'missing number' additions can also be solved with subtraction. (See 'Classifying Problems', page 25.)

Story Problems

Ask students to write a story problem for a given number sentence, e.g. 17 + ___ = 48 or 48 – 17 = ___. Ask: What is in the story that shows it matches the number sentence?

SAMPLE LEARNING ACTIVITIES

Later ✓

Addition and Subtraction

Ask students to use everyday events as a source of addition and subtraction questions or problems. For example: Sam knew the length of a killer whale was about 9 m and wanted to get an idea of what 9 m looked like. He marked off what he thought was 9 m but his estimate was actually 7.5 m. Sam wanted to know how much short his estimate was. Ask: Is this an addition or subtraction problem? How do you know?

Classifying Problems

Repeat activities such as the previous one with the think board (see Background Notes, pages 87 and 88.) Have students provide situations for a number sentence such as 4.6 + _ = 9.9, where the change, that is, the addend or subtrahend, is unknown. Ask students to share and classify their problems into those where amounts are joined, compared, made equal or thought of as parts of a whole.

Change Problems

Have students represent change problems that include fractions and decimals. Ask them to say how they decided on an operation and a number sentence. For example:

- Gemma had $4\frac{1}{4}$ lengths of licorice rope. After her brother asked her for some, Gemma broke off $\frac{1}{2}$ of a whole length and gave it to him. How much rope does Gemma have left?
- Gemma has $4\frac{1}{4}$ lengths of licorice rope. She gave some to her brother. Now she has $3\frac{3}{4}$ left. How much did Gemma give to her brother?
- Gemma had some licorice rope. She had given her brother $\frac{1}{2}$ a rope and now has $3\frac{3}{4}$ left. How much did she start with?

Long Jump

Have students decide which operation to use in equalise situations involving decimals. For example:

- Sonya jumps a distance of 3.25 m and Mark jumps 2.38 m. How much longer does Mark's jump have to be to match Sonya's?
- Mark jumps 2.38 m. If he jumps another 0.87 m, he will have jumped the same distance as Sonya. How far did Sonya jump?
- Sonya jumps 3.25 m. If Mark jumps another 0.87 m, his jump will be the same as Sonya's. What was Mark's original jump?

Part-Whole Situations

Ask students to use diagrams, materials (such as paper tape and string), number lines, words or mental images to represent the parts and the whole in situations, in order to decide on the operation. For example, using the previous activity, have students paraphrase the problem to see what it is about—Mark's jump and something will equal Sonya's jump. Students could draw a diagram to represent Mark's jump as a part and Sonya's jump as the whole. Ask: Is it a part or is it the whole that you don't know? How does knowing the missing part help you decide on an operation and write a number sentence?

Fractions and Decimals

Extend the range of addition and subtraction problems students solve to include fractional and decimal quantities. For example: Yesterday the minimum temperature was 15.2°C in the morning. By the afternoon, the temperature rose to a maximum of 38.8°C. How much did the temperature rise?

KEY UNDERSTANDING 2

Partitioning numbers into part-part-whole helps us relate addition and subtraction and understand their properties.

A quantity, while being thought of as a whole, can also be thought of as composed of parts. That is:

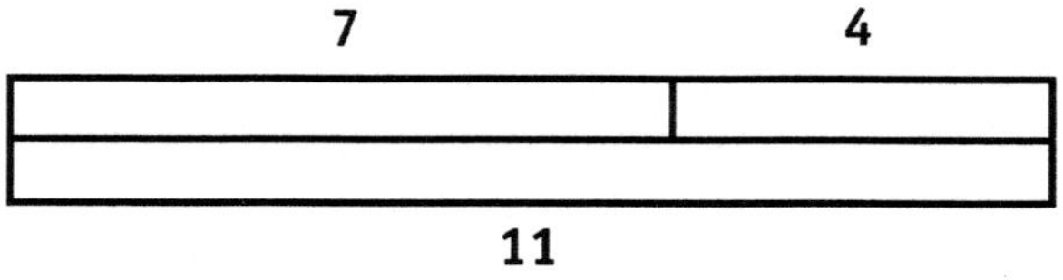

7 + 4 = 11 and 4 + 7 = 11
11 – 4 = 7 and 11 – 7 = 4

The part-part-whole relationship shows how addition and subtraction are related, with subtraction being the inverse of addition. If the whole quantity is unknown, addition is required. If one of the other quantities is unknown, subtraction is required. This enables students to see *why* a problem that they think of as about adding, but with one of the addends unknown, could be solved by subtracting or vice-versa. (See Key Understanding 7, page 66, and Background Notes, page 91.) Linking the joining and separating of the parts that make the whole to a variety of situations also helps students to see *why* subtraction can be used to solve a take-away problem and also a comparison problem. Understanding part-part-whole relationships to represent a problem in different ways, so they can choose the most helpful.

The part-part-whole relationship is also the key to students seeing *why* addition is commutative and *why* subtraction is not. The commutativity of addition is of obvious practical use in calculating, but knowing that, and understanding why, addition is commutative and subtraction is not, helps students represent word problems with appropriate addition and subtraction sentences.

Students who have achieved Level 1 of the outcome can solve simple addition and subtraction problems for whole numbers, mostly by modelling strategies (see Key Understanding 1, page 12, and Background Notes, page 89). However, they may not link addition to subtraction or the types of subtraction to each other.

At Level 2 they link the types of addition (from Key Understanding 1) to the part-part-whole idea and so understand why the addition symbol works in each case.

Similarly, they link subtraction types to the part-part-whole idea and to the subtraction symbol. With the aid of diagrams, they can use part-part-whole relationships to link addition to subtraction and so, given 16 + □ = 34, they could work out a related subtraction and so find the 'hidden number' on their calculator.

At Level 3, students use the inverse relationship between addition and subtraction routinely for large whole numbers, e.g. they readily say that if 35 + 65 = 100, then 100 – 65 *must be* 35, although they may still rely on imagining it in diagrams. At Level 4 this relationship has been generalised so that students can use the inverse relationship in an abstract way for any numbers including decimals and fractions. Students at Level 5 can use the relationship to solve more abstract 'algebraic' problems such as: half my number, add one, is 43, what is my number?

SAMPLE LEARNING ACTIVITIES

Beginning ✔✔✔

Number Combinations

Ask students to represent and record all of the combinations of a given number using everyday materials (e.g. beans, bottle tops, straws, leaves), story contexts and games. Display the addition number sentences and discuss, focusing on two at a time. For example, ask: Is 4 + 3 the same as 3 + 4? Use your bears to show how it is the same and how it is different. Ask: If Ben has three bears and Fran has four, will there be the same number of bears if they swapped, so that Ben has four and Fran has three? Why?

Part-Part-Whole

Have students use MAB blocks and Unifix cubes to represent part-part-whole situations. Ask them to write all the number sentences represented. For example:

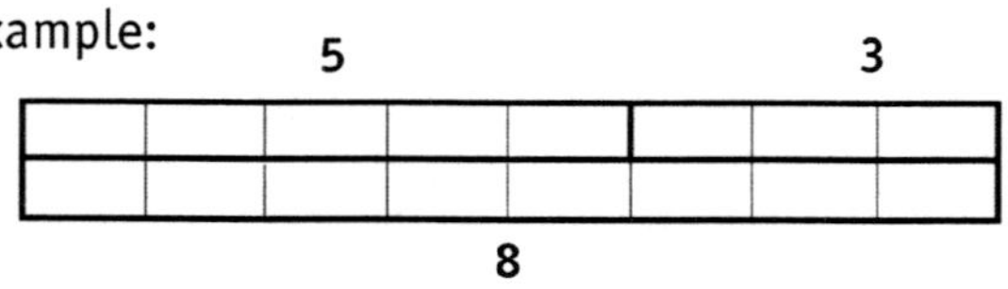

5 + 3 = 8
3 + 5 = 8
8 – 3 = 5
8 – 5 = 3

Discuss, focusing students on:

- the two additions
- the two subtractions
- the relationship between the additions and the subtractions.

Ten in Bed

Read familiar stories to students, e.g. *Five Little Monkeys* (Hanzl and Gardner, 1998) and *Ten in the Bed* (Dale, 1988). Check addition and subtraction calculations by inverting the problem. Use the characters and events in the story to make up problems, e.g. ten in the bed and one fell out: 10 – 1 = 9. Check this by adding one to nine to see if it is ten. What number sentences could we use if there were ten in the bed and two fell out? What about if three fell out?

Inverse Relationships

Have students use materials (e.g. beans, play people, toy animals) and diagrams to model inverse relationships through stories. For example: Have students visualise nine sheep in a paddock. They have to separate them into two groups. Ask: If five sheep move to another paddock, how many will be left here? How do you know? Focus on the idea that knowing how many sheep are in one paddock enables us to know how many are left in the other. (Link to Calculate, Key Understanding 2.)

Think Board

Ask students to use a think board to create three different representations of one operation starting from a story (e.g. model with materials, draw the situation in a picture, use numbers and symbols). For example: There were 15 bears in the zoo enclosure, but I could only count nine. How many were hiding in their cave? Ask them to compare their representations with those of other students. Ask: What is the same/different about the things/pictures? What is the same/different about the number sentences? Can you use both addition and subtraction to show what you did? (See Background Notes, page 87, for an example of a think board.)

Number Sentences

Ask students to write two different number sentences for a combine situation, e.g. there are five students in our class with curly hair; how many do not have curly hair? (They could write 5 + _ = 27 or 27 – 5 = _.) Ask: What is the difference between the two sentences? How does each number sentence tell the story? How would you solve each one?

Number Line

Have students use a number line to solve word problems and then record them in their own way. For example: I had 12 cards and I gave four to my brother. How many cards do I have left? Ask: Can you go both forwards and backwards to solve the same problem and write it as a number sentence? Why? How many cards altogether? Is this the whole number?

Secret Numbers

Show students how to play a calculator game, Secret Numbers, to practise inverting number sentences. Organise the students into pairs. One student secretly enters a number into a calculator and then adds a number they both agree on, e.g. five. The student with the calculator shows their partner what the new number is. The partner says what the original number was and checks it on the calculator by entering a subtraction. For example: the first student secretly enters seven, adds five and gets 12. The partner says 'The number was seven', but must check on the calculator by entering a subtraction (12 – 5), not by entering 7 + 5.

SAMPLE LEARNING ACTIVITIES

Middle ✔✔✔

Related Addition

Ask students to draw pictures showing the whole numbers and part numbers in related addition situations:

- James has 26 marbles and his brother Cameron has 38. Altogether they have 64 marbles.
- James has 38 marbles and Cameron has 26 marbles. Altogether they have 64.

Ask: How are these situations the same or different? How are the number sentences the same or different?

Number Relationships

Invite students to use Unifix cubes, MAB blocks, Cuisenaire rods or a number line to show a relationship such as 14 + 6 = 20. They can then write as many addition and subtraction sentences as possible. Ask: If I know 14 + 6 = 20, what else do I know? Include examples such as 20 = 6 + 14 and 16 = 20 – 4. (Link to Calculate.)

Think Board

Using a more complex think board with one box on each line filled, students work out the other representations for each problem. Ask: Which problems have two ways of writing the number sentences? Why? (See Background Notes, page 87, for an example of a think board.)

Addition and Subtraction Links

Focus on the link between addition and subtraction. Pose this problem: Molly and Hasibee were measuring the height of two chickens. One was 29 blocks high and one was 24 blocks high. Molly worked out the difference in the chickens' height by counting from 24 up to 29, and wrote down 24 + 5 = 29. Hasibee counted down five places from 29 until he got to 24 and wrote down 29 – 24 = 5. Ask: Why can we do this problem in two ways. Is one way more correct than the other?

Modelling Problems

Have students use materials (e.g. beans, bottle tops, counters) to model problems involving comparison. For example: If one penguin ate 18 fish and another ate 22, how many more fish did the second penguin eat? Ask students to show two ways it could be recorded, using addition and subtraction. Ask: Will either do? Why? Which fits the way you worked it out? Which is easier to work out?

Which Operation?

Ask students to review a collection of stories demonstrating combine, change, compare and equalise situations (see Background Notes, page 89, for example). Ask them to decide which numbers are being joined and which are being separated, which are the parts and which are the whole. Ask: If the whole is known, which operation can you use to find the missing part? If the whole is unknown, which operation can you use to work it out?

Backwards and Forwards

Following the previous activity, ask students to represent one of the story problems on a number line. Ask: Do the numbers represent the parts or the whole? Do you locate the numbers directly onto the number line? Does one of the numbers tell you to move a number of spaces along the line? Do you need to move forwards or backwards on the number line to find the solution? Which operation is represented by forwards movements? Which operation is represented by backwards movements? Repeat for other problems. Ask students to write a number sentence for each story.

Unknown Number

Have students decide what number is unknown in a problem: is it one of the parts or the whole? Present a story problem, where one of the parts is unknown. For example: A new computer game costs $76. Jo has saved $44. How much more does she have to save? Ask students to show how it is possible to use both addition and subtraction to solve the problem. Give a problem where the whole is unknown. For example: Jo has saved $44. She received a total of $32 for her birthday. How much does she have altogether? Ask: How can we solve this? Can we use both addition and subtraction? Why? Why not? What is the difference between the first and second problem?

Classifying Problems

Sort a range of addition or subtraction problems into those that can be solved by addition, subtraction, or either addition or subtraction. Look at problems where one part is unknown. For example:

- Twenty-eight students were in the classroom. Some went outside. If there were 16 left inside, how many went outside?
- Garry Smith drove 133 km on the weekend. He drove 86 km on Saturday. How far did he drive on Sunday?

Ask: Why is it possible to solve each of these with both operations? Which operation is most useful for each problem? Why? (See Key Understanding 1, 'Classifying Problems', page 17). Note that the 'missing number' additions can also be solved with subtraction.

SAMPLE LEARNING ACTIVITIES

Later ✔✔

Long Jump

Have students use part-part-whole models to explain why different operations are equivalent. Ask them to examine their representations and number sentences for the long jump problem (see 'Long Jump', page 19). Ask: How did you use the part-part-whole diagram to arrive at 3.25 m – 2.38 m = □ ? How did you use it to arrive at 2.38 m + □ = 3.25 m? Is there another one? Do all these number sentences answer the question? Use your diagram to show why.

Choosing Operations

Have students use what they know about the parts and the whole to practise deciding on operations. Repeat activities where students represent the whole and the parts for a range of addition and subtraction problems using part-parts whole models. For example:

- Sam was saving for an aquarium which cost $176. He was given $85 for his birthday. How much more did he have to save?
- The total rainfall for the three months of summer was 514 mm. In December, 105 mm fell, and 213 mm fell in January. What was February's rainfall?

For each problem ask: What operation is possible if we don't know what the whole is? What operation/s are possible when either of the parts is unknown? Students use their representations to justify their answers.

Inverse Relationships

Ask students to use their understanding of inverse relationships to solve equalising problems. Pose this problem: Sam saw that his brother and friend had eaten most of the pack of ten doughnuts. There were only four left. Sam said that he should have the rest of the pack. Would that be fair? Ask students to represent the problem with materials or diagrams. Invite them to record the number sentences they could use to solve the problem. Talk about the variety of possibilities. Ask: What if there were 5297 doughnuts left out of a bin of 12 942? Are the operations the same or different than before? Use your calculator to try to solve this number sentence. What do you find out?

Increased Quantities

Repeat the previous activity with other addition and subtraction problems where the quantities are increased. The numbers can also be changed to decimals, including those less than one, and fractions.

Focus on Operations

Focus on the relationship between the operations to more easily solve a problem using large numbers. For example: The area of Australia is 7 682 000 square kilometres. The area of the United Kingdom is 244 000 square kilometres. How much greater is the area of Australia than the area of the United Kingdom? Ask students to write and share number sentences to represent the problem:

7 682 000 – □ = 244 000

244 000 + □ = 7 682 000

7 682 000 – 244 000 = □

Ask: Which of these number sentences is useful when using the calculator to solve the problem? Extend to other problems with decimals and fractions.

KEY UNDERSTANDING 3

Multiplying numbers is useful when we:

- ***repeat equal quantities***
- ***use rates***
- ***make ratio comparisons or changes, e.g. scales***
- ***make arrays and combinations***
- ***need products of measures.***

Students should learn to recognise a wide range of problem types to which multiplication applies. They need to be helped to see how these apparently different types of problems are related and can all be solved using multiplication. Examples of the five problem types listed in this Key Understanding are provided in the Background Notes on page 90. Students who understand the meaning of multiplication can also represent number sentences such as 18 x 3 or 27.6 x 3.2 in materials, a drawing, or a sensible story.

Students are usually introduced to multiplication as 'repeated addition'. This requires a big shift in thinking from addition or subtraction. To interpret 5 + 2, students can show five blocks and two blocks and then think about what the + means. Interpreting 5 – 2 is a little more complex, but they can show five blocks, then think about what the – and the 2 mean and push two blocks aside. The parts and the whole are visible and the 5 and 2 each refer to a number of blocks. However, for 5 x 2, the 5 and the 2 do not each refer to a number of blocks. One refers to a number of blocks, but the other refers to a number of sets of blocks. If students begin by counting out five blocks and two blocks, they will run into problems when they try to process the x sign. The notion that 5 x 2 refers to five groups of two requires careful development. Students should be helped, from the earliest years, to think multiplicatively about these situations, since repeated addition does not address all situations in which multiplying is helpful.

Students who have attained Level 2 of the outcome can model problems involving 'repeating equal quantities' with materials and diagrams. For example, to make flowers we need to make five petals for each flower. How many petals do we need for three flowers? Students are likely to think of it as the addition: 5 + 5 + 5. Given continuous access to calculators, they may think of the x sign in the calculator as a shortcut way of telling the calculator to add three lots of five. Those who have achieved Level 3 can choose multiplication to solve repeated addition problems and also to solve simple familiar rate and combination problems such as: We have four shirts and three pairs of pants; how many outfits can we make? These problems do not explicitly involve repeating equal units. However, students' explanations of why multiplication works for rate and combination problems are likely to draw on ideas about repeated addition.

Students who have achieved Level 4 of the outcome have begun to understand multiplication as involving more than repeated addition. They will choose to multiply in situations involving familiar everyday rates (such as shopping) and scales, although these will still tend to involve whole number multipliers or numbers that they think of as 'like whole numbers'. However, those at Level 5 have developed multiplicative thinking to the extent that they consistently recognise multiplication as appropriate in situations involving familiar rates, areas and combinations, including where fractional multipliers are required. Such students consistently solve problems of this type regardless of the size of the multiplier, as long as the situation is sufficiently familiar that they recognise that a rate is involved.

SAMPLE LEARNING ACTIVITIES

Beginning ✔✔

Rate Problems

Have students devise simple rate problems, e.g. one ant has six legs, how many legs do three ants have; if each child has half a slice of bread each, how many slices are needed for four people. Ask students to model the situations using materials such as toothpicks or diagrams to record six for one, 12 for two, 18 for three, etc.

Describing

Encourage students to use summaries to describe their groupings from the previous activity as 'three sixes', 'three lots of/groups of/sets of six', and record them as 6 + 6 + 6 and later as 3 x 6. Ask: How many sixes/groups of six are there? How many times did you make a group of six?

Arrays

Have students arrange materials (such as beans and counters) in arrays to find how many will be needed, e.g. seats in a bus or seats for a puppet play, seeds in a vegetable garden. Ask: How many in each row? How many rows? Focus students on noticing and describing the array and how many there are altogether. Students can later draw some other arrays and set out materials, use pegboards or draw diagrams and describe different arrays.

Planning

Ask students to collect materials, and focus on equal groups. For example: You need three beads each; how many must you get for a group of five? Ask those who count by ones to try to count by threes; ask those who skip count how many threes they need. Ask students to write a number sentence and use a calculator to check the result.

Twice as Many

Invite students to use drawings and diagrams to investigate the meaning of 'twice as many' in response to reading stories such as *Fifteen Pigs on a Pirate Ship* (Edwards and Parkin, 1987), which illustrates 'double the number of ships'. Ask: What did you do to the group to show twice as many? Is there a way we could work it out on the calculator? Repeat for 'three times as many'. Ask: How much bigger is that than twice as many?

Five Times as Many

Have students use materials and drawings to model the meaning of 'five times as many'. Pose the following problem. Sam had three beads and Becky had 12. The teacher said 'Becky! You've taken five times as many as Sam.' Was the teacher right?

Combinations

Ask students to work out possible combinations where there are two sets of variables, e.g. two pairs of shorts and six shirts; six ice-cream flavours and three cones. Students can use models of the items and diagrams to work out a solution. Focus on 'how many times?' Ask: How many times did you use chocolate ice-cream?

Money

Have students use repeated addition to find the total when buying multiple copies of the same item. Ask them to work out the total cost using money or diagrams. Explain how they know it costs that amount. Students can use their calculator to check each other's totals.

Array Problems

Have students explore arrays to discover that, e.g. 6 x 3 = 3 x 6. For example: Katy said we planted the peas in rows of three. Tim said they were in rows of six. Could they both be right? Students can use materials (e.g. beans) and/or diagrams to try to solve the problem.

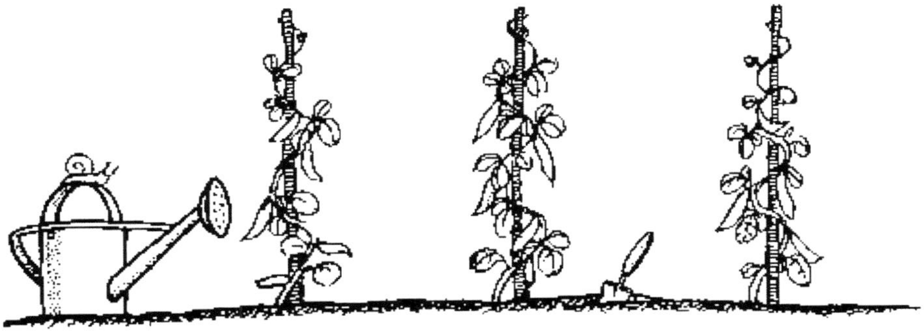

SAMPLE LEARNING ACTIVITIES

Middle ✔✔✔

Collections

Have students investigate collections of everyday objects and say how their arrangements help them to see how many there are, e.g. egg cartons, muffin trays, packets of stock cubes. For example, they might say: *I saw four rows with three in each row.* (Link to Calculate, Key Understandings 1 and 3.)

Equal Groups

Have students solve problems involving equal groups, e.g. how many straws will be needed to make five pentagons, five hexagons, etc. Ask students to write an addition number sentence and a multiplication sentence for each example. Talk about how each sentence shows the same situation.

Grouping and Counting Objects

Have pairs of students take a quantity of blocks. One partner groups or partitions the blocks; the other quickly looks at the arrangement and says how many there are, e.g. *I knew it was 32 because I saw four in each group and I know 8 x 4 =32.* Extend the activity to large numbers, using MAB blocks, and fractional numbers, using Pattern Blocks. (Link to Calculate.)

Classifying Problems

(See Key Understanding 1, 'Classifying Problems', page 17.) Pose new problems for the students to classify into those that can and can't be solved by using multiplication. Ask students to explain their thinking.

Think Board

Provide two multiplication stories, using the same numbers but one involving equal groups and one involving rates. (See Background Notes, page 90.) Ask: How are these the same/different? What was it about the stories that told you they were multiplication problems? What does the x sign mean in each example? What number sentence could be used for both? What does each number in the sentence show? Why are they in that order? What does the x sign show? (See Background Notes, page 87, for an example of a think board.)

Lunch Time

Have students plan a healthy lunch for the class by drawing a picture to work out how much of each item they need to buy and how much it will cost. For example: How much juice will you need to buy if each student drinks 200 ml? If the juice costs $4.70 for 2 litres, how much will it cost altogether? Discuss how the multiplication sign can be used to write a number sentence for each drawing.

Combination Problems

Have students use materials or diagrams to solve combination problems, e.g. how many different types of sandwiches can be made from three types of bread and four fillings? After students complete a number of combination problems involving the same numbers, discuss how the diagrams or arrangements of materials are similar and why multiplication can be used to write a number sentence for each.

Multiplication

Have students decide what the numbers in a multiplication sentence mean in relation to the situation. Use a problem such as 'There were nine people coming to the barbecue and we bought three sausages for each', and a number sentence (9 x 3 = 27). Ask: Why can we use 9 x 3 = 27 to represent this problem? How do you know that it is nine groups with three in each and not three groups with nine in each? Could the number sentence 3 x 9 = 27 also represent this story? Why?

Rate Problems

Have students write and compare number sentences to solve rate problems. For example: A zoo visit costs $5 per student and $10 per adult, with one adult free for every five students. How much will it cost for 32 students and eight adults? Ask: What number sentences did you choose? Why? What order did you place the numbers in the sentence? Does it matter? What does the x sign show in your number sentence?

Soup for Everyone

Have students solve multiplicative change problems to convert a soup recipe for eight to cater for 16 people and then for 12.

Potato Soup (serves 8)

8 small potatoes
4 cups of water
4 chicken stock cubes
2 tablespoons of butter
1 cup of cream

Ask: What number sentences could be used? In what order should the numbers in the sentence be? Does it matter? Why?

SAMPLE LEARNING ACTIVITIES

Later ✓✓✓

Combination Problems

Have students solve combination problems. For example: You bought four different coloured shirts and three different coloured pairs of trousers at a sale. Would you be able to wear a different outfit every day for two weeks? How many different coloured shirts would you need to wear a different outfit every day for a month? What would happen if you bought two different hats? How would that increase the number of outfits you could wear? Ask students to write a number sentence in each case.

Comparing Sizes

Have students investigate changes of size. For example:

- Sam uses an overhead projector and enlarges a diagram eight times its original size. The original diagram is 4 cm high. How high will the enlarged image be? How do you know?
- Sam projects a rectangle 13.5 cm wide and 11 cm high onto the blackboard. The enlarged image is about 44 cm high. How wide will the rectangle appear on the board? How do you know?

Changes in Ratio

Have students use multiplication to solve ratio change problems where the quantity for one measure is not given. For example: Examine a muffin recipe where the quantities given are for 12 muffins. Ask students to adjust the recipe to make six, 18 or 30 muffins. What would you need to multiply by in each case?

Rate Situations

Have students write number sentences for rate situations using money, decimals and fractions. For example:

- Helen's pace rate is 1.4 paces per metre. How many paces will she take to walk 100 m?
- When Larissa went to Bali the exchange rate was 2000 rupiah to $A1. When Tom went, the exchange rate was 6000 rupiah to $A1. They both went with $A150. How many rupiah did they each get?
- A recipe required $\frac{1}{3}$ cup of butter per one cup of flour. How much butter will be needed for six cups of flour?

Compare Quantities

Have students compare quantities such as distances multiplicatively. For example: Jenny's balloon-powered car went 2.75 m. Shane's went three times that distance. How far did Shane's car travel? June's car went about $\frac{2}{3}$ the distance of Jenny's car. How far did June's car go? How did you work it out?

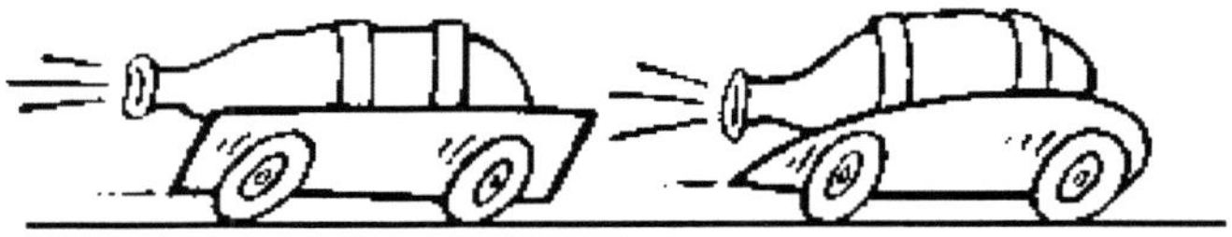

Calculating Area

Have students identify where multiplication can be used to calculate areas. For example: A painter needs to calculate the area of a wall to know how much paint to order. The wall is 7 m long and 3.5 m high. Ask students to write the number sentence and say why multiplication works in that case.

Decimals

Have students solve multiplication problems involving decimals above and below one. For example: One litre of unleaded petrol is 89.9 cents. Ben needs to fill his car. How much will 43 litres cost? He also needs to top up his lawn mower. How much will 0.7 litre cost? Talk about what operation is required. Ask: Was it the same operation for both situations? Why?

Scales

Have students use multiplication for scales. For example: Tom draws a scale map of the streets around his school. His scale is 10 cm to 1 km. If he lives 2.5 km from school, what should be the distance on his map? His friend lives 0.8 km away. What will the distance on the map be?

Choosing Operations

Have students choose suitable operations for this problem. Ty set up a stall selling cherries from his tree to earn some extra money. He charged $8.50 per kilogram. Circle the operation he would key into his calculator as he weighed each of these amounts of cherries:

- For 3 kg
  8.50 ÷ 3   8.50 – 3   8.50 + 3   8.50 x 3
- For 3.25 kg
  8.50 + 3.25   8.50 x 3.25   8.50 – 3.25   8.50 ÷ 3.25
- For 1.75 kg
  8.50 ÷ 1.75   8.50 + 1.75   8.50 – 1.75   8.50 x 1.75
- For 0.75 kg
  8.50 + 0.75   8.50 – 0.75   8.50 ÷ 0.75   8.50 x 0.75

SAMPLE LESSON 1

Sample Learning Activity: Beginning—'Messages', page 14

Key Understanding 3: Multiplying numbers is useful when we:

- repeat equal quantities
- use rates
- make ratio comparisons or changes, e.g. scales
- make arrays and combinations
- need products of measures.

Working Towards: Levels 2 and 3

Motivation

My students had been playing a 'Messages' game (see page 14). This game is played in pairs. One student constructs an arrangement of blocks behind a barrier and writes a summary message (in diagrams or symbols) for their partner. The partner then tries to reproduce the arrangement without having seen it. The purpose is to enable students to connect different forms of representation. Inconsistencies between the students' arrangements provide the conflict needed to motivate them to clarify their thinking about the operations and how they represent them.

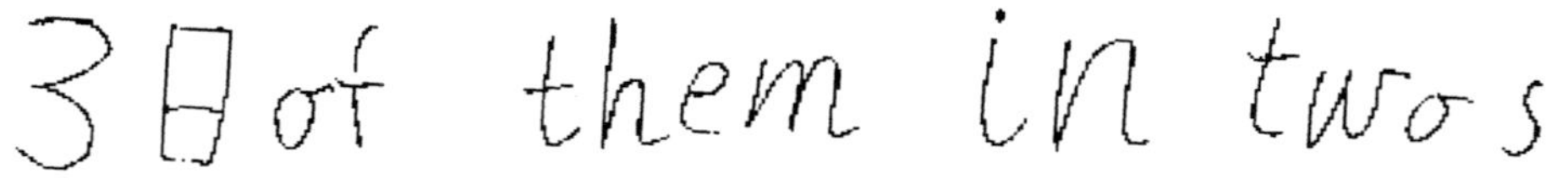

Connection and Challenge

I thought the students would mostly use addition and subtraction situations, but some produced repeated sets and used a multiplication sign to show their arrangement. For example, Anthony's note read 3 x 5 + 2. His partner, Chloe, set out three then five then two blocks, apparently interpreting the x as +. When they compared arrangements, Anthony pointed at the x and told her: *This means three lots of five, not three add five.*

While only a few students used the multiplication sign, I decided that it was a good opportunity to reinforce what some already knew about multiplication, and to develop some preliminary ideas for the others. During the sharing session, students were invited to explain and sort their notes into 'Adds' or 'Take-aways'. I called on Anthony.

Anthony: *Mine's a sort of add but I wrote it the short way. It's a times—3 x 5.*

Chloe: *Yeah, and it tricked me.*

Me: *Anthony, which group does your number sentence belong in?*

Anthony: *Well, it needs another group. It's a times.*

Me: *Chloe, how was it tricky?*

Chloe: *Well, I thought he put three add five, but it was really three times five.*

Me: *What did your blocks look like, Chloe? Draw them on the board.*

Chloe drew both arrangements of blocks on the board. *Mine was like this, but Anthony had his like this—three groups of five.*

Me: *So, how are they different, Chloe?*

Chloe: *I had ten and Anthony had 17.*

Opportunity to Learn

I asked students to 'click' their Unifix blocks together in twos to make seven little bars. Then I asked one student to draw this on the whiteboard, and another to write the quantities for each little bar and to show how he would represent this as a message to his partner. Richard drew arrows between the twos to indicate addition:

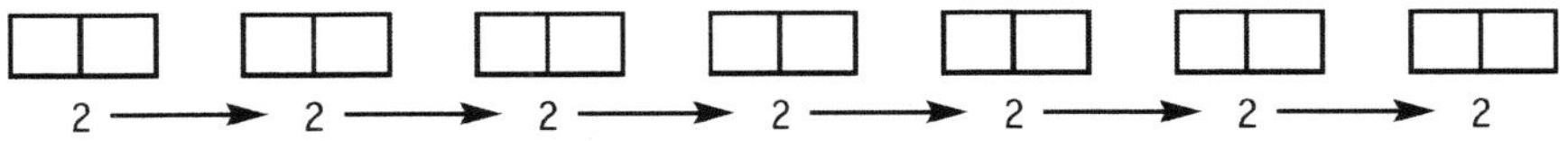

I asked Marilla if she could write a number sentence for her calculator to say how many blocks. Marilla put '+' signs below Richard's arrows:

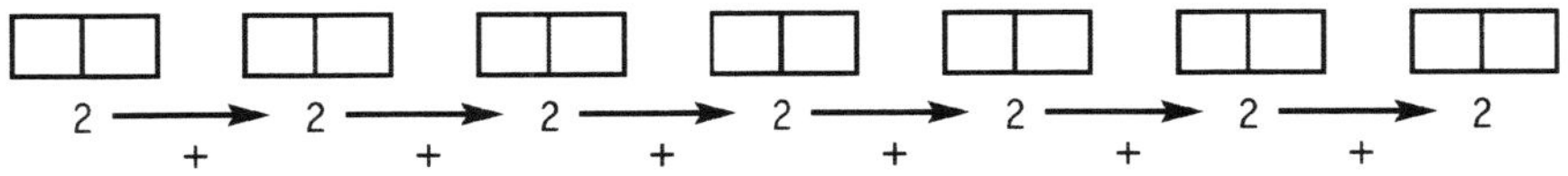

I asked the class how many twos Richard had to write down to show all the blocks, and how many times Marilla had to press **2** on her calculator to add all the blocks. In responding to their count, I took the opportunity to model multiplication language: Yes, there are seven twos; seven lots of two; two taken seven times; so seven times two. I wrote 7 x 2 on the board.

Anthony explained: *That's a short way of writing adds. Instead of two add two add two add two add two add two add two, you just write seven times two, and it's like seven lots of two and you don't get tired when you write it.*

Drawing Out the Mathematical Idea

I wanted the students to focus on the replication rather than simply addition, to emphasise the multiplicative nature of the process.

Me: *What did we do first?*

Students: *We made little bars.*

Me: *Yes, we made little bars. When we made a little bar, how many blocks did we take from the block pile?*

Students: *Two blocks.*

Me: *So, for each little bar you had two blocks. And how many times did we make a little bar?*

Students: *Seven times.*

Me: *We made the little bars seven times altogether. So, you know each little bar is two blocks. How many times did we take two blocks?*

Students: *Seven times.*

Me: *Yes, we took two blocks at once, seven times.*

I then moved on to ask the class to think about how many table legs there were in the classroom. Marilla demonstrated her idea by moving around the room touching each table and saying: *Four, four, four ...*

I asked Marilla if she remembered how many she was up to. She stopped, looked back and counted the tables: *That's one four, two fours, three fours ...* and continued on to seven fours. I then went through a similar conversation for the pairs of blocks, emphasising that the fours were replicated seven times, that there were seven lots of four.

Students recorded 4 + 4 + 4 + 4 + 4 + 4 + 4, and then I asked Chloe if there was a shorter way to write the same thing. Chloe looked confused briefly, but then she wrote 7 x 4. *That means it's there seven times*, she explained. She pointed to the numbers and symbols. *See. Seven times four.*

Did You Know?

Changing the numbers in problems will often expose underlying gaps or misconceptions in students' understanding. For example, students find the following four problems progressively more difficult, even when they can use a calculator for the actual calculation.

Grapes cost $4.90 a kilogram. How much will 4 kilograms cost?

Grapes cost $4.90 a kilogram. How much will 4.2 kilograms cost?

Grapes cost $4.90 a kilogram. How much will 1.2 kilograms cost?

Grapes cost $4.90 a kilogram. How much will 0.3 kilograms cost?

Thinking about multiplication as repeated addition works for the first problem and students at Level 3 will readily multiply by four. Given a calculator, they may also try multiplying for the second problem because it has a 'feel' of repeated addition. That is, it can be thought of as 'four lots and a bit more' and imagined as 'skipping along' or adding four lots and a bit more.

However, the same thinking can act as an obstacle to solving the third and fourth problems, and prevent students from seeing multiplication in the situation. Thus, students at Level 4 will try multiplication for the second grape problem. Given a familiar context where they have a sense of the sort of answer to expect, they will also solve problems like the third but many will struggle with the fourth. Those students at Level 5 consistently solve problems of the above type regardless of the size of the multiplier, as long as the situation is sufficiently familiar that they recognise that a rate is involved.

(**Note:** For diagnostic purposes, the four types need to be presented separately to students, at different times and in different contexts. This way it should be possible to find out whether students recognise multiplication in each situation when there are no other clues to help them.)

KEY UNDERSTANDING 4

Dividing numbers is useful when we:

- ***share or group a quantity into a given number of portions***
- ***share or group a quantity into portions of a given size***
- ***need the inverse of multiplication.***

Students should learn to recognise a wide range of problem types to which division applies. They need to be helped to see how these apparently different types of problems are similar and so can all be solved using division. Examples of these problem types are provided in the Background Notes on page 90. Students who understand the meaning of division can also represent number sentences like $6\overline{)24}$ or 7 ÷ 14 or 4.5 ÷ 0.9 in materials, a drawing, or a sensible story.

Students should learn that the division operation is appropriate for problems where you know the quantity and the number of portions to be formed from it, and you want to find how many or how much will be in each portion. For example: I shared 18 cm of licorice equally between three people. How much did I give each person? These are called partition problems because you know how many parts. They are also informally called sharing problems.

Students should also learn to use division for problems where you know the quantity and how many or how much is to be in each portion, and you want to find out how many portions there will be. For example: I had 18 cm of licorice and gave each person 3 cm. How many people could get licorice? These are called quotition problems because you know the quota. They are also informally called grouping, measuring or repeated subtraction problems.

In the first situation above, the pieces of licorice are 6 cm long. In the second, they are 3 cm long. The situations look different if represented with materials but in each case 18 ÷ 3 is the correct calculation. Students should be helped to see how the situations are linked and, hence, *why* division works for each. For example, the sharing problem, 'Share 18 sweets between three people', can be solved by a grouping strategy. Take out a group of three sweets and say 'one each', take out another group of three and say 'two each'. Continue until the sweets are all gone. Ask: How many lots of three did I take out? That is how many each person gets.

If students associate division mainly with sharing and think of 15 ÷ 5 only as '15 things shared into five groups', they may resist the notion of dividing by fractional amounts. If they associate it mainly with grouping and think of 15 ÷ 5 only as 'how many fives in 15', they may resist dividing a smaller number by a larger number. It is important that problem types vary and different language patterns are used from the beginning.

All multiplication problem types have corresponding division problems. The following problems could be set up as a 'missing number' multiplication or as a division.

- If I ask for $40 worth of petrol and petrol costs 75 cents a litre, how many litres should I get?
- Only 50 people came last week but 125 this week. How many times as many came this week?

The inverse relationship between division and multiplication should receive careful attention. There are division problems associated with rates, ratio comparisons or changes, arrays and combinations and products of measures. Students need experience of all of them.

Students who have achieved Level 2 use materials and diagrams to represent sharing and grouping situations involving whole numbers, and solve simple division problems. However, their thinking may be on the basis of counting and/or subtracting equal quantities and they may not connect the two types of situation. Students at Level 3 have begun to link these two types of division but they may not recognise or even accept the possibility of division where the divisor is the bigger number.

At Level 4, students have enlarged their repertoire and apply their knowledge of division to decimals (for money and measurements), although this will still largely be restricted to whole number divisors. At Level 5, students have developed flexibility with division, and use its inverse relationship to multiplication for each of type of multiplication situation. They use division in situations where the divisors are decimal and fractional numbers, and may be bigger than the number being divided into.

SAMPLE LEARNING ACTIVITIES

Beginning ✔✔

Sharing Situations

Have students use materials or diagrams to model sharing situations, e.g. there are 24 students for six groups, how many students will be in each group; share 15 shapes among five students. Focus on words and strategies such as 'dealing' the 'same amount each time' to 'make equal groups'. Ask students to explain how they shared the quantity. Repeat these activities, grouping collections into small equal groups to find how many groups can be made.

Counting a Collection

Have students count a collection of 25 to 35 objects, and then scatter it. Ask them to then organise and label equal-sized groups, such as threes.

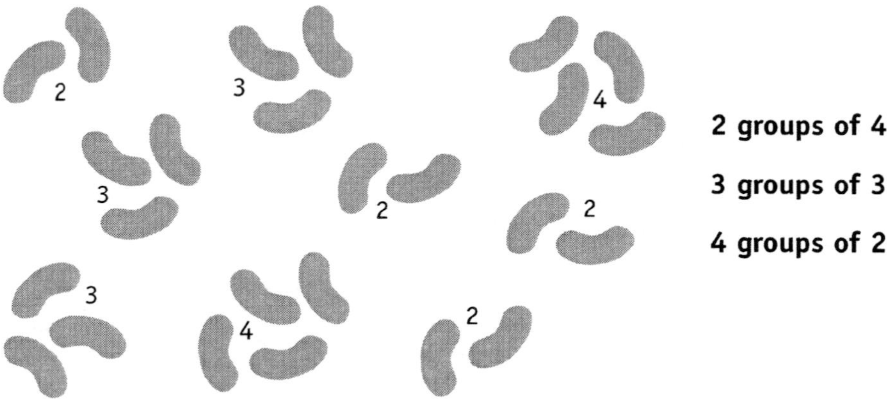

Lead them to summarise the groupings. Ask: How many groups of three/four/one are there? Use this to count again.

Sharing

Use diagrams in real sharing situations to work out group sizes. For example: There are 30 students at school today. We need six new groups. How many will be in each group? Help students to use a diagram, e.g. circles and tally marks to represent the groups and students. Focus on 'share out' and 'deal out'. Ask: What size are the groups? Help students decide on a sensible way to deal with the extras when, for example, only 29 students are at school, and record the result of sharing, say, 29 into six groups.

Grouping

Repeat the previous activity for grouping. For example: 32 students need to work in groups of six. How many groups will there be?'

Sharing Problems

Use grouping to solve sharing problems. For example: Share this chocolate (12 pieces in a 4 x 3 array) between three students, with no leftover pieces. How many pieces will each get? Make the link by asking: How many pieces will I break off to give one piece each? If I break off another three pieces, how many will they each have now? How many strips of three can I break off to share it all out? How many pieces will each have altogether?

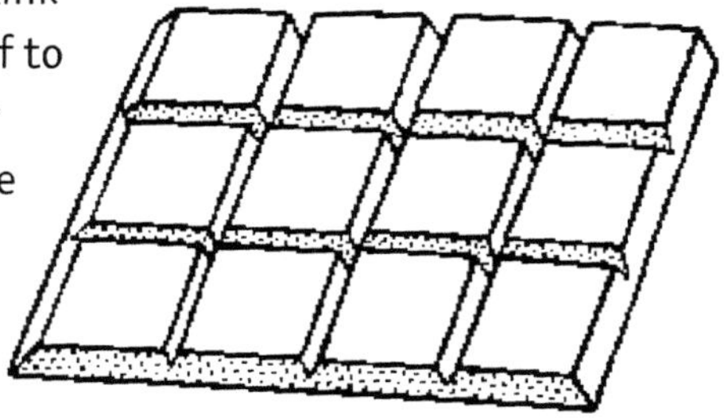

Describing

Look at these problems: We need three straws to make one triangle; how many triangles can I make from 12 straws? I can see eight wheels; how many bicycles? Have students use diagrams and tables to find how many groups.

Recording

Have students read and use both symbols for division:

- For $6\overline{)18}$, read: How many sixes in 18?; sixes into 18; how many sixes make 18?
- For 18 ÷ 6, read: 18 grouped into sixes; 18: how many sixes? Help them to use the division key on the calculator.

Modelling

Have students use materials that closely model sharing and grouping situations, e.g. peg boards or grid paper for array word problems. For example:

- When James packed away the 30 tissue boxes he made each stack five boxes high. How many stacks did he make?
- James made six stacks when he packed away the boxes. How many were in each stack?

SAMPLE LEARNING ACTIVITIES

Middle ✓✓✓

Think Board

Using a think board (see page 87), have students solve problems beginning with a story. For example: 30 students need to form five equal groups, one for each table. How many students should be in each group? Ask: What was it about the story that told you it was a division problem? What does the ÷ sign mean in each example? At other times, begin with a number sentence. Extend into problems involving rates and change. (See page 90 for examples of problems.)

Sharing and Grouping

Ask students to use a think board to solve these problems.

- Sharing: 48 emus are placed into six paddocks. Find out how many emus are in each paddock.
- Grouping: organise 48 emus into paddocks, with six emus per paddock. Find out how many paddocks will be needed.

Ask: How are these two problems are the same and different? What number sentence could be used? Why are the numbers in that order? What does the ÷ sign show?

Calculator

Have students use a calculator to solve sharing and grouping problems (see page 90 for examples). After they have done several, ask them to pretend the ÷ key is broken and find another key to use to solve the problems. Ask: How does the symbol you chose relate to the division operation?

Less in a Group

Ask students to use materials to see that when sharing there will be less per group as the number of groups increases. For example:

- Would you rather be in a group of five students who share 30 sweets, or a group of three students who share 30 sweets?
- In *The Doorbell Rang* (Hutchins, 1986), look at how the number of biscuits changes each time more people arrive and why.

Sharing Strategies

Have students use groups of materials such as beans and cubes to solve a sharing problem. For example, to share a raffle prize of $36 between four students, make one group of four (saying 'that's $1 each'), make another group of four ('that's $2 each'). Continue grouping in this way. Ask: How much does each student get? Is the answer the number of groups or the number of dollars in each group? Ask students to use a division sentence to represent the original sharing problem and then a division number sentence to represent the grouping strategy. Draw out that thinking about the problem as a sharing or a grouping problem will give the same division number sentence and the same result. Repeat activities such as this by having students use a grouping strategy to solve similar problems.

Array Model

Use an array model to help students see how one problem can be solved by grouping or sharing. For example: There are 24 trees planted in four rows. How many trees in each row? There are 24 trees with six in each row. How many rows of trees? Both problems can be represented by a 4 x 6 array.

Changing Quantities

Have students work out the effect of changing either the total number to be shared, or the number of groups needing a share. For example, after reading *The Doorbell Rang* (Hutchins, 1986), ask students if you would get more biscuits if there were:

- 3 students sharing 12 biscuits or three students sharing 15 biscuits
- 3 students sharing 12 biscuits or six students sharing 12 biscuits.

Ask: Which situations will always give more per student? Why?

Relay

Challenge students to investigate a problem where division could help but is not obvious, e.g. find out the distance each member of a relay race would have to run in a 26 km marathon relay. Students choose the size of their relay team but it should have between three and ten runners. (See Sample Lesson 2, page 48.)

Sharing Diagrams

Have students draw a diagram to help solve problems such as sharing three bars of chocolate among four students. Ask them to write a number sentence to show what they did. Ask: Why is the answer a fraction?

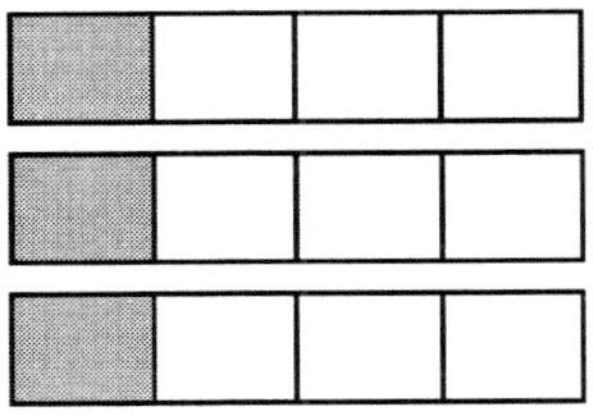

$\frac{1}{4} + \frac{1}{4} + \frac{1}{4} = \frac{3}{4}$

so $3 \div 4 = \frac{3}{4}$

Different Views

Pose the following problem. James saw 9 ÷ 3 and 3 ÷ 9 written on the board and said, *That is nine divided by three, and three divided into nine, so they are the same*. Is he right? Carrie said, *You can't do 3 ÷ 9 because nine is bigger than three*. Is she right? Sam said, *You can do both but they are not the same*. Ask students to say who they agree with, and to explain their thinking.

SAMPLE LEARNING ACTIVITIES

Later ✔✔✔

How Many Each?

Have students group to solve sharing problems, e.g. predict what each share will be if 420 sweets are to be shared between 12 students. Ask: How many will I need to pull out for students to get one sweet each? What if I pull out another round of 12, how many each? How many have I used up so far? How many groups of 12 will I need to pull out to share all the 420 sweets? How many will each student have? (Note the number of groups gives the number in each share.)

Catering Problem

Ask students to use the grouping approach to sharing described in the previous activity to solve catering problems, e.g. there are 125 mini pizzas and 30 students. How many each pizzas for each student? If they have one each, that is 30 gone (pull out a group of 30); if they have two each, that is 60 out (pull out another group of 30) and so on. Ask students why a caterer might prefer to pull out groups of 30 rather than make 30 piles.

Multiplication and Division

Have students use the relationship between multiplication and division to represent sharing problems in symbols. For example: How many pens will each student get if 24 are shared between six students? Ask students to paraphrase to come up with each of the following number sentences: $24 \div 6 = \square$; $\square \times 6 = 24$; $6 \times \square = 24$. Ask: Which number sentence best matches the question? Which number sentence matches the way you might calculate the answer using your tables? Which matches the way you'd get your answer using your calculator? Explain how one relates to the other.

Sharing or Grouping

Ask students to investigate division problems to distinguish the actions of sharing and grouping. Include decimal fractions and common fractions and numbers between zero and one. Have a range of division word problems written on cards:

- If 21 litres of juice is bought for the class of 28 students, how much will they get each?
- How many students will get 0.75 litres of juice from a 21-litre container?

Ask pairs of students to classify the cards according to whether they are sharing or grouping situations, and give reasons for their classifications. Have them say the number sentence required to solve the problem.

Target Division

Play the game in the 'Did You Know?' activity on page 61, varying it by only using the division sign.

Think Board (1)

Present a range of problems requiring a number sentence such as 5 ÷ 8. Ask students to use materials (e.g. paper strips, modelling clay, straws) or a diagram to solve the problems, and to give their answer as a fraction. For example:

- Jana needs to cut a 5 m length of wood into eight equal parts. How long will each part be?
- Mario is serving five pizzas equally to eight people. How much will each get?

Ask students to explain how they thought about breaking up the materials. Why is the answer $\frac{5}{8}$ in each case? Is it a coincidence that the numbers in the question are the same as those in the answer? Draw out that five things shared into eight parts is $\frac{5}{8}$ each, $5 \div 8$ is $\frac{5}{8}$, and $\frac{5}{8}$ means $5 \div 8$. Ask students to present the link between sharing division and the fraction notation on a think board (see page 87).

Think Board (2)

Have students explore the link between grouping division and the fraction notation on a division think board (see page 88). Ask them to write sensible problems for:

$1 \div \frac{1}{2}$	$1 \div \frac{3}{4}$
$1 \div \frac{2}{3}$	$1 \div \frac{5}{8}$

Students should then draw diagrams to represent the problems and explain their thinking. For example, for $1 \div \frac{2}{3}$, they write 'How many $\frac{2}{3}$ m lengths of ribbon are there in one metre?' and draw:

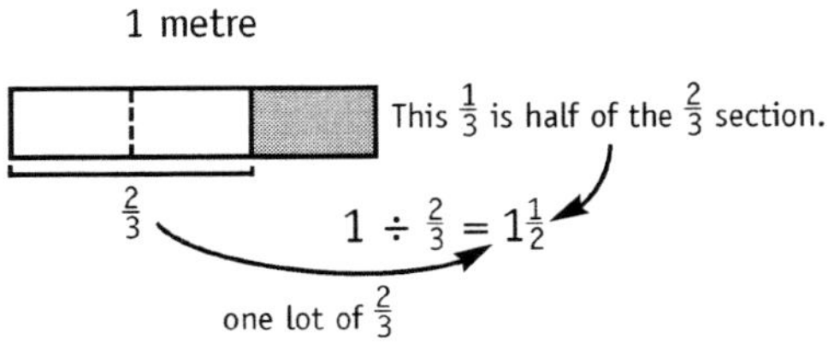

They explain: *There is one full $\frac{2}{3}$ m length, and a third of a metre left over, but that is half of a $\frac{2}{3}$ m length. So there are one and a half lots of $\frac{2}{3}$ m.* $1 \div \frac{2}{3} = 1\frac{1}{2}$ or $\frac{3}{2}$. Students investigate other problems and explain why $1 \div \frac{2}{3} = \frac{3}{2}$, $1 \div \frac{3}{4} = \frac{4}{3}$ and $1 \div \frac{5}{8} = \frac{8}{5}$.

KU 4

SAMPLE LESSON 2

Sample Learning Activity: Middle—'Relay', page 45

Key Understanding 4: Dividing numbers is useful when we:

- share or group a quantity into a given number of portions
- share or group a quantity into portions of a given size
- need the inverse of multiplication.

Key Understanding 9: We make assumptions when using operations. We should check that the assumptions make sense for the problem.

Working Towards: Level 3

Teacher's Purpose

I gave my Year 5 class the following task because I wanted to extend their understanding of division to situations in which division was not explicit.

> *Find out the distance each member of a relay race would have to run in a 26 km marathon relay. You may choose the size of your relay team but it should have between three and ten runners.*

The task was designed so that:

- whatever the size of the team, there would be a remainder to deal with
- it could be easily completed using division and a calculator, but would be difficult using materials and trial and error
- it had two unknown aspects (the number in each team, the distance each runner would travel), which the students had to deal with.

Action

I was surprised by what students did. Adam decided each runner should travel 4 km. He marked off lots of 4 km on a number line and counted the number of runners, but was then baffled by the extra two kilometres.

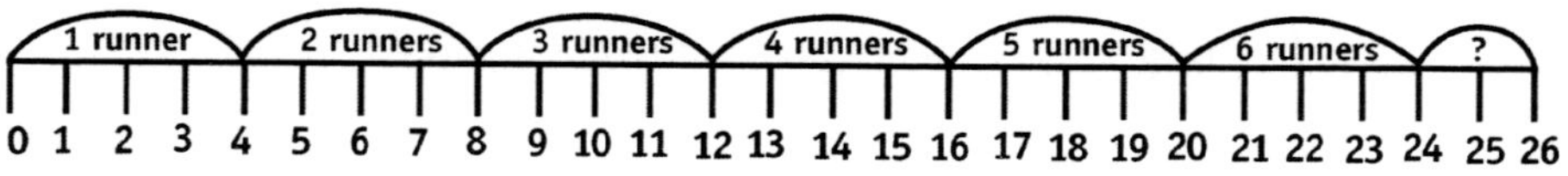

Shari used a tape measure, pretended centimetres were kilometres and skip-counted in 5 km lots, tallying the number of runners as she went. When she had 1 km left over, she started again with 4 km, then 6 km and 7 km. She finally decided 5 km was closest and asked if she could change the length of her marathon so that five runners ran 5 km each.

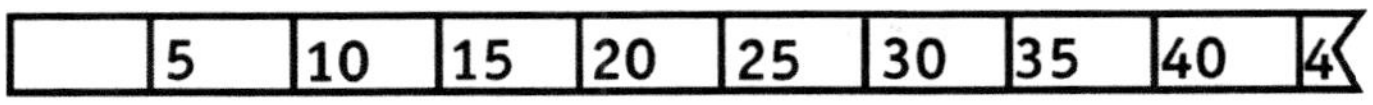

5, 10, 15, 20, 25... ~~||||~~ 5 runners (1 km left)
4, 8, 12, 16, 20, 24... ~~||||~~ | 6 runners (2 km left)
6, 12, 18, 24... |||| 4 runners (2 km left)
7, 14, 21... ||| 3 runners (5 km left)

Raymond chose blocks to represent kilometres, and attempted to group these so that he could choose a team of runners who would do the same number of kilometres each. He became frustrated after exhausting all the possibilities, saying: *It doesn't work out evenly. There's always leftover bits.*

I had assumed students would decide the team size and share the distance among the team. But most chose a whole number of kilometres for each runner and then tried to work out how many runners there would be. They didn't think about their assumptions or about what made sense in the situation. My second surprise was that, although most knew a division procedure with remainders, and all could confidently use a calculator, only one saw right away that division would help.

A few students did take a sharing approach. They folded a 26 cm tape in two, then refolded it to make four or eight equal sections, saying four runners or eight runners would go 'that far' each. But even they didn't start with the idea of choosing the number of runners. It was more that folding the tape seemed like a good thing to do.

Connection and Challenge

I asked the students to think about what they could do with their 'leftover bit'. Some thought one runner could run a bit more or less than the others, but I explained that in relays everyone had to run the same distance.

I suggested they explain to their partner how many people would be needed if each ran 6 km. I asked for comments and we agreed that four people would be too few but five too many. *Oh well,* I said, *We'll make the teams have four and a bit runners!*

This comment got a laugh. When I asked what was funny, several students said: *You can't have part people.*

Well, I said, *if we know the number of people has to be a whole number, couldn't we start with that?*

We thought about what would happen if there were just two runners, and students easily concluded each would run 13 km. At this point, students started to see that splitting the distance equally between the runners was a possibility. *Maybe all the runners could run a tiny bit further to make up the extra*, Casey suggested. Everyone seemed to see the sense of this. To focus their thinking I asked them to tell their partner what we had decided and why, and then to write it down in their own words. Most were able to say that the number of runners had to be a whole number but, to my surprise, still did not recognise that division could help.

I asked them to write it in their own words because I wanted all the students to think about the assumptions they were making and whether they made sense.

Further Action

I asked the students to use paper tape marked in 26 units to approximate the distances run for teams of three, four and five runners. As soon as they all had some results, I wrote on the blackboard a consensus of the distances each runner would have to travel, using students' own language.

3 runners — 8 and a half km and a bit more

4 runners — 6 and a half km

5 runners — 5 km and a tiny bit

To deal with the fact that they didn't choose division, I wrote my big question on the board:

Is there a way to use numbers instead of the tape to share out the kilometres between the runners?

As the students began working, I noticed that many brought out their calculators and a few had actually divided 26 by the team size. I decided not to draw attention to this yet, but asked everyone to use their calculators to help them find a 'mathematical instruction' that would work for this.

In this classroom, the students used calculators that dealt with both decimals and fractions. This made this task much simpler than if the calculator only dealt with decimals. However, depending upon their previous experience, students may be able to check the fractions by adding along a number line, or by changing the fraction to a decimal. These strategies may be more suitable for students requiring 'Later' activities.

Reflection

After a short time, I asked if anyone had anything to share. Sharon volunteered and wrote 4 x 6.5 = 26 on the board. She explained: *It's what my four-runner race is. The 6.5 is six and a half and that's how far the runners did, and I timesed it by four and got 26, and 26 is the whole race. But, I don't know how to do it for the other one. I can't put in 'five and a bit'.*

Kim was keen to show that 26 ÷ 4 = 6.5 worked better. I asked him to explain what he meant.

It's like sharing out, dividing out like 26 between four, that's how many on the team, and then it tells you 6.5 km they go. It's better because you can do it for the other ones, too. When you divide, you don't have to know what that number is [i.e. the distance each runner travels]. *The calculator will do it.*

Students should also develop the more general idea that whenever a quantity is divided into equal parts, the number of shares or parts must be a whole number but the size of each share or part need not.

Drawing Out the Mathematical Idea

We then jointly wrote Kim's instruction on the board: 'Number of km in the race ÷ Number of runners = Distance each runner goes. For this problem: 26 ÷ Number of runners = Distance each runner goes.'

Everyone tried it out for their three- and five-runner teams and we wrote the results in decimals and fractions. I then focused the students' attention on whether the numbers made sense. I used their tapes and a fraction number line to help them connect 8.6666 to their earlier approximation of '8 and a half and a bit more', and 5.2 to '5 and a tiny bit'.

The students used division to find the distances for other team sizes and compared their results with approximations using the 26-unit tape. So that the key mathematical points were not lost in all the calculating, I gave the students a minute to decide on two or three things that really helped us solve the problem in the end. Then, I drew out two points through discussion:

- First, thinking about what made sense in the situation was important because it helped us realise that it was the runners rather than the distance that had to be a whole number.
- Second, using division was much easier than trying to do it with tape and other materials.

Did You Know?

Students may think that $6 \div 18$ is the same as $18 \div 6$, read them as 'six into 18' and '18 shared into six' respectively, and think the answer to each is three. The rule they use is 'you always divide the bigger by the smaller'. Many resist dividing a bigger number into a smaller number. Other students will read division statements in the order in which they come so that they think $6\overline{)18}$ is the same as $6 \div 18$.

A Diagnostic Activity

Make a set of cards using two different pairs of numbers (say, 5 and 15; 12 and 4) with cards for each of the four possible division sentences for each pair of numbers: $5 \div 15$, $5\overline{)15}$, $15\overline{)5}$, $15 \div 5$, $12 \div 4$, $4\overline{)12}$, $12\overline{)4}$, $4 \div 12$. Make cards with a variety of word problems involving either 5 and 15 or 4 and 12 (see Background Notes, page 90). Ask students to sort the word problems into piles. Then ask them to put the number sentences that can be used to solve that pile on top of each.

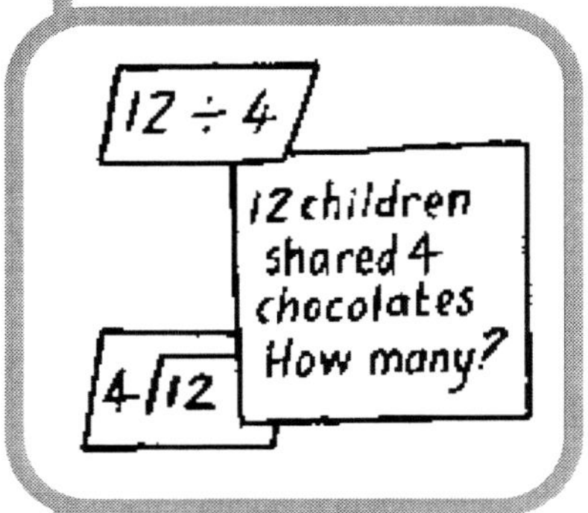

Some students will only have two piles, others four and others eight. If students put all the problems involving the same pair of numbers together, suggest that they think about whether the answer to these problems should be bigger than or smaller than one and sort according to that. Use the conflict this may produce as a basis for discussion. If students correctly sort the problems but label them with the inappropriate number sentences, have groups of students debate what each of the signs mean, how they are entered on a calculator, and so on.

KEY UNDERSTANDING 5

Repeating equal quantities and partitioning a quantity into equal parts helps us relate multiplication and division and understand their properties.

Linking the two ideas of repeating equal quantities and partitioning a quantity into equal portions can help students to understand the connection between multiplication and division. Therefore, it is an important component of their being able to use multiplication and division flexibly to solve problems.

Early understanding of multiplication and division with whole numbers requires students to think about three quantities: the whole (or total) quantity, the number of equal groups, and the amount in each group. If the whole quantity is unknown, multiplication is required. Students have to think about forming equal groups or quantities and then repeating or replicating those quantities a given number of times. If one of the other quantities is unknown, division is required. Students then have to think of taking a whole quantity and partitioning it into a given number of portions or portions of a given size. When we are dealing only with whole numbers, these processes produce the multiples and factors of numbers that are developed in Reason About Number Patterns, Key Understanding 6, and Calculate, Key Understanding 3.

Multiplication is more difficult to conceptualise when the multiplier is not a whole number. Students have to be able to expand their thinking about multiplication from three lots of four, or three of a quantity of four, to include the idea of one-third lot of four, or one-third of a quantity of four. Even though multiplication is formally involved, the operation becomes essentially one of division. Finding one-third of four is the same as dividing (partitioning) four into three equal portions. In practical terms, sharing four chocolate bars between three people could be done by giving each person one bar, splitting the remaining bar into three parts and giving each person one part. We might give each person one-third of each bar.

Other practical partitions are also possible:

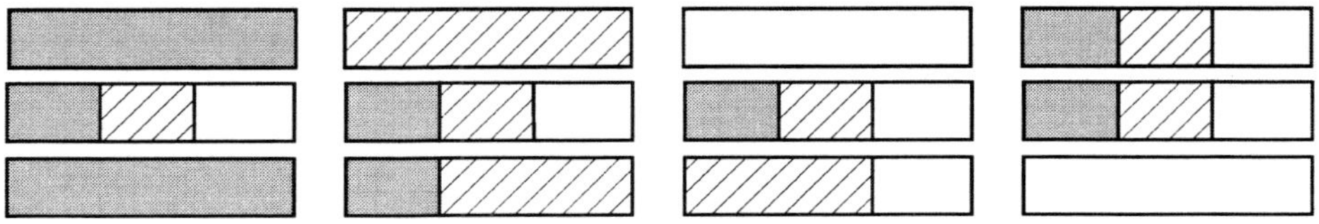

So: $\frac{1}{3}$ x 4 is $\frac{4}{3}$ or $1\frac{1}{3}$

Thus, multiplying by a number that is less than one produces a 'smaller' answer. The three ideas of multiplication, division and fractions are closely related.

In the following arrangements, the amount in each portion and the number of portions are different, so that two different multiplications are involved—eight taken three times and three taken eight times:

Nevertheless, the products are equal. That is, the operation of multiplication is itself commutative. In concrete terms, three groups of eight is different from eight groups of three, but the total quantity 3 x 8 will always be, *must be*, the same as 8 x 3. An array diagram can help students to see why it must be so:

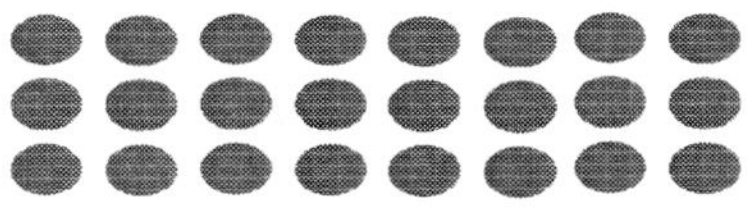

Arrays can also help students understand the distributive property. Thus, students can see that an array can be split into parts without changing the total:

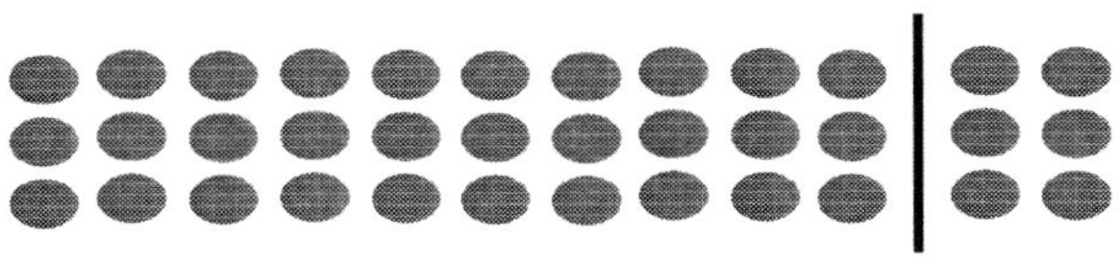

3 x 12 = (3 x 10) + (3 x 2)

Experimentation and recording alone is unlikely to be enough to develop this Key Understanding. The joint idea of repeating equal groups and partitioning into equal groups, and the associated idea that a number can be decomposed and recomposed into its factors in a number of ways without changing the total quantity, must be drawn from the activities.

SAMPLE LEARNING ACTIVITIES

Beginning ✔✔

Describing Arrangements

Have students make arrays to show commutativity. Ask students to make cards showing coloured squares, dots, stars or animals arranged in equal rows and columns. They should then describe the arrangements and write a label for each card, e.g. Colin has made five rows of three. Ask students to rotate each card and describe the arrangement from that view. Ask: How do you know if there are still the same number?

Describing Quantities

Ask students to group materials such as beans and cubes to count more efficiently and describe quantities in different ways. For example, when making arrays, ask students to describe the numbers of rows and columns, e.g. *I saw four rows with three in each row. I've used four, three times.*

Composite and Prime Numbers

Have students arrange materials such as beans and cubes to work out all the possible different equal groups that can be made from a given number. For example: There are 30 students here—could we have equal groups for news telling today? What size groups could there be?

Grouping Summaries

Following the previous activity, ask students to make diagrammatic displays of the possible groupings if some students are absent. Have students summarise the groupings, e.g. *For 29 we can only have a group of 29 or groups of ones. There are no other equal groups in 29. For 27 we can have groups of nines, and threes.*

How Many?

Have students investigate collections of everyday objects and say how their arrangements help them to see how many there are, e.g. egg cartons, muffin trays, packets of stock cubes. For example, they might say, *I saw four rows with three in each row.* (Link to Calculate, Key Understanding 3.)

Halves and Quarters

Investigate practical situations where a smaller number of items is to be shared between a larger number of people. For example: Here are two slices of bread. If each student gets a half a slice, how many students will this feed? Will there be more pieces or fewer pieces if we cut the two slices into halves? Ask students to model the problems and explain what they did and found. Repeat for quarters and for other situations. For example: Eight children need to have an equal share of two apples. How much of an apple will each child get?

More or Less

Have students use materials such as play dough to model simple situations that connect multiplication and division. For example: Sven ate four sandwiches. Nikki ate twice as many sandwiches as Sven. Sharn ate half as many sandwiches as Sven. Ask: Who ate more and who ate less than Sven? How do you know? What did you have to do to find out? (Link to Understand Fractional Numbers, Key Understanding 3.)

Retelling

Retell or make up class versions of stories about giants, for example, *Jack and the Beanstalk*, adding bits that describe how many steps Jack has to run for each giant step. Students mark out three giant steps by making one giant step equal to, say, four of their own. Ask: How many steps will you take to show six giant steps (e.g. six lots of four steps)? What about half a giant step? Have students then represent these, using little cubes for their own feet.

SAMPLE LEARNING ACTIVITIES

Middle ✓✓✓

Jugs

Organise students into groups, and have each group work out how many little cups it takes to fill a jug. They then take a number (say, seven) of identical jugs and fill them. Ask: Is it possible to say how many cupfuls that would be? Model the process with students by asking: Do you need to measure the cups in each jug? How many cups are there in each jug (say, four cups)? So there are four cups in each jug, and how many times did we take four cups (seven times)? So we took four cups, seven times; we took seven lots of four cups. Have students draw a picture and record: Seven lots of four cups. 7 times 4. 7 x 4.

2D Shapes

After completing the previous activity, have students say how many hexagons will cover a pattern block shape (e.g. an outline of a shape produced by tracing around five hexagon shapes placed together), then how many trapeziums fit on the hexagon. Use this to say how many trapeziums will fit on the original shape. Focus on the five times two, rather than counting by 2s. Repeat to find out how many blue rhombuses (five times three) and how many triangles (five times six) will cover the same shape.

More or Less than One

Pose the following problem: Six students divide 18 bars of chocolate between themselves. How much will each one get? More or less than one bar? Do you need to work out how many each gets in order to answer the question? What if some students leave early and do not share the chocolates, so there are only four left to share the 18 chocolates? Will those remaining get more or less now? What if the four students had only six chocolate bars to divide between them? Would they get more or less than one each? What if four students had three chocolate bars to share? Discourage students from doing the calculation in order to decide.

Constructing Arrays

Have students construct arrays for a given number using grid paper, geoboard or blocks. Ask them to record each array using two multiplication sentences, e.g. 6 x 4 = 24, 4 x 6 = 24, and two division sentences, e.g. 24 ÷ 6 = 4 and 24 ÷ 4 = 6. Ask: What do each of the numbers show in the array? How is 6 x 4 = 24 the same as 4 x 6 = 24? How is it different? Can we say 24 ÷ 6 = 4 and 24 ÷ 4 = 6 are the same? Why not?

Unknown Number

Ask students to write open multiplication sentences to solve problems, and then say whether the unknown number is the number of groups or the amount in each group. For example: Tanya has five times as many marbles as Jill; if Tanya has 70, how many does Jill have? Or: Jill has five marbles; how many times as many marbles does Tanya have if she has 70? This could be written either as 5 x ☐ = 70 or as ☐ x 5 = 70. Ask students to read their number sentence to others and say how it represents the situation. Ask: What does the missing number represent in each case?

Fraction Problems

Have students use materials, such as paper, or diagrams to solve multiplication problems involving fractions. For example: If 32 students need half a piece of paper each, how many whole pieces of paper will be needed? Ask students to reflect on what they did and record this by writing a description of their thinking. Ask: Which sign can be used to show how you found your answer? How can you decide between multiplication and division? For example: Is it $\frac{1}{2}$ x 32 = 16 or 32 ÷ 2 = 16, or can it be both?

Multiplication and Division Stories

Have students review a collection of different multiplication and division stories (see Background Notes, page 89) and decide whether the unknown number represents the whole, the number of groups or the quantity in each group. Ask: If the whole is the unknown, which operation can be used to work it out? If the number of groups or the quantity in each group is unknown, which operation can be used? Why?

Halving Quantities

Students extend 'More or Less' (see page 55) by using the calculator to work out the results of halving quantities. Ask: What keys can you use to find a half of six? How can you multiply by a half using the calculator (multiply by .5)? How is 6 ÷ 2 the same as .5 x 6?

SAMPLE LEARNING ACTIVITIES

Later ✔✔✔

Small Units

Extend the 'Jugs' activity (see page 56). Have students create groups to count large collections or measure quantities with small units. Present situations where students have to say how many dots there are in a large array, how wide the classroom is in centimetres, or how many eyedroppers of water there are in a jug. Ask students to decide how they could efficiently work out the amount without counting the single units by ones or repeatedly counting the number of units in each group. How would knowing the number in a row and the number of rows in the array help? How would knowing that a medicine cup holds eight eyedroppers help? How would knowing that a metre ruler is the same as 100 cm help? Encourage students to use multiplication to find out how many or how much.

Multiplication and Division

Encourage students to recognise the relationship between multiplication and division. Ask them to draw a 7 x 8 array, and then record multiplication and division number sentences about the array. Ensure that a range of examples are drawn out, e.g. 7×8, 8×7, $56 \div 8$, $56 \div 7$, $\frac{1}{7} \times 56$, $\frac{1}{8} \times 56$.

Arrays

Have students use materials such as beans and cubes to construct arrays, then partition them in different ways and record a number sentence for each. For a 10 x 3 array, they might write $10 \times 3 = (6 \times 3) + (4 \times 3)$ or $30 = (6 \times 3) + (4 \times 3)$. Ask: How can you check that your partner's number sentences match the array they have made without calculating the answer? Which numbers did you use—the number in each row or the number of rows?

More Arrays

Extend the previous activity by posing problems such as: If you had four rows of three blocks and added some more rows to make 11 rows altogether, how many rows did you add? How many blocks did you add? If you had some rows of five and added four more rows of five to make 12 rows of five, how many rows did you start with? How many blocks did you start with?

Which Operation?

When solving the following problems, have students say what is missing—the whole quantity, the number of groups or the number in each group—to justify their choice of operation:

- The grandstand at the show can hold 525 people and has 15 rows of seats. How many seats are there in each row?

- How many students can have six felt pens if there are 55 in the container?
- If 28 students drink about $\frac{3}{4}$ litre of juice each, how much juice will have to be ordered for the party?

Ask: What operation is required when you know the number of groups and the number in each group, but not the whole? What operation/s can be used when you know the whole amount and the number of groups, but not how many in each group? What operation/s can be used when you know the whole amount and the number in each group but not how many groups? Why can some situations be represented with both division and multiplication?

Division Questions

Have students write division questions from multiplication problems. Begin with a multiplication situation such as: Shane's car travelled three times as far as Jenny's. Jenny's car travelled 2 m, so Shane's car travelled 6 m. Ask students to construct two division questions from this multiplication situation. What questions could you ask if you know the whole amount (Shane's distance) but don't know the number in each group (Jenny's distance)? What question could you ask if you know the whole amount but don't know the number of groups (how many times more)?

Equivalent Operations

Encourage students to use equivalent number sentences to make calculating easier. For example: Lizzie needed to work out 56 ÷ 8. She knows her multiplication tables well but does not know her divisions as well. How could Lizzie use multiplication to help her solve the division sentence? Ask students to draw an array or a diagram to show which piece of information is missing (the whole amount, the number of groups or the number in each group) and explain why they can work it out either way.

Fractions

Use pizza-sharing activities where three pizzas are shared between four people to draw out the idea that if anything is shared between three people, each person gets one third of it. Therefore, 2 ÷ 3 is the same as $\frac{1}{3}$ of 2. Have students demonstrate with materials (e.g. paper, fruit, modelling clay), diagrams and a calculator with fraction functions, that 4 ÷ 5 is the same as $\frac{1}{5}$ of 4 and $\frac{1}{4}$ of 3 is the same as 3 ÷ 4.

Factors

Set students a target number such as 105 and ask them to use their calculator to test whether various numbers are factors. Many will use 'guess and check', that is, to test whether 13 is a factor they will guess what you would multiply 13 by to get 105 and test it with their calculator. Challenge them to find an easier way and draw out that they can use the inverse relationship between division and multiplication, e.g. 105 ÷ 13 = 8.07 so 13 is not a factor; 105 ÷ 15 = 7, so 15 is a factor. (Link to Reason About Number Patterns, Key Understanding 6.)

Later ✔✔✔

Sharing Problems

Have students group to solve sharing problems, e.g. predict what each share will be if 420 sweets are to be shared between 12 students. Ask: How many will I need to pull out for 12 students to get one sweet each? What if I pull out another round of 12, how many each? How many have I used up so far? How many groups of 12 will I need to pull out to share all the 420 sweets? How many will each student have? Note that the number of groups gives the number in each share. (See 'Sharing Problems', page 43.)

Rewriting Number Sentences

Pose problems with larger and more complex numbers so that students see a reason for rewriting a number sentence in a different but equivalent form. For example: two 2 L (4000 mL in total) containers of juice were emptied into 16 large glasses. How much was in each glass? Students record the possible number sentences and say which they prefer to use and why: $16 \times \square = 4000$ or $4000 \div 16 = \square$.

Did You Know?

Many students have a strong conviction that multiplication makes bigger and division makes smaller. This early and partial understanding is reasonable for multiplying or dividing by whole numbers, where multiplying does make bigger and dividing smaller. It can, however, develop into a misconception when students continue to believe and apply these rules in situations where they need to multiply or divide by fractional numbers less than one.

Target—A Diagnostic Game

How to Play:

- Player 1 enters any number onto the calculator.
- Player 2 has to multiply this by another number so that the answer will be as near to the target number, 100, as possible.
- Player 1 multiplies this new number, trying to get nearer to 100.
- The players take turns until one player hits the target by getting 100.------.

Player	Keys pressed	Display
1	64	64
2	x 1.5	96
1	x 1.2	115.2
2	x 0.9	103.68
1	x 0.9	93.312
2	x 1.08	100.7769
		WINNER!!

Many students playing this game for the first time will believe that Player 1 has lost as soon as he or she gets 115.2, since they cannot conceive of being able to 'get smaller' through multiplying. The game itself helps students to overcome this misconception if you challenge them to find a way to continue.

Other students, when they have to act on a number such as 96, will think that, since they only need a 'little bit' more, they need to multiply by a little bit. They may choose something like 0.4 and be very shocked to find the answer is 38.4. They expect the answer to always be bigger and in this case, be bigger by a little bit. They are probably thinking additively rather than multiplicatively.

'Target' can also help overcome the related division misconceptions by using division only (see 'Target Division', page 47). This game is also an excellent tool for improving students' estimation skills. (See Calculate, Key Understanding 8.)

KEY UNDERSTANDING 6

The same operation can be said and written in different ways.

The concise way in which mathematics is written has many advantages. However, it makes it different from and, in some ways, more difficult to read and write than more narrative forms of text. Learning to read, write and say mathematics is an important part of learning mathematics. Students need to:

- relate special mathematical forms and symbols to everyday language
- recognise the various symbols used to represent the operations of addition, subtraction, multiplication and division
- know when and how the symbols are used, e.g. $35 \div 7$, $\frac{35}{7}$ and $7\overline{)35}$ all mean the same thing, but $35 \div 7$ is not the same as $7 \div 35$.

Students need to practise moving in both directions between the reduced symbolic forms and the various alternative everyday language forms, both oral and written, for example:

12 – 5
twelve take away five
twelve subtract five
the difference between 12 and 5
5 from 12

6 x 4
six multiplied by four
six times four
the product of six and four
four lots of six
four groups of 6

Students who have achieved Level 2 can use the range of alternative everyday expressions for addition and subtraction; those at Level 3 can do this for each of the four basic operations interchangeably.

SAMPLE LEARNING ACTIVITIES

Beginning ✔✔

Packing Away

Focus students' attention on the words that describe the actions they use when packing away equipment and materials. For example: put with, took out, added, missing, two more, another, as well as, separate, subtract, plus, and, the same. Help students link their terms for joining, separating and equalising to 'add', 'put together', 'subtract', 'take away', 'make equal' and 'make the same'.

Equal Groups

Have students make a poster of things that occur in equal groups, e.g. rows, bunches, lots, stacks, lines. Draw attention to different situations with the same numbers. For example, say: Three groups of four students make 12—that's three lots of four; three stacks of four boxes makes 12 boxes altogether—that's three lots of four as well.

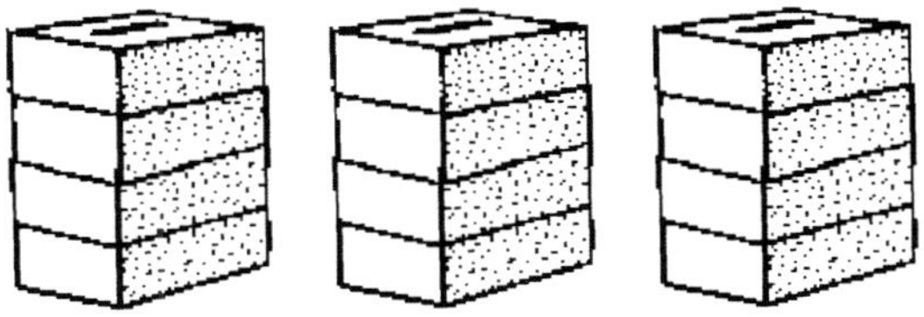

Number Stories

Have students make up a story for a given number sentence, e.g. 6 x 4, 2 + 4, 6 ÷ 3, 6 – 5. Some students may need to be given a context. For example, after reading *Six Foolish Fishermen* (San Souci and Kennedy, 2000), students could write a story about the fishermen that is represented by one of those statements.

Two for Each

Pose problems that can be described as 'two for each'; 'two, two, two and two'; 'that's four twos'. For example: How can you show how many legs the four birds have? How can you show how many shoes in your group? How can you show how many eyes on the teddies? Have students draw or make models. Focus on 'groups of' and 'lots of'.

Alternative Expressions

Have students use alternative expressions in questions. For example: You had $10 and you spent $6; $10 subtract $6; $10 take away $6; the difference between $10 and $6; $6 from $10.

SAMPLE LEARNING ACTIVITIES

Middle ✔✔

Maths Language

Have students build a chart of language expressions for each of the operations: +, −, x and ÷. For example, for multiplication students might suggest *groups of, half of, times, multiply, lots of, twice as big.*

Read Aloud

Organise students to work in pairs. One reads aloud various number sentences from either a textbook or a card and the other writes the number sentence. Include examples such as 7 + □ = 27 and 12 = □ − 5. Compare the written version with the original to see if they are the same. If not, why? Create a list of the words used for the operation signs. Compare lists with others' to find more words.

Story Problems

Have students work in pairs. One reads aloud a number sentence from a textbook and together, they write a related story problem. Ask students to use different words for the operation by referring to the list made during the previous activity.

Saying Symbols

Ask students to show problems such as 'How many 19s in 677?' in symbols, and read what they have written. Draw attention to how 677 ÷ 19 may be said as '677 divided by 19' but is also sometimes said '19 divided into 677' or '19s into 677'. This is NOT written as 19 ÷ 677. (You can also link this to the other division symbol.)

In Other Words

When working on operations, model the use of different words. For example, use 'add, and, plus, with' when reading or saying number sentences involving the addition sign.

SAMPLE LEARNING ACTIVITIES

Later ✔✔

Which Goes with Which?

Provide students with cards that have symbolic expressions and phrases for division using the same pair of numbers (e.g. $100 \div 5$, $5 \div 100$, $\frac{5}{100}$, $\frac{100}{5}$, $5\overline{)100}$, $100\overline{)5}$ five into a hundred, how many fives in 100, five divided by 100). Have students sort these into matching sets. Draw out that there are only two different divisions represented.

Matching Pairs

Ask students to write number sentences or symbols for situations such as: How much juice will each student in a group of eight get from a two-litre container? Which of these is correct: $2 \div 8$, $8 \div 2$, $2\overline{)8}$, $8\overline{)2}$, $\frac{2}{8}$, $\frac{8}{2}$? Draw out which ones match the problem and which do not, and the different order of the digits in the matching pairs.

Everyday Language

Have students read and use alternative everyday language to say what a number sentence means. For example: $3\overline{)18}$ and $\frac{18}{3}$ could each be expressed as 'how many threes in 18' or '18 divided by three'.

Lucky Dip

Play a lucky dip game to read number sentences. Organise students to work in groups of three. Have them make cards to go in three containers:

- one container has cards numbered from zero to five, including fractions and decimals
- one container has cards numbered from ten to 50
- one container has cards showing the four symbols +, −, x and ÷.

Place the three containers of cards in the centre of the group. Each student chooses a card from a different container and together they arrange the cards to make a number sentence. Each student says the number sentence in a different way, e.g. three times 12, three multiplied by 12.

KEY UNDERSTANDING 7

Properties of operations and relationships between them can help us to decide whether number sentences are true.

By using the properties of operations, and connections between operations, we can anticipate the general *effect* of operations on numbers without carrying out the particular calculations involved. This is important for two reasons. Firstly it is an important aspect of number sense. For example, the fact that multiplying by a number less than one makes smaller means that you don't need to calculate to know that 32 x $\frac{1}{2}$ is less than 32, or that 0.3 x 0.2 must be smaller than 0.2 and so cannot possibly be 0.6. This helps us to decide whether results are reasonable and to pick up errors. (See Calculate, Key Understanding 8.) Secondly, it is the basis of algebraic thinking and is therefore an important foundation for further mathematical progress. For example, using *properties of operations* and *relationships between them* means that we can construct and rearrange number sentences into simplified forms that help us solve equations and simplify computations.

Students should use their understanding of properties and relationships to:

- **complete** mathematical statements (without finding the 'answer' to the calculations), for example:

  392 x 5 = □ x 392 (Put in the missing number.)

  14 ÷ 0.7 □ 14 (Put in < or = or >.)

Students should also generate numbers or pairs of numbers that fulfil some constraint, such as, □ – ○ = 17 or □ x ○ = 72, without relying simply upon trial and error (e.g. if 27 – 10 = 17, then 28 – 11 also equals 17 and so too does 29 –12, 30 – 13, 31 – 14 and so on. Students should consider whether they have all the possible numbers or pairs, how many there might be and how they could be sure that they have them all.

- **construct** mathematical statements, for example:

  5 x 26 = 5 x (20 + 6) = 5 x 20 + 5 x 6

  25 x 16 = 50 x 8 = 100 x 4 = 200 x 2 = 400

  I have to solve □ + 47 = 93. It's the same as 47 + □ = 93 and that's easier to work out!

- **check** the truth of mathematical statements, for example:

  273 x 5 = 1065 cannot be right because 273 x 5 > 260 x 5 = 130 x 10 = 1300.

  1024 x □ < 1000 can only be true if □ < 1.

  375 x 18 = 6745 cannot be right because the answer has to be even.

Many students interpret the = sign as 'makes' or as a signal to 'find the answer'. Asked to complete □ + 7 = 12, they may place 5 in the box but nevertheless say that 12 is the answer. Some will find a sentence like □ + 5 = 12 + 3 a nonsense and others will place a 7 in the box. In drawing out this Key Understanding, it is important to emphasise that the = sign means 'is equal to' and that it indicates that both sides of the equation represent the same number.

SAMPLE LEARNING ACTIVITIES

Beginning ✔

Inverse Relationships

See Key Understanding 2 ('Ten in Bed', page 22) for checking the truth of addition and subtraction statements without actually working them out.

Addition

See Key Understanding 2 ('Number Combinations', page 22) for showing that numbers may be added in any order without changing the result.

Missing Number

Have students use materials (e.g. beans, grid paper, cubes) to model open sentences such as 14 + □ = 8 + ○ and say what the missing quantities have to be. Ask: What does the = sign mean?

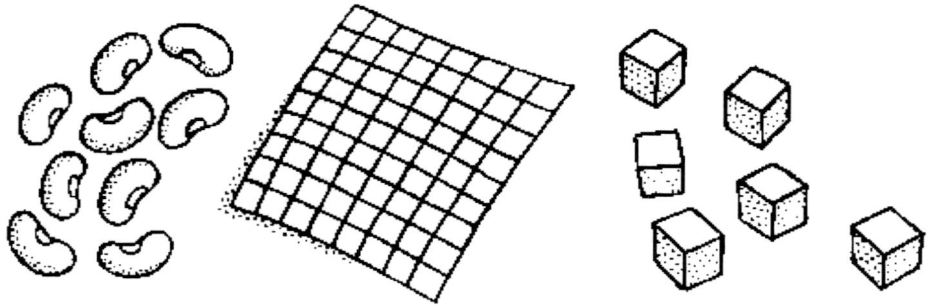

SAMPLE LEARNING ACTIVITIES

Middle ✔✔

Missing Number

Have students use inverses to find a missing number. For example: Use 327 – 118 = 209 to solve 327 – 209 = __; 118 + 209 = __; 209 + __ = 327; 118 = __ – 209 and so on. Ask: How do you know what the numbers must be? (Choose large numbers that discourage students from calculating the answers.)

Inequality Statements

Ask students to write inequality statements such as 4 + 16 < 5 + 16 and show each side using materials. Ask them to decide whether statements involving large numbers (e.g. 197 + 385 < 200 + 400) are true without using materials or calculating.

Equals

Have students read the = sign in open number sentences as 'is equal to'. For example, 18 = __ + 13 is read as, *18 is equal to something add 13*; __ + 6 = 14 + 2 is read as, *something add six is equal to 14 add two*. Ask: What does the = sign mean? What does the missing number have to be?

Extension Activity

Extend the previous activities, and ask students to create complex open sentences for others to solve, e.g. 14 + □ = ○ – 25. Ask: How can you make both sides of the = sign equal the same amount?

Choose Your Numbers

Write numbers on the board, for example:

12	20	21	5	16
4	8	13	26	18

Ask students to choose any three of these numbers to write a true addition or subtraction sentence. Have them share their number sentence. Ask: Does it work? Could you use your numbers again to write other addition or subtraction number sentences? Repeat this activity using multiplication and division.

Today's Number Is...

Have students write different number sentences to make the same total. Encourage them to use what they know about the operations instead of calculating each example separately. For example: If we know 117 – 100 = 17 and 118 – 101 = 17, what would the next one be?

Middle ✓✓

Bigger or Smaller

Ask students to complete number sentences such as:

19 + 32 is .... 20 + 32   47 + 49 is .... 45 + 45

19 + 32 is .... 19 + 30   156 – 19 is .... 156 – 20

47 + 49 is .... 50 + 50   156 – 19 is .... 160 – 19

by writing 'bigger than' or 'smaller than' without carrying out the calculation. Ask them to justify their reasoning to a partner, then check the calculations and revise their thinking if needed.

Easy Check

Extend the previous activity by asking students how they could use sentences like those above to estimate answers. For example: 47 + 49 is less than 50 + 50 and more than 45 + 45, so it is between 90 and 100. Ask: how could this help you check your work? What would you say to a friend who did this:

$$\begin{array}{r} 47 \\ +\ 49 \\ \hline 86 \end{array} \quad \text{or this} \quad \begin{array}{r} 47 \\ +\ 49 \\ \hline 816 \end{array}$$

Bigger, Smaller or Equal (1)

Extend activities such as 'Bigger or Smaller' to include 'equal to' examples formed by rearranging parts. For example:

47 + 49 + 3 is ...... 47 + 3 + 49   56 + 37 is .... 56 + 4 + 33

Bigger, Smaller or Equal (2)

Extend 'Bigger or Smaller' to include 'equal to' examples formed by compensating. For example:

47 + 49 is .... 46 + 50   56 – 19 is .... 57 – 20

72 + 73 + 74 is ....73 + 73 + 73

Have students generate sets of equivalences, e.g. for 47 + 49. Ask: Which changes to the number sentence help calculation? Help students describe the difference between the addition and subtraction lists. Ask: How do you change the numbers for addition? Is this the same or different for subtraction? Think of a simple rule for each.

Multiplication and Division

Repeat the 'Bigger, Smaller or Equal' activity for multiplication and division.

47 x 19 is .... 47 x 10   400 ÷ 19 is .... 400 ÷ 10

47 x 19 is .... 47 x 20   400 ÷ 19 is .... 400 ÷ 20

Checking Work

Give students a set of calculations completed by an imaginary student and ask them, without doing the full calculations, to find those which can't be right (include errors commonly made by students).

SAMPLE LEARNING ACTIVITIES

Later ✓✓✓

What Do You Know?

Have students use relationships between operations to answer: If we know that, what else do we know? Ask them to work out 41 + 41 + 41 = 123. Challenge them to find other number sentences that say the same thing in another way, e.g. 123 ÷ 3 = 41, 123 ÷ 41 = 3, 3 x 41 = 123, 41 x 3 = 123, 123 – 41 – 41 – 41 = 0.

Broken Keys

Invite students to use connections between the operations to deal with a broken calculator key. For example: The division key on your calculator has broken. How can you find the answer to 210 ÷ 7?

Shortcuts

Ask students to check the truth of calculating shortcuts. For example: Sue said to calculate 57 + 99, she says 56 + 100, and to calculate 58 x 99 she says 57 x 100. Is she correct? Why or why not?

Bigger or Smaller

See 'Bigger or Smaller' (page 70) for addition and subtraction, and extend to include decimals and fraction.

For example:

4.73 + 3.56 .... 4 + 3

4.73 + 3.56 .... 4.5 + 3.5

4.73 + 3.56 .... 5 + 4

$\frac{2}{3} + \frac{3}{4}$ .... $\frac{1}{2} + \frac{1}{2}$

$\frac{2}{3} + \frac{3}{4}$ .... 1 + 1

$\frac{2}{3} + \frac{3}{4}$ .... $\frac{3}{4} + \frac{3}{4}$

Bigger, Smaller or Equal

Extend activities such as 'Bigger or Smaller' to include 'equal to' examples formed by rearranging factors.

For example:

25 x 19 x 4 .... 25 x 4 x 19

25 x 36 .... 25 x 4 x 9

Multiplication and Division

See 'Multiplication and Division' (page 70) and extend to include decimal and fraction multipliers and divisors.

For example:

236 x 1.3 236

236 ÷ 1.3 236

236 x 0.3 236

236 ÷ 0.3 236

236 x $\frac{3}{4}$ 236

236 ÷ $\frac{3}{4}$ 236

Later ✔✔✔

Equivalent Statements

Ask students to construct equivalent statements by multiplying or dividing both sides of a number sentence. For example: Continue: 64 x 124 = 32 x 248 = 16 x 496 = ☐. Ask: What is happening to the multiplication sentences? Write a rule about what you have discovered. How does knowing this rule help you work out 5 x 384? Why does it work?

Number Line

Have students use a number line to predict the results of operating on decimals, including those less than one. For example: Draw a large number line from zero to five. Randomly place points labelled A, B, C and D between zero and two. Ask: What numbers could the letters represent? Have students work out approximate solutions to 'letter sentences' such as A + B, D ÷ A, C x D and so on. Ask: What helped you to do this? When did you know that an answer was going to be larger or smaller?

Target Multiplication

Use calculator games to show that multiplication does not always make numbers bigger. For example, play the 'Target' game described in 'Did You Know?', on page 61. Have students play the game and after several rounds, ask: Does multiplying always make numbers bigger? What do you have to multiply by to make your number smaller? What do you multiply by to make your number bigger? Write the rule so you will remember next time you play the game. (See 'Did You Know?', page 61.)

Target Division

Use calculator games to show that division does not always make numbers smaller. Play the same Target game as in the previous activity, but use division and make the target number 30. Vary it by changing the target numbers. Ask: How does the size of the numbers affect the size of the answer? Write the rule so you will remember next time you play the game. (See 'Did You Know?', page 61.)

The Same As

Have students use number strips to interpret the = sign as 'is equivalent to' or 'is the same as'. Begin by writing a number sentence such as 41 + 41 + 41 = on the left side of a long strip of paper. Ask students to write as many equivalent number sentences, e.g. (3 x 40) + (3 x 1) = as they can before writing the answer. Ask students to share their strips by reading their equivalent sentences to others.

Equivalent Statements

Have students use an array representation of a multiplication sentence to construct equivalent statements that will make calculating easier. For example:

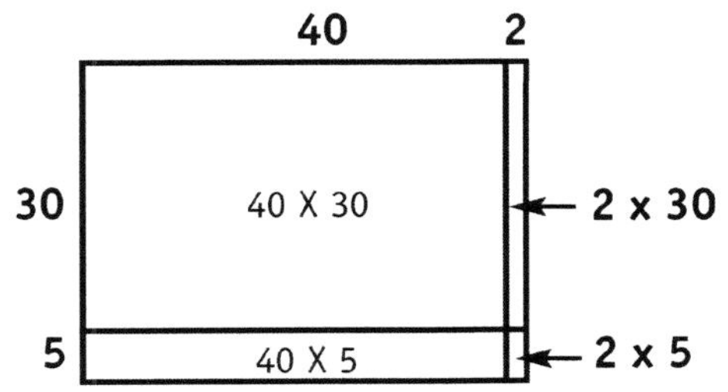

Students divide the grid into sections and label the multiplication needed for each section. Compare number sentences and representations for 42 x 35. Is it easier to calculate a 42 x 30 and a 42 x 5 section or 40 x 30, 40 x 5, 2 x 30, and a 2 x 5 section. Ask: Are there other ways to section your array to make calculating the product easier? (See Background Notes, pages 90 to 93.)

True or False

Ask students to decide why number sentences cannot be true, without doing the calculations. For example: Why is 0.3 x 0.2 not 0.6? (It has to be smaller than either.) Why is 1.2 x 100 not 1.200? (It has to be bigger than 1 x 100.) Why is 3.0 ÷ 10 not three? (It has to be smaller than three.) Why is 3.05 ÷ 10 not 3.5? Why is 1.23 + 3.4 not .157? Ask: What might a student have been thinking to give those answers?

KEY UNDERSTANDING 8

Thinking of a problem as a number sentence often helps us solve it. Sometimes we need to rewrite the number sentence in a different but equivalent way.

To solve everyday problems involving numbers, we have to represent the problem as a number sentence. For example, when we buy two things that cost \$35 and \$17 we have to think of it as '35 add 17 is what?' Students need a lot of experience in representing problems in ways that enable them to be dealt with mathematically. However, for common situations, the process will eventually become almost subconscious.

In some cases, the number sentence we use is a standard one that shows what operation we have to do, e.g. 16 + 7.3 =; 22 x 4 =; 105 ÷ 5 =; 3.9 – 2.4 =. That is, we choose the operation and the solution can be found right away by a calculator (machine or human). The reason we want students to understand the operations is so that they can choose the right one to apply in a range of situations.

In other cases, the number sentence we choose has the unknown quantity embedded within it. For example, for the problem

The 2.5 kg pack of minced meat cost \$12. How much per kilogram is that?

the student might think: *What did they multiply 2.5 by to get to 12?* or *2.5 times what gives 12?* (that is, 2.5 x □ = 12). Here the 'missing multiplier' can't be found by entering the number sentence into a calculator or doing a single mental or written computation. Nevertheless, the number sentence represents the problem and can be solved (see Background Notes, page 90). We could solve it by trial and error or rearrange the sentence. For example, we could use the relationship between multiplication and division to rewrite the sentence: if 2.5 x □ = 12 then □ = 12 ÷ 2.5. This process is the basis of generalised (or algebraic) thinking and its development should be a high priority (see Key Understanding 7, page 66).

Of course, another student might think of the problem immediately as a division, seeing that the price per kilogram is the total cost divided by the number of kilograms (12 ÷ 2.5). It is important that students see these two ways of thinking about the problem as equivalent so they can choose the best approach (see Background Notes, pages 91 to 92). This flexibility depends on students understanding (indeed, trusting) the following:

- Two number sentences are equivalent (that is, mathematically the same) when they represent the same situation.
- It is not necessary to go back to the original situation to know that two number sentences are equivalent; instead we can use properties of operations and relationships between them.

Students need to practise representing problems in reduced symbolic forms. Sometimes, it is complex. For example, the statement 'Dave is six years older than Kim' does not have any obvious linguistic cues to indicate what operations are involved. Students need to be able to say to themselves: *If you take Kim's age and add six, you have Dave's age, so Kim's age + 6 = Dave's age*. Many students will follow the sentence sequence and incorrectly write: *Dave's age + 6 = Kim's age*. They need to learn to make sense of the whole expression and be discouraged from using cue words or translating word for word. (See Background Notes, pages 91 to 94.)

SAMPLE LEARNING ACTIVITIES

Beginning ✓

Money

Re-price the items on a page from a shopping catalogue into whole dollars. Nominate an amount of money for students to spend, and have them choose items from the catalogue. Ask them to use number sentences to show how much they have, what they have bought and what they have left to spend.

Identifying Operations

Have students listen to word problems and identify the operation in the problem. For example: Fran had seven sweets. Tom gave her some more. Now she has 19. How many did Tom give Fran? Ask students to hold up an 'add' or 'take away' sign to show what kind of problem it is. Ask: What was the clue that made you think it was an add/take away? Could we write an addition number sentence for it?

Inverse Relationships

Organise students into pairs so they can practise writing open number sentences using inverse relationships. One student secretly enters a number into a calculator and adds an agreed number, e.g. five. The other student writes the number sentence used, e.g. $\square + 5 = 9$ and rewrites it in a way that can be solved on the calculator, e.g. $9 - 5 = \square$.

Did You Know?

Students require real experience in deciding what operation is needed. Practise on 'word problems' might only appear on pages labelled, say, 'Addition'. Or, there may be other obvious cues so that students do not need to think much about the situation or really choose the operation. In daily life, there may be extraneous information and we have to choose the relevant numbers as well as the operation. Ask students to do the following activity.

Tick the problems for which 379 – 280 would give the answer. Give reasons for your choices.

- ❑ 379 sheep had to be put through the dip. 280 sheep had been dipped by lunchtime. 80 of the sheep were black and 200 were white. How many sheep have still to be dipped?
- ❑ There was 379 kg of dog food stored in the factory's freezer. 280 kg of it was sold to local shops. How much dog food was left for other places?
- ❑ 379 posts are needed for the eastern boundary of the fence line and 280 posts are needed for the northern boundary. How many posts are needed altogether?
- ❑ Maxine finished the car rally in 379 minutes. Her older sister, Jane, finished the rally in 280 minutes. How much longer did Maxine take?

SAMPLE LEARNING ACTIVITIES

Middle ✔✔

Signs

Ask students to hold up a sign that shows the appropriate operation as word problems are read out. Discuss variations when they arise, e.g. if some students show the x sign while others show the + sign. Encourage students to justify their choice. Ask: Could they both be right?

Classroom Situations

Have students write number sentences for situations that arise in the classroom. For example: Everyone needs half a sheet of paper; how many pieces of paper do we need? Ask: How many different ways can this be written as a number sentence?

Best Buy

Have students use a calculator to determine which of several sizes of an item would be the best buy. For example: Is it cheaper to buy two small jars of peanut butter or one large one? Ask students to justify the operations they choose.

Choose the Operation

Ask students to match word problems with given operations. For example: 105 + 7, 105 x 7, 105 – 7, 105 ÷ 7:

- Seven trucks carried 105 sheep each. How many sheep altogether?
- Out of the 105 sheep, seven had not been shorn. How many had been shorn?
- 105 sheep were put into small pens of seven. How many pens were needed for all of the sheep?
- A farmer bought seven sheep to put with his flock of 105. How many sheep does he have now?

Discuss with students the information in each problem that signalled the correct operation.

Numbers and Signs

Have students use numbers and signs to solve problems and compare their strategies with others. For example: If one penguin ate 18 fish and another ate 22, how many more fish did the second penguin eat? Discuss the different number sentences created and how each is related to the original situation. For example, ask: How is $18 + \square = 22$ the same as $22 - 18 = \square$? Which sentence would you use on the calculator? Why?

Middle ✓✓

Fractions and Operations

Extend the 'Choose the Operation' activity (page 77) to include fractions. For example, sharing out three pies among four students. (See 'Sharing Diagrams', page 45.) Ask: How is 3 ÷ 4 the same as □ x 4 = 3? Which sentence would you use on a calculator? Why?

Classifying Problems

Have students look at problems that can be solved using either addition or subtraction and the two number sentences generated for each. Ask: How are the sentences the same? Which operation is most helpful if you were solving these problems with a calculator? Which would you use if solving it in your head? Why? (See 'Classifying Problems', pages 17 and 25.)

Related Numbers

Give students three related numbers and ask them to write as many number sentences as possible. For example, for three, six and 18 students might write 3 x 6 = 18, 18 = 6 x 3, 3 = 18 ÷ 6 and so on. Ask: If the 18 is unknown, which of these can be solved using a calculator? Which cannot? Why? What if the three is unknown, can you solve the same ones with the calculator?

Clarifying Problems

Have students rephrase a problem to clarify it. For example: Casey earns $4.50 per hour for working between 9 a.m. and 5 p.m., and $5.50 per hour when working after 5 p.m. How much did she earn when she worked from 2 p.m. to 10 p.m.? This can be rephrased as: Casey worked three hours at $4.50 per hour and five hours at $5.50; how much did she earn? Ask students how they arrived at a number sentence from the rephrased problem and which sentences are easier solved with a calculator. Ask students to compare their different sentences and say how each is the same.

Story Problems

Invite students to choose a number sentence that could be used to solve a story problem. For example: Jenny finished the car rally in 369 minutes, while her brother Phillip finished it in 283 minutes. How much longer did Jenny take?

369 + 283 = □	□ = 369 – 283	283 + □ = 369
369 – 283 = □	369 + □ = 283	

Ask: Why can the number sentence/s be used to solve the problem?

SAMPLE LEARNING ACTIVITIES

Later ✓✓✓

Equivalent Sentences

Have students use equivalent number sentences to make calculating easier. For example: Lizzie needed to work out 56 ÷ 8. She knows her multiplication tables well but is not fast at division. How could Lizzie use multiplication to help her solve the division sentence?

Problem Solving

Ask students to use different but equivalent number sentences to solve a problem. For example: Two students were trying to solve Miles's problem. He was saving for a CD player costing $169. He had $97 and he wanted to know how much more he needed. Guy worked on this calculation: 97 + □ = 169, while Miles had this: 169 – 97 = □. Ask students to explain to their partners why the calculations were chosen and whether they can both be correct.

Larger Numbers

Pose problems with larger and more complex numbers so that students see a reason for rewriting a number sentence in a different form. For example: A 2 L container of juice was emptied into six large glasses. How much was in each glass? Ask students to record the possible number sentences and say which they prefer to use if an approximate answer is required: 6 x ____ = 2000 or 2000 ÷ 6 = ____ .

Rewriting Problems

Have students rewrite a problem in their own words. Then ask them to progressively find shortcuts to write it: first with words, then with words and symbols, and finally, with symbols alone. For example, for the problem 'The grandstand at the show can hold 525 people and has 15 rows of seats, how many people in each row?', a student might write:

- *The grandstand holds 525 people in 15 rows. How many in each row?*
- *That's 15 rows of how many people are in 525.*
- *15 lots of ____ = 525*
- *15 x □ = 525*
- *525 ÷ 15 = □*

How Much? How Many?

Repeat the previous activity with more complex problems, such as:

- Jesse paid off his computer game on layby, with a $12 deposit and five $16 payments. How much was the game?
- The bus for the excursion will hold 77 adults. If three students can take the place of two adults, how many students will the bus hold?

KU 8

SAMPLE LEARNING ACTIVITIES

Later ✔✔✔

Sorting Sentences

Extend the previous activities to a wider range of problems. Present a problem: Guy's mum told him to cook a roast. She said it needed to cook for 20 minutes, and then 30 minutes for each kilogram. The roast weighed 4.5 kg. How long should Guy cook it for? Have students write a number sentence for the problem on a card. Collect, sort and display the variety of number sentences. Ask students to explain how they paraphrased the problem in their head to come to their number sentence. Ask: Which number sentences will solve the problem?

Matching

Have students decide which number sentences match a word problem. For example: Amanda works at the supermarket for an hour a day for five days of the week and four hours on Saturdays. The pay is $5.50 per hour during the week and $7 per hour on Saturdays. How much does she earn?

(7 + 5.50) x (4 + 5)   (4 x 5) + (5.50 x 7)

(5 x 5.50) + (4 x 7)   (7 x 5) + (5.5 x 4)

Checking Solutions

Invite students to use a different but equivalent number sentence on a completed problem as a good way to check solutions. For example:

- The lawn mower cost $467. Jemma only had $275. How much more did she need? 275 + ___ = 467. Answer 192.
- I have a photo that is 75 cm high, but I want to put it into a photo frame that is only 15 cm high. By how much will I have to reduce my photo? 75 x ___ = 15. Answer $\frac{1}{5}$.

Ask: What number sentences could you key into your calculator to check that your solution to each problem is correct?

Everyday Problems

Have students ask mathematical questions from everyday situations and write number sentences to fit the questions. For example: The year 6s had a 25 L container of cordial to sell to raise money for their school camp. They wondered if they would make more money by using 300 mL cups and charging 50 cents per cup, or by using 200 mL cups and charging 20 cents per cup. The cups were donated. Ask students to list the questions that need to be answered, along with the number sentences required to answer each question.

Choose the Operation

Have students match word problems that use the same pair of numbers to different operations. For example: match 23.5 + 13, 23.5 – 13, 23.5 x 13 or 23.5 ÷ 13 to a set of six or seven problems that use 23.5 and 13 (see 'Did You Know?', page 76).

Exploring Word Problems

Ask students to decide which word problems match a given number sentence and explain why. For example, 12.6 ÷ 3:

- 12.6 L of juice is shared between three groups. How much for one group?
- If you have 12.6 L of juice, how many groups could have 3 L each?
- A marble rolls 12.6 m in three seconds. What is its average speed in metres per second?
- If the marble travels at 12.6 metres per second, how long will it take to travel 3 m?
- Eva put 12.6 mL of red food colouring into a test tube. This was three times as much as the blue. How much blue did she put in?
- A picture has been enlarged three times its original size. If it was originally 12.6 cm high, how long is it now? (Link to Key Understanding 4, Later Sample Learning Activities.)

How Old?

Have students write shortened sentences that combine numbers and words to represent simple relationships between two variables. For example: Maria is two years older than Sam; Andrew is two years younger than Despina; Cameron is twice as old as James.

Unknown Quantity

Ask students to write number sentences to match more complex 'unknown quantity' problems. For example: Two teams of students had 24 balls to share between them. The teacher said that the bigger group was to get six more balls than the other group. How many balls should each group get?

Solving Problems

After solving problems like those in the previous activity, challenge students: You have been asked to write instructions to another class on how to solve problems like this. Their problem will have different numbers, so you have to explain how to solve the problem without using any numbers.

KEY UNDERSTANDING 9

We make assumptions when using operations. We should check that the assumptions make sense for the problem.

Students should think about the assumptions they need to make in order to use an operation. It should be treated incidentally, and questions like those in the Sample Learning Activities asked regularly as students go about their everyday mathematical work. That is, on the whole, special activities will not be needed. Students should be asked such questions, such as: Does multiplying make sense here? What would we need to assume? Will two people really cost twice as much as one? If it is not likely to be exactly right, will it be close enough?

To decide whether using an operation makes sense, students need to understand the operation. For example, they may know that 18 students in the class like pizza and 14 like sausage rolls. But this does not mean that 32 students will be happy so long as both pizza and sausage rolls are provided—as few as 18 might be! Students need to understand that when we add the number in one collection to the number in another collection, the answer will be the number in the combined collection *only* if the two original collections had no overlap. Another example of having to be careful in adding relates to the different uses of the fraction symbol. When we write $\frac{7}{10}$ on a test paper we say 'seven out of ten' and really think of it as two numbers. If we get $\frac{7}{10}$ for Section A and $\frac{8}{10}$ for Section B, we cannot add the numbers $\frac{7}{10}$ and $\frac{8}{10}$ to get the total test result because the two ratios do not show fractions of the same whole. Rather, we add the number right in each section (7 + 8), and the possible number of marks in each section (10 + 10) and record the two results as $\frac{15}{20}$. Students need to understand that adding fractions assumes that the two fractions are each a single number that show parts of the same whole.

Students also need to think about what is sensible or realistic in real life. How well they are able to judge this will depend on how familiar they are with the context in which a problem is set. For example, in deciding whether to multiply, students may need to decide whether it makes sense to assume that it would take ten times as long to run 1000 m as it would to run 100 m. They may think about their own running, or they may do some research and investigate the pace set by sprinters, middle-distance runners and marathon runners.

Thinking about and checking assumptions are important components of the achievement of the Working Mathematically outcome 'Choose techniques and models which fit the constraints in a situation and check and verify their use'. It is also included here as a Key Understanding for two reasons. First, you do not understand the meaning of an operation unless you can tell when you can and cannot use it. Second, on the whole, Working Mathematically outcomes will be developed in the context of learning experiences for each of the other mathematics outcomes.

SAMPLE LEARNING ACTIVITIES

Beginning ✓

Rainy Day

Pose an everyday problem, such as: There are 12 raincoats and four unmbrellas outside. How many people came to school ready for the rain today? Ask students if adding the raincoats and umbrellas will tell them how many students were ready for the rain. Ask: What could we be sure about?

Graphs

When students are graphing, ask questions that focus on whether categories overlap. For example, when graphing pet ownership, ask: How many students have cats or dogs? Some students are likely to add the groups of pets together to find the total. Display the results and ask students to stand if they have cats or dogs at home. Ask: How can that be? Your answer was 18 but only 15 students are standing. Is something wrong?

Remainders

When sharing cakes, sweets and so on, have students decide how to deal with remainders. For example:

- When sharing out the chocolate-coated sultanas between five, would it make sense to cut up the two left over? What should you do with them?
- What could you do if you had four pieces of toast to share between three children? What could you do with the remaining piece of toast?

SAMPLE LEARNING ACTIVITIES

Middle ✔✔

Cats and Dogs

Have students create a book of crazy additions or subtractions showing nonsensical situations. For example: In our class of 25 students, 15 students have a cat and 12 students have a dog. That means at least 27 students have a pet.

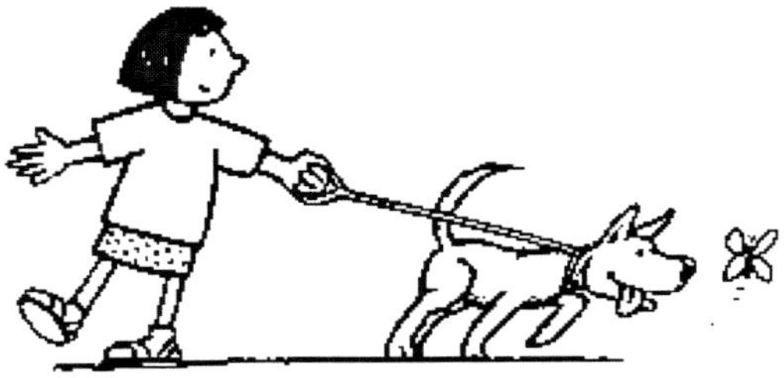

Remainders

Ask students to investigate ways of dealing with remainders. For example:

- Share 48 cans of drink between 23 students.
- 136 students are going on an excursion; how many buses do we need if each one carries 50 students?
- You need 9 m of fabric to make 6 flags; how much fabric for each flag?

Students discuss what to do with the remainder in each case.

Venn Diagram

Have students produce a Venn diagram to show the sports they play out of school hours. Ask: Can we find the total number of students playing sport out of school hours by adding all of the numbers? How can we find what we are looking for when the information provided overlaps?

SAMPLE LEARNING ACTIVITIES

Later ✔✔

Correct Operations

Ask students to identify 'hidden' assumptions in using an operation and decide whether they are sensible. For example, Julia used multiplication for these problems:

- A man can run 1 km in three minutes. How long will it take him to run 6 km?
- One 125 g jar of coffee costs $3.45. How much will a 1 kg container of the same coffee cost?

Ask: What did Julia assume? Are the assumptions reasonable? Can you give a more realistic answer?

Sense or Nonsense?

Have students decide if it is sensible to operate in situations such as: In this illustration, would it make sense to add the shaded parts? Why? Why not?

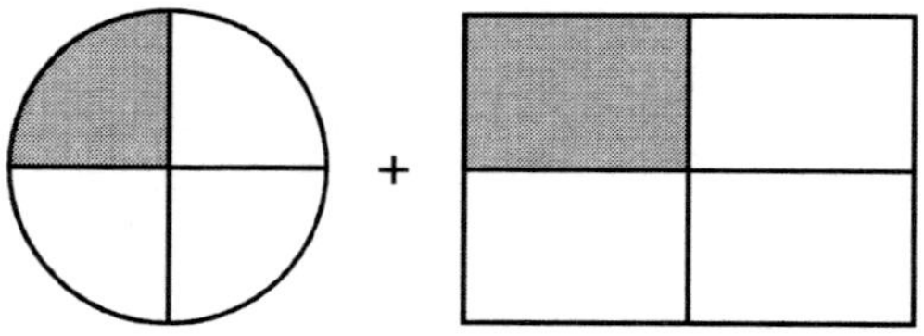

(NB: It is not sensible!)

Or: If you got half of last week's spelling words correct, and a quarter of this week's spelling words correct, would it make sense to add $\frac{1}{2}$ and $\frac{1}{4}$ and say you got $\frac{3}{4}$ of your spelling words correct altogether? Why? Why not? How could you find out what fraction of words you got correct altogether? (NB: You would need to find the total number of words you got correct in the two tests and write that number over the total number of words tested. This ratio tells you the fraction you got correct altogether.)

BACKGROUND NOTES

Representing Word Problems in Ways

Students need to develop a deep understanding of the meaning and use of the four basic operations—of their links to each other and to real-world applications. In order to build up conceptual links between the various types of situations and the addition, subtraction, multiplication and division operations, a rich and flexible variety of representations is needed over an extensive period of time. It should not be rushed.

These various forms of representation include[1]:

- experience-based scripts of real world events or dramatic play
- manipulatives
- pictures and diagrams
- spoken language
- written symbols in number sentences.

Thus, students should describe, represent and explore both additive (addition and subtraction) and multiplicative (multiplication and division) situations dramatically, physically, diagrammatically, verbally and symbolically.

Many teachers have found a 'think board' helps students to link various ways of representing the operations. There are many different versions of, and ways to use a think board. With the simple versions, one problem is dealt with at a time.

Story	**Materials**
If one penguin ate 18 fish and another ate 22, how many more fish did the second penguin eat?	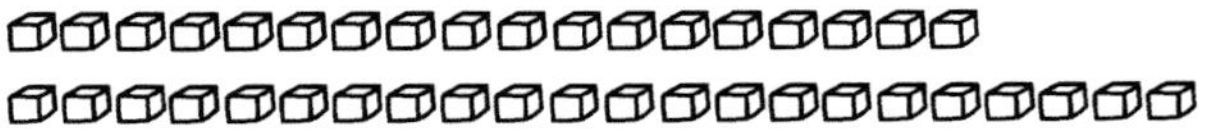
Picture/Diagram	**Number sentence**
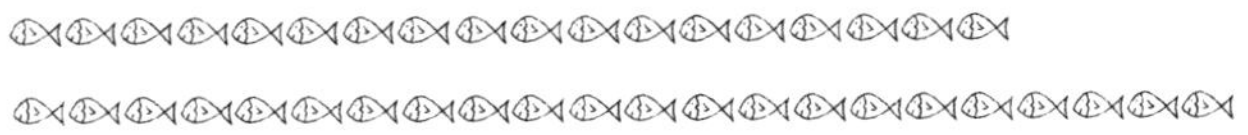	$18 + \square = 22$ 

[1] This list is adapted from Verschaffel, L. & De Corte E. 1996, 'Number and arithmetic', in A. Bishop, et al (eds) *International Handbook of Mathematics Education*, Kluwer Academic Publishers, Netherlands, pp99–137.

Students in the early years might work with a think board similar to the one above[2], or a simplified version of this. They work in small groups around the different sections of the think board. Teachers might start them with a story and the students then decide which section to work in next. They might decide to start with the materials section and as a group decide to get out blocks to represent the penguins in the above story, manipulating them until they find the answer.

The students then choose to move to the pictures section and as a group, decide to draw a picture of the 18 fish and the 22 fish. Many students will choose to use a diagram instead of drawing something that looks like the real thing. This is appropriate as children need to move to more abstract representations.

They then work together to decide what number sentence they could write that connects to the way that they have solved the problem. For the above story this might be 22 – 18 = ☐ or 18 + ☐ = 22, depending on how they solved it. This section might include a calculator for the students to use. In this case the focus of this section is on deciding which buttons they need to push in order to solve the problem, that is, the operation.

Students in the later years might work with more complex think boards like the division think board below[3]. In this version, students may be provided with cards that they place into the appropriate squares. They can then work in small groups to discuss and debate their views on the appropriate placement of cards.

The focus of the think board is on finding the connections between the different ways of representing the problem. This helps students to focus on the meaning of the operation rather than on just calculating to find an answer.

The think board

Story	Dramatisation (Story picture)	Things	Diagram	Number sentence	Answer
We ate 16 biscuits and there are 18 left in the packet. How many were in the packet to start?					

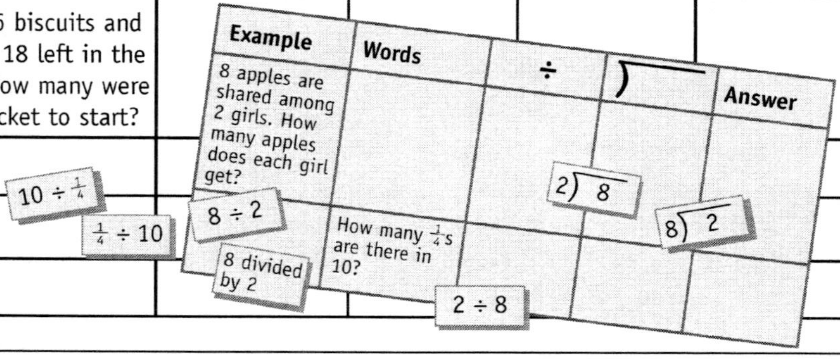

[2] Haylock, D. W. 1984, 'A mathematical think board', *Mathematics Teaching*, 108, pp.4–5.
[3] Swan, M. 1990, 'Becoming numerate: developing conceptual structures', in *Being Numerate: What Counts?*, Sue Willis (ed), ACER, Hawthorn, Victoria.

Addition and Subtraction Problems

Students need experience with all the common types of addition and subtraction problems. They *do not* need to learn to name different problem types—the vocabulary of 'change', 'combine' and 'compare' is used here simply to help you ensure that the full variety of addition and subtraction situations are provided. However, this is just one of many possible classifications. Sometimes the same problem can be thought of in different ways and may not obviously belong to one type. The examples below involve small whole numbers and discrete quantities that can be counted. However, students should experience all problem types in contexts involving larger whole numbers and measured quantities, including with decimals and fractions.

CHANGE

where students have to transform one quantity by adding to or taking from it

Join

- Anna had 7 bears and then her brother gave her 3. How many does she now have? (result unknown)
- Anna had 7 bears but would like to have 10. How many more does she need to get? (change unknown)
- Anna had some bears and then her brother gave her 3. Now she has 10. How many did she have to start with? (start unknown)

Separate

- Anna had 7 bears and then she gave her brother 3. How many does she now have? (result unknown)
- Anna had 10 bears and then she gave her brother some. She now has 7. How many did she give her brother? (change unknown)
- Anna had some bears and gave her brother 3 of them. Now she has 7 left. How many did she have to start with? (start unknown)

COMBINE

where students have to consider two static quantities either separately or combined

- Anna has 7 brown bears and 3 white bears. How many does she have in all? (whole unknown)
- Anna has 10 bears. 7 are brown and the rest are white. How many are white? (one part unknown)

EQUALISE or COMPARE

where students compare or equalise two quantities

Students tend to find EQUALISE problems easier because they suggest an action that students can carry out or imagine carrying out.

- Anna has 10 brown bears and 7 white bears. If all the white bears take a brown bear as a partner, how many brown bears won't get a partner?
- Anna has 7 white bears and some brown bears. All the white bears took a brown bear as a partner, and there were 5 brown bears left without a partner. How many brown bears does she have?
- Anna has 10 white bears and some brown bears. All the white bears tried to take a partner but there were 4 brown bears too few. How many brown bears does Anna have?

Students tend to find the matching COMPARE problems harder, because they are static and so don't immediately suggest an action.

- Anna has 10 brown bears and 7 white bears. How many more brown bears does she have?
- Anna has 7 white bears and some brown bears. She has 5 more brown bears than white bears. How many brown bears does she have?
- Anna has 10 white bears and some brown bears. She has 4 fewer brown bears. How many brown bears does Anna have?

Multiplication and Division Problems

Students need experience in modelling all the common types of multiplication and division problems. The naming of types is used here to help teachers ensure that the full variety of situations are provided for students. It is **not** intended that students are taught to name different problem types.

The two divisions for each multiplication are of different types		
Multiplication	**Division (partition/sharing) —know how many portions**	**Division (quotition/grouping) —know the size of the portions**
	REPEAT EQUAL QUANTITIES	
• There are five tables and six students can sit at each table. How many students can we seat? • Nine flags will each need two-thirds of a metre of fabric.How much material do we need?	• Thirty students need to form five equal groups, one at each table. How many students should be in each group? • We have six metres of fabric to make nine flags. How much fabric can we use for each flag?	• There are 30 students in our class. Our new hexagon tables each seat six students. How many tables will we fill? • Each flag needs two-thirds of a metre of fabric. How many flags can we cut from nine metres?
	USE RATES	
• Apricots cost $4.90 a kilogram. How much will it cost for 2.5 kilograms?	• If a 2.5 kilogram sack of apricots costs $12.25, what is the price for one kilogram?	• Apricots cost $4.90 a kilogram. If a sack of apricots costs $12.25, how much must it weigh?
	MAKE RATIO COMPARISONS or CHANGES, e.g. scale	
• Tanya has five times as many marbles as Jill. If Jill has 14, how many does Tanya have? • A picture is 60 cm high. If it is reduced to 0.8 of its original size, what will its height be?	• Tanya has five times as many marbles as Jill. If Tanya has 70, how many does Jill have? • A picture that has been reduced to 0.8 of its original size is now 48 cm high. What was its original height?	• Jill has 14 marbles. How many times as many marbles does Tanya have if she has 70? • A 60 cm high picture is reduced to 48 cm. What is the reduction ratio?

The two divisions for each multiplication are not of different types	
MAKE ARRAYS AND COMBINATIONS	
• There are three different types of ice-cream cone and six ice-cream flavours. How many different types of (single) ice-creams can we make?	• There are several different types of ice-cream cone and six ice-cream flavours. If 18 different (single) ice-creams can be made, how many different types of cone must there be? • There are three types of ice-cream cone and various ice-cream flavours. If 18 different (single) ice-creams can be made, how many different flavours are there?
NEED PRODUCTS OF MEASURES	
• What is the area of a rectangle 16 cm by 13.6 cm?	• A rectangle of area 217.6 sq centimetres has one side 16 cm long. How long is the adjacent side? • A rectangle of area 217.6 sq centimetres has one side 13.6 cm long. How long is the adjacent side?

Representing Word Problems in Number Sentences

Initially students will solve problems by 'playing out' or modelling them in various ways—dramatically, physically, mentally and with drawings—and then counting. However, they do need to learn to represent problems in number sentences containing the operation symbols. Being able to represent problems symbolically helps students to see the connection between apparently quite different problems that can be solved with the same mathematics.

Students need to learn to write number sentences for simple word problems.

An important aim is to teach students to represent problems mathematically. One of the earliest forms of this is to write number sentences to represent simple addition and subtraction word problems.

Most students readily learn to write addition and subtraction number sentences for simple Join and Separate problems where the result is unknown. However, they often have difficulty writing standard number sentences ($3 + 5 = \square$; $8 - 4 = \square$) for other addition and subtraction problem types, even when they can solve the problems by modelling and counting. Researchers[4] have found that even after months of teaching, fewer than half of Year One/Two students could represent a simple Compare problem in the standard form, even though almost all could solve it. They did not connect the sentence writing and the problem solving. The difficulty is that the standard representations often do not match the modelling or counting processes they use.

What these researchers and teachers have also found is that young students can learn to represent the problems if they are taught to use representations such as $3 + \square = 5$; $\square - 7 = 4$. These are not standard but they more closely fit the meaning of a problem and the way the student thinks about it. Once they are familiar with this form of writing sentences, young students are able to represent the structure of new problems where they have not been taught that particular problem type. That is, they can learn to write number sentences where the representations match *their* understanding of the meaning of the problem.

Students should first learn to write number sentences that match the semantic structure of the problem (its meaning), even though this may produce a non-standard number sentence.

This is surprising at first because we think of standard number sentences as being easier to solve than non-standard number sentences, which first

---

[4] Carpenter, T. P. 1985, 'Learning to add and subtract: An exercise in problem solving' in Silver, E. (ed) *Teaching and Learning Mathematical Problem Solving: Multiple Research Perspectives*, Lawrence Erlbaum Associates, Hillsdale, New Jersey.

have to be rearranged. But if the problem is not standard, then in order to write the standard number sentence, students have to rearrange the problem in their head, which is much harder. Thus, given a problem like this:

We had eight mice but some escaped and now we only have five left.
How many escaped?

students who think of it as *eight and some ran away leaving five* will find it easy to represent it as: 8 – □ = 5. It is much harder for young students to think of the above problem as the standard subtraction: 8 – 5 = □. If a student cannot solve 8 – □ = 5, it is unlikely that he or she will have been able to rearrange the problem in his or her head in order to get 8 – 5 = □.

For simple word problems, students do not write a number sentence in one phase and then solve it in a second phase. Much of the solution process is carried out on the semantic representation, not on the mathematical and physical representation of it. That is, students use their understanding of the situation itself to transform the problem before they represent it mathematically—they rearrange the problem in their heads. *After* students have solved a problem, they may write a number sentence that reflects their understanding of what happened in the situation. For the mice problem, many will write 8 – 3 = 5 and say, *three mice went away and there were five left.* In order to write the 8 – 3, they need to have *already* solved the problem.

We do eventually want students to be able to write number sentences before they have solved the problem. This will help them solve problems where the numbers are not easily represented in materials or diagrams and where they cannot rely on known number combinations. However, expecting students to begin with the, to us, obvious and easy subtraction 8 – 5 actually makes it harder. Students should learn to write sentences like 8 – □ = 5 (see Key Understanding 8, pages 74 to 75) and, over time, develop their part-part-whole understanding (see Key Understanding 2, pages 20 to 21) to link equivalent addition and subtraction sentences, e.g. 8 = 3 + 5, 8 – 3 = 5, 8 – 5 = 3. We need to help them talk about these links so that they can move between the various ways of representing the situation.

Students should imagine the situation and try to find a helpful way to think about it.

Students should be encouraged to think flexibly about problems and helped to see that we can often think about the same situation in different ways and so represent it differently. For example:

We ate 16 biscuits between us and there are 18 left in the packet. How many were in the packet to start with?'

could be thought of as:

The number in the packet take away 16 leaves 18, what is the number?
$\square - 16 = 18$

(A change problem with the start unknown)

or as:

The 18 left together with the 16 eaten gives the number in the packet.
$18 + 16 = \square$

(A combine problem with whole unknown)

The two number sentences are equivalent because they represent the same problem; they ask essentially the same question.

Students should paraphrase the problem in a way that makes sense to them.

Many textbooks encourage students to try to represent problems using a syntactic translation of words into symbols. This is unfortunate. It causes many problems and leads to many errors. Good problem-solvers use the semantic structure of the problem, not a syntactic translation. Thus, the process described above of paraphrasing the problem to 'see what it is saying' is an essential part of good problem solving and students should be encouraged to do this rather than focusing on key words or phrases.

Students need to link the number sentences from the various ways of thinking about a problem. We need not necessarily go back to the original problem to link them. If we begin with a number sentence such as $\square - 16 = 18$, we can use the inverse relationship that exists between addition and subtraction to rewrite it as $\square = 18 + 16$. The transformed number sentence is easier to solve than the original.

If the student has thought of the *actions* in the biscuit problem in the first way described above, then the number sentence $\square - 16 = 18$ is a direct representation of the actions, but the transformed version is not. As was suggested earlier, working with a number sentence that is not a direct representation of the *actions* in the problem is usually more difficult, even though the computational demands may be easier. Unless students are confident (that is, trust) that such transformed number sentences are always 'asking the same question', they will not be able to use strategies flexibly to find unknown quantities and will be forced to use trial-and-error or rote procedures.

Students should learn to transform problems to assist in problem solving.

In developing skill in solving addition and subtraction problems, students pass through several stages. The less skilled or younger problem-solvers are limited to directly representing the problems. Older or more skilled problem-solvers conduct a more elaborate semantic analysis of the problem and often transform to a form that is easier to solve before they represent it mathematically. Students' solutions to multiplication and division problems follow much the same pattern, although generally not as early.

CHAPTER 4

Calculate

This chapter will support teachers in developing curricula that relate to this outcome in Number:

Choose and use a repertoire of mental, paper and calculator computational strategies for each operation, meeting needed degrees of accuracy and judging the reasonableness of results.

Overall Description

Students are justifiably confident of their capacity to deal, correctly and efficiently, with everyday counting and computational situations. They can count a collection one-to-one, recognise skip counting in twos or threes as more efficient, and combine collections using strategies such as counting on.

They know the addition facts to 10 + 10 and multiplication facts to 10 x 10. They extend these with a flexible repertoire of mental strategies for each of the four operations on whole numbers, money and simple fractions. They use written approaches as a back-up for calculations they cannot store completely 'in the head'. These may include diagrams, jottings, standard routines, and supporting technology for students with disabilities.

They understand that calculators or computers are the sensible choice for repetitive, complex or lengthy calculations. They use them efficiently, correctly interpreting calculator displays.

Students judge the appropriate level of accuracy, are accurate when necessary, and otherwise estimate and approximate.

As a matter of course, they check that the results of their computations make sense both in terms of the numbers and operations involved and the context in which the calculation arose.

Levels of Achievement	Pointers Progress will be evident when students:	
Students have achieved Level 1 when they use counting and other strategies to mentally solve self-generated or orally presented questions from stories involving small numbers.	• use their own mental counting strategies to add and subtract small numbers generated from stories • decompose numbers and represent them in a variety of ways to assist in adding and subtracting, e.g. think of five and three more as the same as two fours	• use imagery to mentally add and subtract small numbers generated from stories, i.e. see 'how many' in their 'mind's eye' • find hidden numbers mentally with sums to at least ten, e.g. watch as seven dinosaurs are counted into a box and as five are removed one at a time, and say how many are left in the box
Students have achieved Level 2 when they count, partition and regroup in order to add and subtract one- and two-digit numbers, drawing mostly on mental strategies for one-digit numbers and a calculator for numbers beyond their present scope.	• use counting strategies such as combining collections and counting the lot, counting on from the first number, counting on from the largest number • use materials and diagrams to solve story problems and symbolically expressed additions and subtractions, e.g. work out how to represent 24 + 37 • use multiples (i.e. equivalent groups) to count and compare collections • remember many basic addition facts and work	out the others, e.g. *I don't know 7 + 9 but 7 + 7 is 14 and this will be two more* • count forwards and backwards in tens from a provided starting point, e.g. *16, 26, 36, ...* • use informal methods based on partitioning to solve two-digit addition and subtraction problems, e.g. write 24 + 37 as 20 + 4 + 30 + 7, which is 50 + 11 = 61; for 34 – 27, think of it as 30 – 27 and add back the four • use a calculator to add and subtract numbers, entering subtractions in correct order
Students have achieved Level 3 when they add and subtract whole numbers and amounts of money, and multiply and divide by one-digit whole numbers, drawing mostly on mental strategies for doubling, halving, adding to 100, and additions and subtractions readily derived from basic facts.	• remember basic addition facts and many multiplication facts and mentally calculate multiplication facts they don't recall, e.g. *three eights is 24 so six eights would be double that, so 6 x 8 = 48* • partition two-digit numbers to assist in adding and subtracting them mentally • use their own methods or a conventional algorithm to multiply whole numbers by single-digit numbers • estimate sums and products by rounding to single-digit numbers, e.g. the mugs cost $4.95 so $30 will be enough for six • mentally estimate the results of a calculation to	check the reasonableness of calculator results • use their own methods or a conventional algorithm to divide a whole number by a one-digit number and express results with remainders or fractions • add and subtract whole numbers using their own written method or a conventional algorithm, explaining the method by reference to place value, e.g. write 457 – 361 = 157 – 61 = 100 – 4 = 96 • explain why the multiplication/division method used works, e.g. *For 127 ÷ 7, I thought of sharing the 12 tens first, that's one ten each and five tens left, so I had 57 left ...*
Students have achieved Level 4 when they calculate with whole numbers, money and measures (one-digit multipliers and divisors), drawing mostly on mental strategies to add and subtract two-digit numbers and for multiplications and divisions related to basic facts.	• remember most basic multiplication facts (to 10 x 10) and mentally extend to multiply one-digit numbers by multiples of ten • estimate sums and products by rounding to single-digit multiples of ten and give upper and lower bounds • add and subtract money and measures with equal numbers of decimal places • partition double-digit numbers in order to mentally multiply and divide by small single-digit numbers	• multiply and divide measurements and amounts of money by a one-digit number • enter divisions in a calculator and interpret the part after the decimal point in answers, e.g. enter 37 ÷ 3 to answer: Three children in a family shared $37, how much did each receive? • plan sequences of calculations using a calculator memory facility e.g. enter (2.75 x 35) + (0.54 x 27)
Students have achieved Level 5 when they calculate with whole numbers, decimals and fractions (well-known equivalences, whole-number multipliers and divisors), drawing mostly on mental strategies for whole numbers, money and readily visualised fractions.	• mentally multiply double-digit by single-digit numbers using partitioning strategies • mentally add and subtract fractions using well-known equivalences where the proper fraction parts do not add to more than one • mentally calculate unit fractions of whole and decimal numbers • choose appropriate estimation strategies, e.g. 'front end' such as $16.67 + $4.12 + $0.97 + $0.46 is more than $16 + $4 + $0 + $0 = $20; rounding 'to the nearest' is about $17 + $4 + $1 + $0 = $22 • add and subtract decimals including with unequal numbers of places • use informal methods to multiply two-digit numbers	• multiply and divide decimals by one-digit numbers, interpreting remainders and deciding whether to round up or down • record stages in finding proper fractions and percentages of quantities that they cannot complete mentally, e.g. to find three-quarters of $48, find one-quarter mentally, record $12 and multiply by three • record stages in adding and subtracting fractions that they cannot complete mentally • convert between fractions, decimals and percentages • use a calculator to express one quantity as a percentage of another and to find fractions and percentages of numbers

Key Understandings

Teachers will need to plan learning experiences that include and develop the following Key Understandings (KU). These Key Understandings underpin achievement of the outcome. The learning experiences should connect to students' current knowledge and understandings rather than to their year level.

Key Understanding	Stage of Primary Schooling—Major Emphasis	KU Description	Sample Learning Activities
KU1 The same number fact will be true no matter how you count the objects or what the objects are.	Beginning ✔✔✔ Middle ✔✔✔ Later ✔✔	page 98	Beginning, page 100 Middle, page 102 Later, page 104
KU2 We can think of a number as a sum or difference in different ways. We can rearrange the parts of an addition without changing the quantity.	Beginning ✔✔✔ Middle ✔✔✔ Later ✔✔	page 106	Beginning, page 108 Middle, page 110 Later, page 112
KU3 We can think of a number as a multiplication or division in different ways. We can rearrange the factors of a multiplication without changing the quantity.	Beginning ✔ Middle ✔✔✔ Later ✔✔✔	page 114	Beginning, page 116 Middle, page 118 Later, page 120
KU4 Place value and basic number facts together allow us to calculate with any whole or decimal numbers.	Beginning ✔ Middle ✔✔✔ Later ✔✔✔	page 122	Beginning, page 124 Middle, page 126 Later, page 128
KU5 There are strategies we can practise to help us do calculations in our head.	Beginning ✔ Middle ✔✔ Later ✔✔✔	page 132	Beginning, page 134 Middle, page 136 Later, page 139
KU6 There are some special calculating methods that we can use for calculations we find hard to do in our head.	Beginning ✔ Middle ✔✔ Later ✔✔✔	page 144	Beginning, page 146 Middle, page 148 Later, page 150
KU7 We can calculate with fractions. Sometimes renaming fractions is helpful for this.	Middle ✔ Later ✔✔✔	page 156	Middle, page 158 Later, page 160
KU8 Rounding, imagining a number line, and using properties of numbers and operations help us to estimate calculations.	Beginning ✔ Middle ✔✔ Later ✔✔	page 162	Beginning, page 164 Middle, page 165 Later, page 167
KU9 To use a calculator well we need to enter and interpret the information correctly and know about its functions.	Beginning ✔✔ Middle ✔✔ Later ✔✔	page 172	Beginning, page 174 Middle, page 176 Later, page 178
KU10 Thinking about what makes sense helps us to check and interpret the results of calculations.	Beginning ✔ Middle ✔✔ Later ✔✔	page 182	Beginning, page 184 Middle, page 185 Later, page 187

Key

✔✔✔ The development of this Key Understanding is a major focus of planned activities.

✔✔ The development of this Key Understanding is an important focus of planned activities.

✔ Some activities may be planned to introduce this Key Understanding, to consolidate it, or to extend its application. The idea may also arise incidentally in conversations and routines that occur in the classroom.

KEY UNDERSTANDING 1

The same number fact will be true no matter how you count the objects or what the objects are.

For calculation to make sense to students, they need to understand that numbers and operations have their own consistent meanings apart from any real-world situation. A student may count a collection of five pens and a collection of seven pens, put the pens together, count and conclude that there are 12 pens altogether. The question then arises whether it would still be 12 if counted another way. Or whether it is the same for pebbles? Or for people? Through experimentation the student has to be able to conclude that, no matter how you rearrange them, or from where you start your count, or what the items are, five items together with seven distinct items will (*must*) give 12 items.

Without this key understanding the question 'What is five add seven?' doesn't really make sense and nor does the statement '5 + 7 = 12'. This idea, together with partitioning (See Key Understanding 2, and Understand Operations, Key Understanding 2), is needed for students to see *why* when they add, they can count on from the largest number rather than counting the whole collection. The same idea underpins students' understanding of why the number facts for subtraction, division and multiplication can be relied upon—you do not have to work each one out for each new situation.

In the process of developing this key understanding, students should be assisted to use partitions and other strategies to help work out basic sums (to 10 + 10) and basic products (to 10 x 10), and record their findings in a variety of ways, leading to a systematic collection of facts using conventional notations. Having instant recall of basic number facts is helpful. This does **not** mean that students should learn them by rote, i.e. without understanding. Trying to remember things you do not understand increases the memory demands and makes learning more difficult for all students. This is particularly so for those who have intellectual disabilities, since poor memory is often a characteristic of their learning.

We find it easier to remember and use things that we understand and which are well connected to other things. Students will remember number facts more easily if they understand what the facts are telling them, connect them to each other, and have the confidence and skill to work out those they do not recall by building upon those that they do. With suitable learning experiences that cluster basic facts into meaningful groups and reduce the memory load, most students can remember basic facts and should be helped to do so (see Background Notes, pages 189 to 192).

Students who have achieved Level 1 of the outcome use imagery and mental counting strategies to add and subtract small numbers such as four and three, where the numbers are generated by a story. They may not, however, be confident that four plus three must always be seven. At Level 2, they understand that the same basic addition or subtraction fact will be true regardless of how you count the collection or what the objects are. They will have constructed the addition facts to 10 + 10 and remember many of them. Those at Level 3 work with whole numbers independently of the particular context, including investigating patterns in the numbers themselves. They also remember the basic addition facts, have built up a table of multiplication facts to 10 x 10 and remember many of them. At Level 4, they remember almost all of the basic facts and can work out those they do not remember.

SAMPLE LEARNING ACTIVITIES

Beginning ✔✔✔

How Many?

Have students use materials such as gumnuts or bottletops to model an addition story involving change and then compare their answers. For example: Four emus are in your paddock. If three more come home, how many will there be? Ask: Are the answers all the same? What if we counted them another way? Suppose the emus moved around? Ask students to count the total in different ways. Record in a picture and symbols.

Counting Chickens

Ask students to model stories. For example: Mother Hen gathered four of her chickens. If three more come back, how many will there be? Continue with different examples using the same numbers until students confidently claim it will always be seven. Ask those who claim this to justify to others. When students are convinced, ask them to say it in their own words and record as a number sentence: 4 + 3 = 7. (Link to Understand Whole and Decimal Numbers, Key Understanding 2.)

Imagining

Have students mentally add or take away two from a small collection of objects, e.g. five plastic animals. Ask students to imagine that they have taken away two animals. Ask: How many animals will be left? Repeat by adding three, four and five animals. Focus students on working it out by counting on; thinking of four as two and two and counting on by twos; and thinking of five as three and two.

Addition Table

Encourage students to build up their own table of addition facts, first to 5 + 5. Over time, build up the addition table to 6 + 6, then 7 + 7, etc. (Link to Understand Whole and Decimal Numbers, Key Understanding 2.)

Dice Games

Play games such as the three-dice game. Organise students into pairs. Give each pair three dice. Have students take turns to throw three dice, add the numbers together and keep a running total on a calculator. During the game, ask: Which two numbers did you add together first? Why? At the end of the game (when one reaches a total of, say, 50 or more), ask students to use number sentences to show their working out for at least one turn.

Doubles

Help students develop their repertoire of known facts by building on from the 'doubles', e.g. use 6 + 6 = 12 to work out 6 + 7, 5 + 6 and so on.

Number Line

Have students use a number line to check that their mental counting on and counting back in situations such as the three-dice game (see previous activity) always gives the same result as counting, starting the count from one every time. (Link to Understand Whole and Decimal Numbers, Key Understanding 1.)

Compensating to Ten

Ask students to use two ten-frames (2 x 5 arrays) to find ways of breaking up numbers to calculate. For example, to add 8 + 5, students move two from the five into the frame with eight to make ten and then add the remaining three. Extend so students can visualise the above movements. (See Understand Operations, Key Understanding 7.)

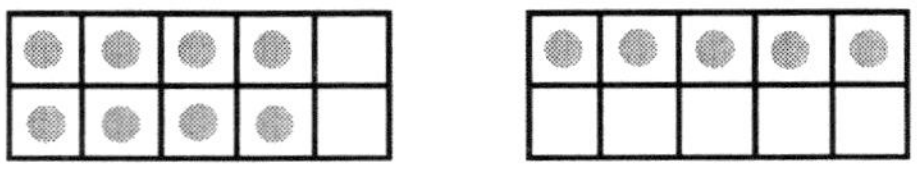

Easy Calculations

Help students find an easy way of working out calculations such as 7 + 4 or 5 + 7 using known combinations to ten. Ask them to share their strategies with the class. Extend later to include calculations with larger numbers by adding or subtracting from one of the numbers to make the other into a multiple of ten.

Double Collections

Have students double collections of materials such as beans and counters to make 'twice as many' or 'two times' and tell others the results. Begin with numbers from one up to four and ask students to extend the numbers themselves. Use a diagram to show the results and describe what the groupings mean, e.g. two sixes and six plus six. Use double and double again for students to work out four times a given collection. (See Understand Operations, Key Understanding 3.)

Number Combinations

Ask students to recall number combinations from contexts where they made different partitions of the same number. For example: Think about when we made necklaces. We made one with eight beads. When five were red, how many were blue? Ask them to recall the situation and 'see' in their mind's eye the parts of the collection.

Basic Facts to Ten

Help students to memorise basic facts to ten. Give each one a set of number facts cards. Ask students to work in pairs and take turns to put out three combination cards, e.g. 6 + 3, 9 + 0 and 3 + 4, two of which are combinations of the same number. If the partner can identify the odd card and say why, they can take the three cards. To vary the game, one student can set out two cards with equivalent totals for the partner to find another card to match the total.

SAMPLE LEARNING ACTIVITIES

Middle ✔✔✔

Animal Patterns

Have students create an animal using pattern blocks, and then say how many blocks were used. For example: *My cow was made with eight triangles*. Ask: How many triangles would you need for five cows? Ask students who did not use materials to solve this, to share with the class how they worked it out.

Same Numbers

Ask students to use their own strategies to solve and record solutions to multiplication problems involving the same numbers. For example: Lawson can only carry seven plastic milk containers at a time to the recycling bin. How many does he take in four trips? Ask students to share the number sentences they used, say why they are the same and why the answers are the same.

Multiplication Facts

Help students to build up sets of related multiplication facts. For example: Ask students to draw one tricycle and say how many wheels; two tricycles, how many wheels; and so on. Encourage students to look for the pattern and say why five tricycles must have 15 wheels. Have students record the number sentences as the pictures are drawn, to list the first five or six multiples of three.

Today's Number

Write a number on the board. Ask students to suggest calculations with that number as an answer. Record their calculations on the board. Ask: Are there any number sentences that belong together? Why? As students mention the four operations, build different groups. Ask: Can we rearrange the number sentences so they are in order? How can each set be extended?

Forgotten Facts

Ask students to explain to a partner how they could work out a fact they don't know or have forgotten. For example: *To find 6 x 5, I know it's 5 x 5 and another five*.

Doubles and Halves

Have students use doubles and halves to multiply and divide. For example: 4 x 7 is double double seven, which is double 14, or 28; 24 ÷ 4 is half of half of 24, which is half of 12, or six.

Multiplication Doubles

Have students relate known multiplication 'doubles' to the harder multiplication facts. For example: As a way of remembering 6 x 8, students could make a 6 x 6 grid and build on until they make 6 x 8. They work out tables they could put together to help work out the original, i.e. 6 x 6 and 2 x 6. Ask: Could you use addition instead of the 2 x 6? Which is easier? (See Understand Operations, Key Understanding 5.)

Extending Doubles and Halves

Extend students' use of doubles and halves to find answers to multiplication such as 8 x 12. For example: Halve eight and double 12 gives 4 x 24; halve four and double 24 gives 2 x 48; halve two and double 48 gives 1 x 96.

Concentration

Have students use addition and multiplication examples to construct cards to play games such as Concentration. Pairs of cards are made by putting together different representations of the same number. For example: 3 x 2 and 2 + 2 + 2 would be a matching pair.

Constant Calculations

Have students use the constant function on the calculator to find multiples. For example: When learning the four times table, press 0 + 4 then = = = to find the multiples of four. Ask students to predict what will be next and then to verify their prediction. Ask: Why can't a number with seven in the ones column be a multiple of four? (See Key Understanding 9.)

Grid Patterns

Have students make a multiplication grid by placing numbers along the bottom and down the side and the answers within the grid. (See Background Notes, page 191.) Look for patterns within the grid. Ask: Why are the numbers above the diagonal the same as below? How can this help find answers to tables you don't know? (Link to Reason About Number Patterns, Key Understanding 6.)

Looking for Patterns

Have students investigate patterns in the answers of times tables. For example: In the nine times table, the digits of each answer add to nine, the numbers in the ones column go up by one and the numbers in the tens column go down by one. (Link to Reason About Number Patterns, Key Understanding 6.)

SAMPLE LEARNING ACTIVITIES

Later ✔✔

Array Facts

Have students cut out arrays to represent different multiplication facts. Ask them to take turns to show an array and write facts about that array. For example: 7 x 9, 9 x 7, 63 ÷ 9 = 7, 63 ÷ 7 = 9, $\frac{1}{9}$ x 63 = 7, $\frac{1}{7}$ x 63 = 9.

Fewer Facts

Encourage students to use turn-arounds to reduce the number of facts to be learned. Present stories such as: Jessica knows her ones, twos, fives and ten times tables. How can she use what she knows to work out 5 x 8? Ask students to show on a 10 x 10 grid how using turn-arounds reduces the number of facts to be learned.

Unknown Facts

Ask students to use known facts to work out unknown facts. For example: How does knowing 9 + 6 help you work out 8 + 6? How does knowing 9 x 6 help you work out 8 x 6? What was different?

Difficult Facts

Have pairs of students use factors to work out the more difficult basic multiplication facts. For example: To work out 7 x 8 you can say 7 x 4 x 2 or go further and say 7 x 2 x 2 x 2. Ask students to sort a range of multiplication facts according to whether using factors helps.

Equivalent Sentences

Have students use equivalent number sentences to make calculating easier. Pose this problem: Lizzie needs to work out 56 ÷ 8. She knows the multiplication facts well but is not as sure of the division facts. Ask: How could Lizzie use multiplication to help her solve the division sentence? (See Understand Operations, Key Understanding 8.)

Checking Calculations

Encourage students to experiment with their calculators as a tool to help them practise basic facts. For example: To practise the eight times table, key in 8 x 2. Now key in 3 =, 5 = and 1 =. Ask: Is your calculator still multiplying each number? Try other numbers, saying the answer before pressing the equals key. Students can experiment with programming different 'times tables' into their calculator.

Choice Bingo

Invite students to play Choice Bingo. This is similar to the normal bingo game except that students make up their own 4 x 4 boards by writing their choice of numbers on the grid. The teacher holds up multiplication facts from 5 x 5 to 10 x 10 on flashcards. The first student to cross off a whole row, column or diagonal is the winner. Ask: Is 37 a good number to use? Why? Ask students to decide which numbers are best for their grid.

42	32	56	27
60	36	50	49
64	90	72	45
48	54	81	70

Constant Quantities

Invite students to use a calculator to explore what happens in multiplication when you double one number and halve the other. Ask: Why doesn't this change the quantity? How does knowing about the effect of doubling and halving help you to work out more difficult multiplication facts?

Squared Numbers

Have students use squared numbers as known facts to work out unknown facts. For example: Ask students to construct a multiplication grid (See 'Grid Patterns', page 103) and locate the pattern of squared numbers. Shade in the facts that could be easily worked out from a squared number. For instance, if you know 7 x 7 you can work out 6 x 7 by saying 49 take seven. You can also work out 8 x 7 by adding seven to 49.

Number Facts

Invite students to use a range of strategies to give calculations that match a given number. For example: A small group of students select the number cards one to nine from a pack of cards. They each start with the same number of cards. The first player turns over two cards and arranges them to make a two-digit number. The next player then states a multiplication or division fact about the number. This continues until the last player who can state a fact keeps the pairs of cards. The person with the most cards at the end of the game is the winner. If a prime number appears, the cards go to the bottom of the pack. Later, primes can be included to encourage the use of fractions.

KEY UNDERSTANDING 2

We can think of a number as a sum or difference in different ways. We can rearrange the parts of an addition without changing the quantity.

As described in Understand Operations, Key Understandings 1 and 2, partitioning into part-part-whole is the basis of students' understanding of the *meaning* of addition and subtraction, and the relationships between them, and of why addition is commutative but subtraction is not. This idea is also included here because it underpins flexibility in calculation with both whole and fractional numbers.

Students should develop the idea that they can partition collections and objects into part-part-whole without changing the total quantity, and that they can often do this in different ways. They should experiment by moving quantities from one part into the other to discover that:

- the quantity does not change when the objects are rearranged
- there are patterns linking pairs of numbers. (Link to Reason About Number Patterns, Key Understandings 1 and 5.)

Thus, they should learn to think flexibly of numbers as the sum and difference of other numbers. This is the basis of skilful calculation because it enables students to see, for example, *why*:

- to find 8 + 274 you *must* get the same result if you start at 274 and count on eight as if you start with eight and count forward 274
- to find 274 + 8 you can think of eight as 6 + 2, use the six to 'fill up' the seventies to get 280 and then add the two
- to find $\frac{4}{5} + \frac{3}{5}$ you can mentally 'shift' one-fifth from the $\frac{3}{5}$ to the $\frac{4}{5}$ to make up a whole (one), which you can then combine with the remaining two-fifths, giving $1\frac{2}{5}$.

Students who have achieved Level 2 of the outcome understand that it makes sense to rearrange the parts of an addition for whole numbers. Hence they can use a known basic fact to work out facts they do not yet know, for example, eight plus nine must be double eight plus one. They also use known basic addition facts to work out subtraction facts. As described in Key Understanding 4, they will use informal written strategies based on partitioning to add and subtract two-digit numbers. At Level 3, they can do this mentally, as described in Key Understandings 4 and 5. They also partition a number into an addition to assist in their multiplication and division, e.g. 27 x 4 can be thought of as four 20s plus four sevens. At Level 4, they do the latter mentally and at Level 5, they also partition fractions to add and subtract them (see Key Understanding 7).

SAMPLE LEARNING ACTIVITIES

Beginning ✓✓✓

Same Amounts

Have students move objects to develop the idea that the same amount can be partitioned into two groups in different ways without changing the quantity. For example: Six students sat down to eat pieces of fruit. At first three had bananas and three had apples. Then two had bananas and four had apples. (See Understand Whole and Decimal Numbers, Key Understanding 2.)

Moving Items

Ask students to model stories about the movement of items from one group to another, e.g. *Ten in the Bed* (Dale, 1988). Ask students to describe each combination of those in and out of bed. There are ten altogether and three are in the bed; how many are on the floor? If you're the only one left out of ten in the bed, how many are on the floor? Students record the combinations.

Hands

Ask students working in pairs to use fingers to show numbers between six and ten as five plus something, that is, show six as 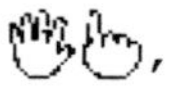, eight as 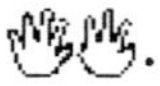. Have one student hold up their hands and then hide them, then their partner says number shown. Practise until students recognise one to ten immediately. (See Understand Whole and Decimal Numbers, Key Understanding 2.)

More Hands

With students working in pairs, ask one student to hold up some fingers on each hand. The partner imagines some fingers from one hand moving over to fill the other hand, and says how many in all. For example,  and  makes 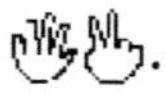.

Practical Partition

Have students create practical partitions of the same number. For example: Read *Edward the Emu* (Knowles and Clement, 1989) and ask students to show the ways they could put eight emus in two yards.

Tosses

Have students take a handful of counters that are red on one side and blue on the other. They record how many in all (say, eight). They then toss the counters and record how many of each colour is showing. Continue and make a record of combinations. Ask: What stays the same (eight in all)? What changes (how many each of red and blue)? Have you got all the possible combinations? How do you know? (See Understand Whole and Decimal Numbers, Key Understanding 2.)

Record Symbols

Extend the previous activity by recording in symbols. For example: Four yellow beads and five red beads make a necklace of nine beards, $4 + 5 = 9$.

Number Combinations

Represent partitions in activities like the previous ones. For example: Provide beads in two colours and ask students to make a necklace of nine beads, then represent it using spots or drawings on cards. They then sort their cards into the same number groups, e.g. put together the cards with four yellow and five red. Make a label for each combination under students' direction. Draw out that all necklaces have the same number of beads but in various number combinations of yellow and red.

Reverse Order

Extend the previous activities to draw out that we can reverse the order of the numbers in an addition. For example: When we looked at the emus we saw eight emus—three in the first yard and five in the second, so $3 + 5$. When we saw the yards from the other side it looked like five emus in the first yard and three in the second, so $5 + 3$. These are the same. Have students rearrange the nine beads on their necklace so that all of one colour is at one end and the other colour at the other end. They hold the necklace and read the number sentence from left to right: $4 + 5$. Their facing partner looks at the same beads and reads the number sentence also from left to right: $5 + 4$.

Three Groups

Extend the previous activities to partitioning into three groups.

Favourite Number

Have students make, describe and display a poster about their favourite number, showing the various number combinations. For example: eight is four and four; it is five fingers on one hand and three on the other, it is four pairs of shoes. (See Key Understanding 1.)

One-to-Ten Partitions

Ask students to show partitions for numbers from one to ten. For example: Make cards with spots in two clusters. Write the total number on the back of cards and use them in games to develop recognition of partitions, e.g. Snap, Concentration.

Combinations to 20

Have students use two ten-frames (see 'Compensating to Ten', page 101) to investigate ways of representing combinations to 20. For example: $14 = 8 + 6$, $7 + 7 = 14$, $20 - 6 = 14$ and so on. Ask: How many different combinations are possible for 14? How do you know? (See Understand Operations, Key Understanding 2.)

SAMPLE LEARNING ACTIVITIES

Middle ✓✓✓

Marble Bags

Have students start with 16 marbles in one bag and work out how many different ways they can put the marbles into two bags. Ask them to record the combinations and look for patterns in the number sentences to help find other possibilities. Extend by asking: If there were 19 in the bag, would your pattern still be helpful? (See Reason About Number Patterns, Key Understanding 3.)

Number Combinations

Use a grid or number line to construct the combinations for a given number. Ask: How do you know you have found all the ways? How do you know you have found all possibilities?

Patterns

Have students drop materials such as beads, blocks and counters onto a card divided into three sections, and record the different combinations for each number up to 18. Ask them to organise the number sentences into a pattern to see if they have found all possible combinations. Ask: Is 7 + 6 + 5 the same as 6 + 5 + 7 or 5 + 6 + 7? (Link to Reason About Number Patterns, Key Understanding 3.)

Dice Patterns

Repeat the previous activity using three dice.

Card Games

Have students play card games, such as Snap or Fish, to make combinations to a predetermined number, rather than pairs. For example: In Fish, they may have four in their hand and need to make 11, so they ask for seven. (See Understand Whole and Decimal Numbers, Key Understanding 2.)

The Answer Is ...

Ask students to make up an addition or subtraction that has a specified answer, e.g. 30. Ask them to make up as many as they can. Help them to put their sums (or differences) in order and fill in any gaps. For example:

1 + 29 = 30 2 + 28 = 30 3 + 27 = 30.

Ask: What happens to the second number as the first goes up by ones? Challenge them: I worked out that 237 + 492 = 729. Make up some other pairs that add to 729, without doing the calculation. If I increase the 237 to 238, what do I need to do to the 492? Repeat for subtractions.

Grid Partitions

Have pairs of students find and record partitions of 100 using a 10 x 10 array on grid paper. To play this game, students choose the left or right side of the grid to score. Together they toss two, ten-sided dice. One die represents tens, the other represents ones. Use the numbers from each turn to partition a 100 square. Students count the tens and ones to find the other number and record each combination of 100. Students add their scores as they go. The first to reach (say) 500 is the winner.

34 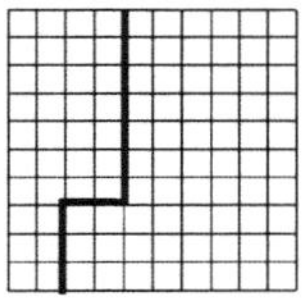 66

Ten-frames

Encourage students to develop a visual image of number partitions to 20 by saying how many counters there are in ten-frames as they are flashed on an overhead projector. Ask students to explain how they were able to see 'that many' on the frame. Extend to two frames or to 100 frames (10 x 10, 4 x 25, etc.). (See Understand Whole and Decimal Numbers, Key Understanding 2.)

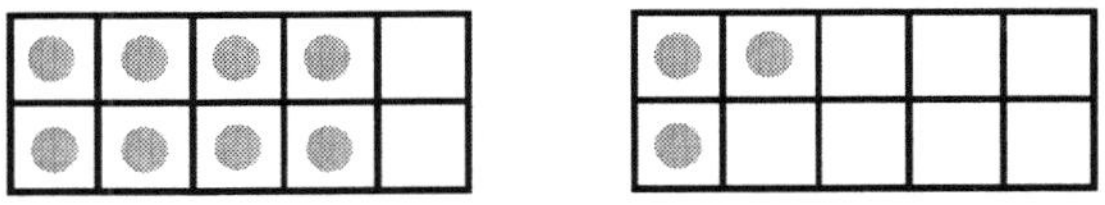

Hide the Blocks

Play Hide the Blocks in pairs, using a given number of blocks. Player One closes their eyes while Player Two hides some blocks under a container. Player One then works out how many are hidden, using the beginning number and how many are left outside the container. Have students record the number sentences as they go. Extend to two- and three-digit numbers by using material bundled in tens and 100s.

Groups of Tens

Invite students to use materials grouped into tens (e.g. Unifix, pop sticks, washers, MABs) to construct as many representations of a given number as possible. For example, 37 could be represented as three tens and seven ones, two tens and 17 ones, one ten and 27 ones, or 37 ones. Have students record their representations and justify each by showing how their groups of materials linked to the representations. Extend to include three-digit numbers.

Breaking Up

Have students use materials grouped into tens (e.g. Unifix, pop sticks, washers, MABs) to show how they might break up a number to calculate. For example: 86 + 47, shown as 86 + 4 to make 90 and then add 43. Have students record the breaking of numbers and movement from one number to the next with a written explanation or with numbers and signs. (See Understand Whole and Decimal Numbers, Key Understanding 6.)

SAMPLE LEARNING ACTIVITIES

Later ✔✔

Grid Partitions

Have students identify partitions of 100 by using 2 mm squared paper and drawing a line to partition a 100 square into two parts. (See 'Grid Partitions', page 111.) Ask: Where would you draw the line so that your partner can say how many in each part at a glance? Using a new 100 square each time, ask students to take turns to quickly recognise the two parts of 100. Have students share strategies that make this recognition easy. Repeat the activity but imagine the 100 square is $1. (See Understand Whole and Decimal Numbers, Key Understanding 2.)

Thousand Grid

Extend the previous activity using a 1000 grid. Ask students to say how they could see at a glance how many hundreds, tens and ones there are in each of the two parts. Ask: How do the strategies differ from the previous activity? (See Understand Whole and Decimal Numbers, Key Understanding 2.)

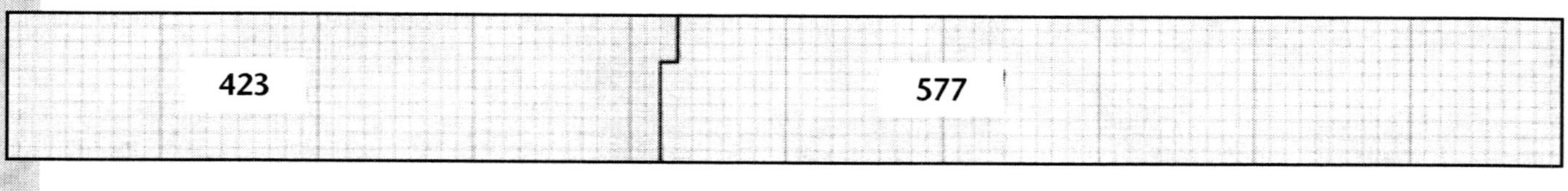

Small Change

Have students partition money to avoid small change. For example: Li's takeaway food came to $10.25. He gave the cashier a $20 note and 25 cents. Why did he give the extra 25 cents?

Number Line Leaps

Ask students to use place value to partition numbers. For example: When showing 48 on a number line, take the least amount of one-unit or ten-unit jumps to get to 48. For instance, jumping five ten-jumps and back two one-jumps is quicker than jumping four ten-jumps and eight one-jumps. Ask students to represent the different jumps as an addition or subtraction to make 48.

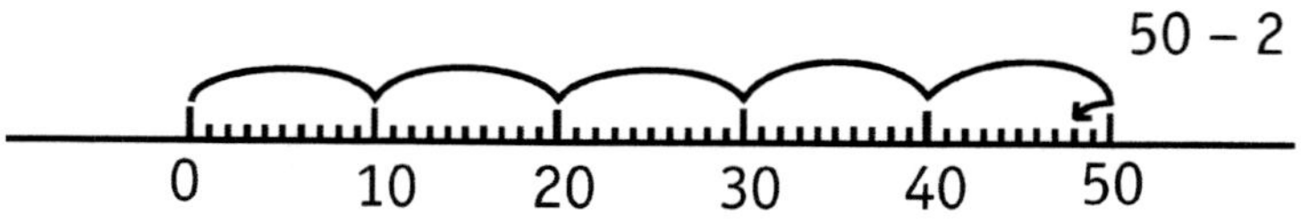

Further Leaps

Extend the previous activity to numbers requiring jumps of 100, 1000 or 0.1.

Pass the Number

Play Pass the Number, where students use partitioning to represent a number in different ways. A number (include decimal and common fractions) is written at the top of a piece of paper and the paper is passed around the class. Each student writes an alternative form of the number using either an addition or subtraction. Students try to circulate the paper without any combination being repeated.

Talk About It

Invite students to share their conjectures about partitioning to make calculating easier. Sue said: *You can add the same number to both numbers in a subtraction problem without changing the calculation*. So, 47 – 16 is the same as 50 – 19 or 51 – 20. Ask students to decide if this is true and talk about how knowing this could be useful to calculate examples such as 78 – 29 and 96 – 17. Ask: Does this conjecture only work for subtraction?

Rewriting Number Sentences

Have students partition numbers and rewrite a number sentence in a variety of ways that do not change the result. For example: 73 – 38 can be written as: 73 – 25 – 13; 73 – 21 –17; (60 – 30) + (13 – 8); 73 – 30 – 8. Ask students to exchange number sentences with a partner who checks that the total has not changed. Ask: Which one of these ways would be most useful when calculating? (See Key Understanding 4.)

Rewriting Addition

Have students partition numbers in an addition number sentence to make calculating easier. Ask: How can 36 + 28 be rewritten in a different way without changing the result? Encourage students to share ways that the parts were rearranged and check that the total stayed the same. Ask: Which arrangement is the easiest for you to calculate this particular example?

Complex Numbers

Repeat the previous activity but with more complex numbers such as: 1499 + 1501; 3000 – 1499; 15.01 + 14.99; 15.01 + 1.499; 1.49 + $1\frac{1}{2}$.

Large Numbers

Ask students to partition large numbers, fractions and decimals in different ways. For example: The answer is 14.25. What could the addition question be? What could the subtraction question be?

Compatible Numbers

Encourage students to recognise pairs of numbers that combine to make one, 100, 1000 or a decimal fraction such as 0.1. Ask students to generate pairs of numbers that add to make a given number such as 1000, and randomly record the pairs on a piece of paper. Have them exchange sheets with a partner and join up all the compatible numbers. Ask: What clues did you use to know how many hundreds to look for? What about the tens and ones?

KEY UNDERSTANDING 3

We can think of a number as a multiplication or division in different ways. We can rearrange the factors of a multiplication without changing the quantity.

Partitioning quantities into equal groups is the basis for students' early understanding of the *meaning* of multiplication and division and the relationships between them and of fractions. (See Understand Operations, Key Understanding 5.) This idea underpins flexibility in calculation with both whole and fractional numbers.

Students should develop the idea that a number can be decomposed and recomposed into its factors in a number of ways without changing the total quantity involved. They can use this to write numbers as products (multiplication) or quotients (division). They should experiment by arranging and rearranging actual collections and objects into equal groups and arrays, skip count either orally or along a number line or with a calculator, and explore the numbers themselves.

For example:

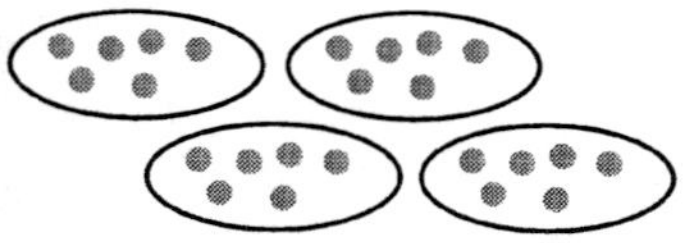

24 is four groups of six

24 = 4 x 6

24 ÷ 4 = 6

24 ÷ 6 = 4

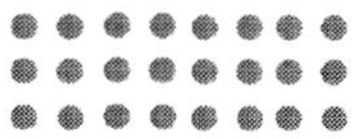

24 is three groups of eight

24 = 3 x 8

24 is eight groups of three

24 = 8 x 3

24 ÷ 8 = 3

24 ÷ 3 = 8

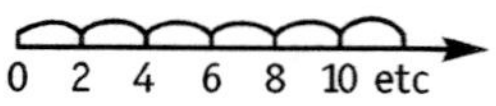

24 = 12 x 2

Numbers can also be written as the product of a number of factors. Thus 24 is 2 x 3 x 4, which can be represented with a two by three by four prism made with cubes. As well, 24 is 1 x 2 x 2 x 6, although this would be difficult to show with materials so we usually rely upon explorations with the numbers themselves.

Being able to think flexibly of numbers as the product of two or more factors is helpful when calculating. It enables students to see that to calculate 24 x 5 we could think of the 24 as 12 x 2, so that 24 x 5 must be the same as (12 x 2) x 5. We can then mentally change the order of the multiplications to 12 x (2 x 5) which is 12 x 10, or 120. Alternatively, we could think of five as 10 ÷ 2 or $\frac{10}{2}$, then multiply 24 by ten and divide by two—a common 'trick of the trade'. Students should not be taught such 'tricks' mindlessly but rather should be helped to develop the flexibility with numbers that leads to the shortcuts.

Students who have achieved Level 3 of the outcome understand that it makes sense to rewrite whole numbers as factors and can do it for numbers for which they know the relevant basic facts, e.g. 20 or 36. They can also further break down these numbers into three or four factors and realise that you can do the multiplications in any order and get the same result. They draw on this idea and known multiplication facts to produce new facts (e.g. since four sixes is 24, eight sixes must be two lots of four sixes, or 48; four 60s is four lots of six tens, which is 24 tens or 240). At Level 4, they can rewrite larger whole numbers into factors and even into prime factors. They understand *why* you can rearrange the factors of a number and do the multiplications in any order. They freely draw upon this understanding for their mental calculations.

SAMPLE LEARNING ACTIVITIES

Beginning ✓

Equal Groups

Have students work with materials that are fixed representations of numbers (e.g. MAB ones and tens, Unifix or Centicubes), using different colours to show equal groups. Ask students to investigate and record the different equal groups that can be made for each given number, e.g. six.

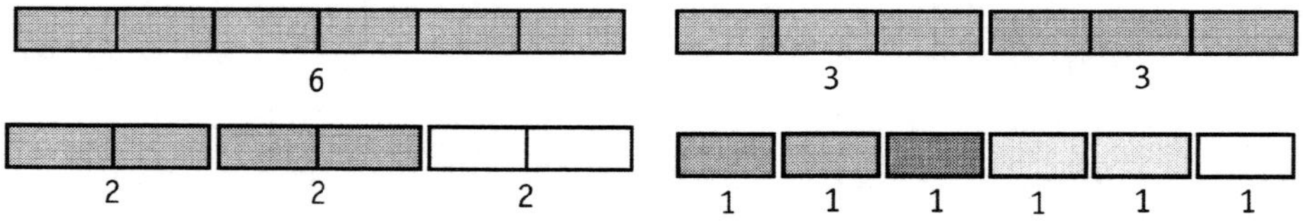

Arranging Objects

Ask students to arrange and rearrange a collection of, say, eight objects into equal groups. Ask: What equal groups can be made from eight things? Ask students to record in their own way using drawings, diagrams or numbers on individual cards and display on a chart about 'eight'. Ask: What about nine things?

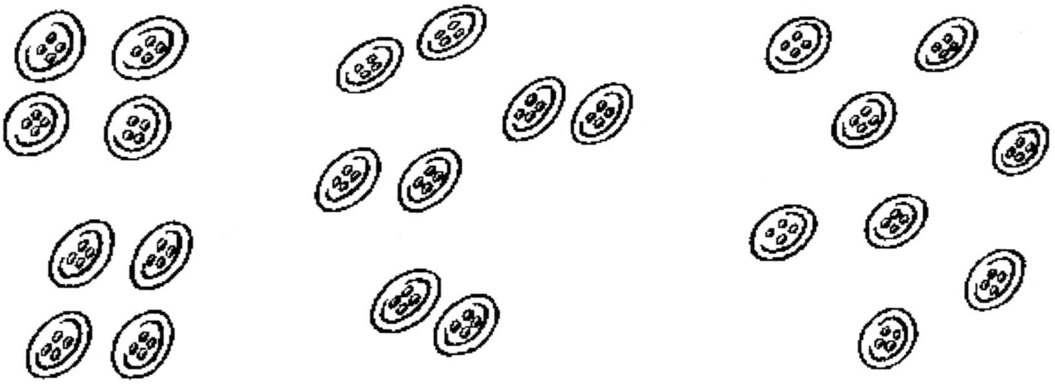

Sharing Biscuits

Have students draw diagrams to show grouping in stories such as *The Doorbell Rang* (Hutchins, 1987). Ask them to share the 12 biscuits into two equal groups and write a matching number sentence, i.e. 2 x 6 = 12. Repeat as each visitor in the book arrives. (See Understand Operations, Key Understanding 4, Middle Sample Learning Activities.)

Number Line

Ask students to skip count to a given number along a number line, using groupings to see that the count always reaches that number. For example: 12 has equal groups of one, two, three, four and six. Draw out that 3 x 4 and 4 x 3 are different partitions of the same collection.

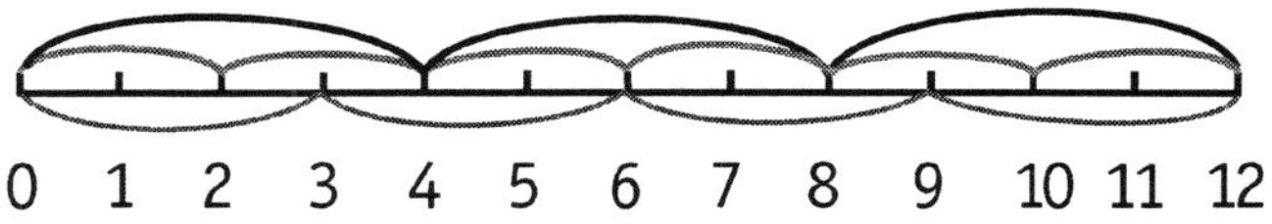

A Different Point of View

Have students investigate arrays from different positions and describe the groupings to see that rearrangement does not change the quantity. For example: A baker had lots of different trays for making 12 muffins. Ask students to draw, on grid paper, all the trays the baker could have, and describe their different arrays, e.g. three rows of four, six rows of two. They can cut them out and sort them to see that some are the same shape, e.g. three by four and four by three. Ask: How do they look different on the paper? Why? Are they both still 12?

SAMPLE LEARNING ACTIVITIES

Middle ✓✓✓

Arrays

Help students develop a visual image of tables to 20. Briefly show an array of dots, e.g. 2 x 4. Ask students to say how many along, how many down and how many altogether. Turn the array 90 degrees and ask again. Ask: How is this array the same/different from the last array? Have students write a sentence for each, e.g. 2 x 4 and 4 x 2 are both eight. (See Understand Operations, Key Understanding 2.)

Making Arrays

Have students construct all arrays for a number using grid paper, geoboard or blocks. Ask them to record each using a multiplication sentence, e.g. 6 x 4 = 24, and a division sentence, e.g. 24 ÷ 6 = 4. Ask: What do each of the numbers show in the array? Why isn't there a sentence using the number five or seven? Draw out that you cannot make groups of five or seven from 24 blocks. They are not factors of 24. Ask students to write a list of factors for 24. (Link to Understand Operations, Key Understanding 5.)

Prisms

Ask students to build rectangular prisms from a set number of blocks. Ask them to record each as they go, e.g. 2 x 2 x 3 = 12. Ask: Is 2 x 2 x 3 equal to 2 x 3 x 2? Can you make a different shape for each? Why is it that some numbers are used (one, two, three, four, six and 12) and some are not (five, seven, eight, nine, ten, 11)?

Planning

Have students partition equipment (e.g. straws and marbles) into all possible equal groups to find out how many groups of students can play at one time. Ask them to list the groupings and keep these with the equipment as instructions, e.g. 12 cards can be shared equally between two, three, four, six and 12 players. (See Understand Operations, Key Understanding 4.)

More Planning

Extend 'Planning' to involve larger numbers in each collection (e.g. 48 straws, 100 marbles). Ask students to predict which numbers of groups will 'work' for the specified collection size. Check by skip counting on a calculator to reach the total number of the collection.

Multiple Pieces

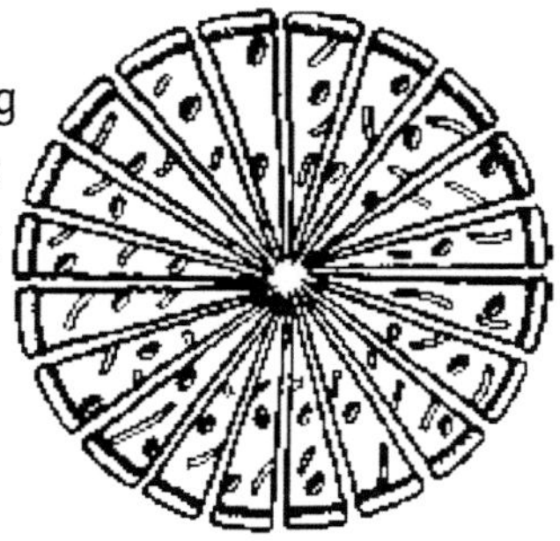

Extend the previous activities to include those involving partitioning a whole into parts. For example: I am not sure whether there will be four or five of us to share the pizza. How many pieces should I cut it into to make sure that either way, we can all take the same number of pieces? Draw out the mathematical idea that the number of pieces has to be a multiple of both four and five.

Sharing Sweets

Ask students to find a number divisible by two other numbers. For example: Dad bought enough sweets to share equally between three children. Then a friend arrived, but luckily the number of sweets we had could still be shared evenly. What is the smallest number Dad could have bought? Draw out that the number has to be a multiple of both three and four. Ask: Are there other numbers of sweets that would work? (Link to Understanding Fractional Numbers, Key Understanding 2, and Understand Operations, Key Understanding 5.)

Using Factors

Have students use factors to solve problems. For example: We have 24 lamingtons to put into trays. How could we arrange them into rectangle shapes? How do you know you have found all possible arrangements? How can you work out factors of numbers without using material?

Finding Multiples

Invite students to use the constant function on the calculator to find multiples of a number and predict whether a given number will be a multiple. For example: Will 51 be a multiple of four? This can become a game by taking turns to predict the next number before pressing the =.

Using Shapes

Have students use shapes to investigate factors. For example: Ask students to take a 'good' handful of straws, and decide how many triangles they can make. How many rectangles? Pentagons? Record using pictures and number sentences. Draw out the idea of factors asking: Why do you get straws left over for some shapes and not for others?

Multiples of Three

Build up multiples using the inverse of the previous activity. Have students make one triangle using three straws, two using six straws, and so on. Ask them to draw their triangles. They then write the list of multiples of three next to their diagrams to show how many straws were used altogether.

SAMPLE LEARNING ACTIVITIES

Later ✔✔✔

Pass the Number

Write a number, say 32, at the top of a piece of paper and pass it around the class. Ask each student to write an alternative form of the number on the paper, using either a multiplication or division, with no combination being repeated. Encourage students to include fractions and decimal fraction examples. Ask them to justify interesting examples such as 0.25 x 128 and 2^5.

Turn-arounds

Ask students to explain scenarios such as: Jodie knows her one, two, five and ten times tables. How does knowing about turn-arounds help her work out 5 x 8? Show on a 10 x 10 tables grid how this reduces the facts to be learned.

Frog Hops

Have students partition quantities into equal-sized fractional amounts. Start by making different fraction number lines. Use them to solve frog-hopping problems. The frog can only make hops of the same length. How many ways can the frog hop to $1\frac{1}{2}$? How many ways can the frog hop to 2? How many ways can the frog hop to $\frac{3}{4}$? Ask students to write a number sentence for each kind of frog hop. For example: $6 \times \frac{1}{4}$, or $3 \times \frac{1}{2} = 1\frac{1}{2}$. Ask: Can you use your number line partitioned into thirds to end up at $1\frac{1}{2}$? Why?

Multiple Slices

Have students decide how many parts they need to partition things into so that they can be shared equally by groups of different sizes. For example: Pop likes to cut the cake so that it can be shared equally by the grandchildren, but he isn't always sure how many will come. Ask: If sometimes three come and sometimes five come, what number of pieces could he cut? What is the smallest number of pieces? Repeat for numbers that have factors in common, such as six and eight (so that 48 works but is not the smallest) Repeat for other pairs of numbers that have no factors in common. Draw out that the number of pieces has to be a multiple of each number of children. (Link to Understanding Fractional Numbers, Key Understanding 2.)

Factor Bingo

Ask students to draw a 5 x 5 grid and fill the grid with numbers. The teacher holds up a number such as 36 and students cross off numbers that multiply to make 36. The student who is the first to cross off a line or a diagonal is the winner. Discuss the most suitable numbers to use in their grid and the strategy for being able to cross off the most numbers. Ask: Why would 36 be a better number to hold up than 37?

Making Factor Trees

Invite students to investigate factors and products by making different factor trees, e.g. for 36.

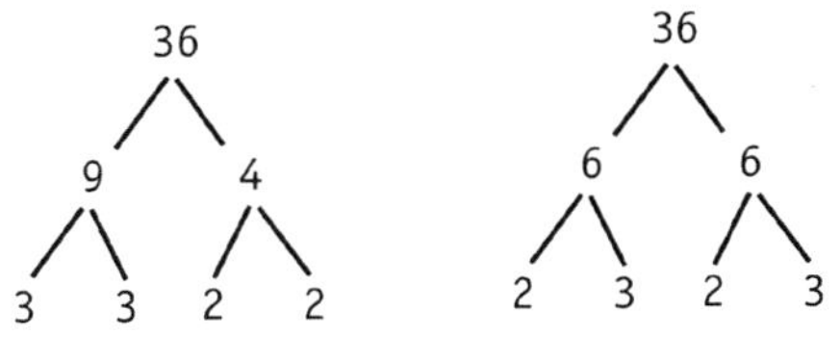

Comparing Factor Trees

Have students compare the different factor trees for the same number. Ask: What is it about the number in the last row that tells you that you have all the factors? (See Understand Operations, Key Understanding 5.)

Divisibility

Ask students to generate multiples of numbers such as two, three, four, five, six and nine, and investigate divisibility rules of each number. Ask: What numbers will divide evenly into 2004? How do you know?

Doubling Strategy

Have students look for multiplications where factorising enables them to use a doubling strategy. For example: 19 x 4 can be solved by saying double 19 is 38 and double again is 76. Ask: Would you be able to use doubling to solve 34 x 2, 45 x 4, 8 x 15 or 16 x 34? Why?(See Key Understanding 5.)

Shortcuts

Extend the previous activity by having students build up a chart of other shortcuts, using factors to multiply. For example: To calculate 36 x 25 you can say 9 x 4 x 25 which is 9 x 100. Ask students to use factors to work out 28 x 25 and compare this way to the way an adult they know works it out. Ask: Which way is easier? Why?

Easier Multiplication

Have students factorise numbers to multiply more easily. For example:

- 8 x 32 can be rewritten as 2 x 2 x 2 x 32. That's double 32, three times.
- 14 x 15 can be rewritten as 7 x 2 x 3 x 5. That's the same as 5 x 2 x 7 x 3, which is 10 x 21.

Multiplying by Ten

Ask students to look for multiplications where factors of two and five enable them to multiply by ten. For example: 15 x 18 is the same as (3 x 5) x (3 x 6), which is the same as (3 x 5) x (3 x 3 x 2), which is the same as 3 x 3 x 3 x 10.

KEY UNDERSTANDING 4

Place value and basic number facts together allow us to calculate with any whole or decimal numbers.

From the earliest years, students should be challenged, through practical problem situations, to calculate with numbers larger than those that they readily do by counting or using known facts. As suggested in Key Understandings 2 and 3, partitioning is the key to calculation. By decomposing and composing numbers into convenient forms, we can turn any required calculation into one involving a series of applications of basic facts.

In most cases, computational strategies rely on the flexible use of place value, where numbers are partitioned in both standard (47 = 40 + 7) and non-standard (47 = 20 + 27 or 47 = 43 + 4) ways. Although numbers can be partitioned in many ways, partitioning involving tens, hundreds, thousands etc. is particularly helpful because these numbers are easy to calculate with. For example, when a student finds 97 + 26 by shifting three across from the 26 to the 97 to make 100 + 23, it is because she or he knows it is easier to add 23 to 100. When a student finds 176 + 206 by jumping along a number line in hundreds first, she or he is also using place value.

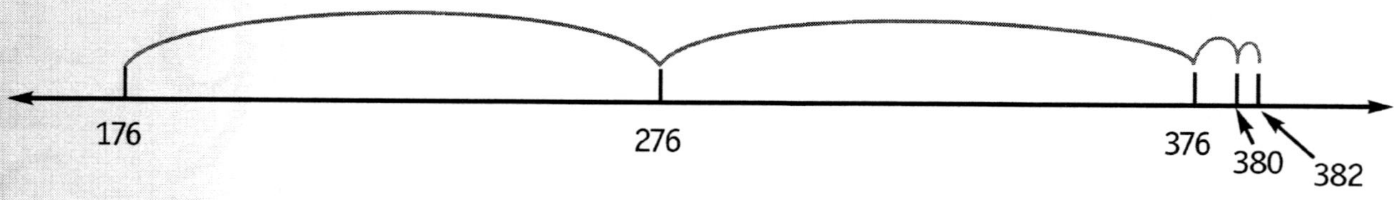

The place-value concepts in Understand Whole and Decimal Numbers, Key Understanding 6, should be extended and deepened as students experiment with ways of computing with larger numbers using manipulative materials, diagrams, calculators, visual images and patterns in the numbers themselves. Teaching place-value concepts separately as a prerequisite to calculation is unnecessary and likely to be ineffective. Rather, students should construct increasingly deeper concepts of part-part-whole and place value as we challenge them with opportunities for making estimates and computations.

Students who have achieved Level 2 partition into tens and units to add and subtract two-digit whole numbers. They may use mental or informal paper-and-pencil methods including diagrams or jottings.

At Level 3, they explain their written or mental method for adding and subtracting in a way that shows they understand *why* they work and they can use standard place-value partitions to help them multiply and divide a whole number by a single-digit whole number.

Those who have achieved Level 4 have the flexibility to partition whole numbers in both standard and non-standard ways to meet the particular demands of the current computational task (link to Key Understandings 5 and 6, and Understand Whole and Decimal Numbers, Key Understanding 6).

At Level 5, they have extended this flexibility to the partitioning of decimal numbers.

SAMPLE LEARNING ACTIVITIES

Beginning ✔

Hands

Have pairs of students each hold up fingers to show a number between five and ten, e.g. six as 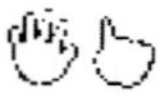 and eight as . To calculate 6 + 8, they put the two fives together to show ten and add to the others to give four more. Practise until students are able to quickly say the sums.

Groups of Ten

Use groups of ten to count large collections. For example: Give students a handful of materials such as beans, buttons or toothpicks. Ask them to arrange these into groups of ten to count by tens then ones, or skip count by twos or threes. (See Understanding Whole and Decimal Numbers, Key Understandings 5 and 6.)

Breaking Up

Encourage students to talk about how they 'break up' numbers to make them easy to work with. Look for responses that show use of basic facts such as: *I know five and three is eight; I thought of five and three as four and four.* With 5 + 4, focus on answers such as *four and four and one more*.

Adding Ten

Suggest students use a number line and calculator to add ten to any number. Have students write 3 + 10 = 13 and 13 + 10 = 23. Ask: Which of the digits in 23 will change when you add ten? Why? What happens when we add ten again? What if you take away ten? What if you add nine? Take away nine? Continue this for one to ten. (Link to Key Understanding 9 and Understanding Whole and Decimal Numbers, Key Understanding 6.)

Partitioning

Have students build on the previous idea and partition numbers to help calculate. For example:

- 'five and something', so with five and eight you know eight is five and three more. So it's 5 + 5 is ten and three more
- expand this later into 'ten and something'
- think of nine as one less than ten so think of nine and eight as ten and eight less one
- eight is two less than ten so eight and seven is 17 minus two
- seven and six could be double six add one.

(See Understand Operations, Key Understanding 7.)

Hundreds

Extend the previous activity to numbers into the hundreds for students to count on and back through the decades by tens. For example:

- 160 – 30: 30 is three tens so it's 160, 150, 140
- 140 + 50: 140, 150, 160, 170, 180, 190.

Students can count how many tens by keeping track on their fingers.

Class Collections

Store class sets of glue, scissors, thick felt pens and so on in rows of ten and have a student check by glancing how many have been collected or need to be collected. Ask: How many tens can you see? Can you combine some to make another group of ten?

Combining Tens

Have students use ten-frames to experiment with ways to calculate with larger numbers. For example: Ask students to set up dots on ten-frames to show 17 + 23. Ask: How does moving your frames to put the tens together help? How can you put the singles together to more easily see what the total is? How can we use numbers and signs to show what you did with the tens and ones? (Link to Understand Whole and Decimal Numbers, Key Understanding 6.)

Orders

Use materials such as paper clips or notebooks—singles, in packs of ten or 100—for solving individual students' orders. For example: At the shop, mini chocolate frogs can be bought as singles, and in packets of ten and 100. Jack wants 72. What packs will be in his order? Mae Win wants 142. What are the different ways we could make up her order? (See Understanding Whole and Decimal Numbers, Key Understanding 6.)

Larger Orders

Expand on the previous activity and ask students to suggest other combinations for filling large orders by using diagrams or referring to the numbers alone, apart from materials, to work out these combinations.

SAMPLE LEARNING ACTIVITIES

Middle ✓✓✓

Building on Basics

Challenge students to build from their basic facts by saying: If I know 3 + 4 = 7 then I also know ... because ... Ask: Does knowing that 3 + 4 = 7 help you know what 30 and 40 is? Have students make personal lists of what they know from the one fact and add to this as they discover more. This activity can later be extended to include multiples, e.g. 3 x 4 and 30 x 4; large whole numbers and decimals, e.g. 0.3 + 0.4 = 0.7.

Problems in Context

Have students visualise or represent problems in a way that enables them to use place value to calculate an answer. For example: Trisha's family has to travel 123 km to their campsite. They have already gone 87 km. How much further is there to go? Students can jump forward along a number line, or visualise the same saying: *87, 90 (that's three) 100, 110, 120, (that's 30) and 123 (three more) so that's 36.* (Link to Understanding Whole and Decimal Numbers, Key Understandings 5 and 6.)

Combinations to 100

Encourage students to solve problems by using combinations to 100. For example: Lawson had $87 and Filomena had $123. How much more does Lawson need to earn to have the same amount? 100 – 87 is 13 so 13 + 23 is 36.

Maths Methods

Present an operation horizontally on the board, e.g. 62 – 23. Allow time for students to calculate in their head and then ask them to explain what they did. Record methods on the blackboard and draw out how most methods break up the numbers. Ask: Why did you break the numbers up in that way? Why did you put those two numbers together first? (See Understanding Whole and Decimal Numbers, Key Understanding 6.)

Non-standard Place Value

Have students solve problems using non-standard place value partitions by moving from one number to another on a 100 chart. For example: We need 74 balloons for a party and we have 36. How many more do we need? This could be solved by counting on by tens: 36, 46, 56, 66, 76, – 2. That's 40 – 2 so the answer is 38. Or counting back from 74: 74, 64, 54, 44, 34, + 2. That's 40 – 2 = 38. Ask: Which do you find easiest? Why? What other methods could be used?

1–100 Grid

Ask students to visualise movements on a 100 chart to solve problems involving addition and subtraction. Discuss how moving up or down a row is the same as adding or subtracting ten and moving back or forth along a row is the same as adding or subtracting one. (Link to Understanding Whole and Decimal Numbers, Key Understanding 5.)

Grid Partitions

Have students explore ways of breaking up numbers for multiplication calculations. For example: Represent 6 x 14 using grid paper and find an easy way of breaking up the grid to help work out the total.

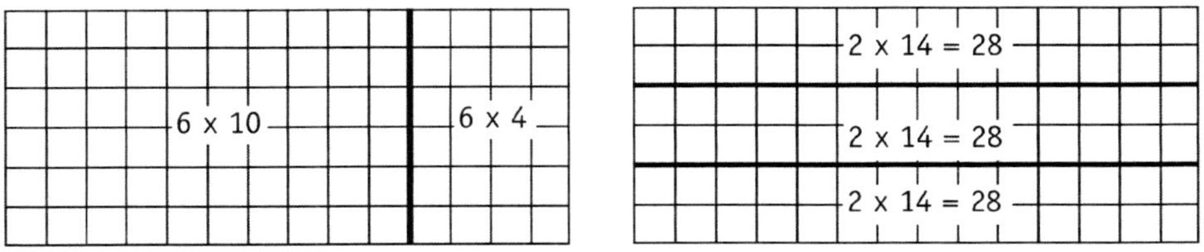

Ask students to share the various partitions and decide which ones make calculating easier. (See Sample Lesson 1, page 130.)

Moving Squares

Have students draw representations of three-digit numbers on ten-squared grid paper to help add or subtract. When adding, ask students to look for ways of 'moving' some squares from one number to the other to make groups of tens. For example: 136 + 248, move two from 136 and add to 248 to make 250.

Bundling Materials

Ask students why it is helpful to bundle materials into tens to solve division problems. For example: When sharing 75 sweets among three students, making bags of ten to begin with means you can share out using groups rather than ones.

Personal Strategies

Have students use their own methods to calculate using strategies such as those in the previous activity. Ask them to show how they have worked it out by writing the way they carried out the calculation, and why they choose to write down those particular numbers. They could do this on an overhead projector.

Explaining Procedure

Show the students a procedure used by 'another class' to solve a calculation. For example: 273 x 4 done as 800 + 280 + 12 = 1092. Ask: What did they do with 273 x 4 to get 800/280/12? How did it help them to solve this problem? Ask students to explain what is helpful about this procedure, and how they would modify it to suit them. Have them use it for similar and other ways of calculating, e.g. 4 x 250 add 4 x 23.

SAMPLE LEARNING ACTIVITIES

Later ✓✓✓

100 Chart

Have students add and subtract numbers by visualising a 100 chart. Show them a 100 chart for a few minutes and then remove it from view. Ask: What number is below 43? How do you know? What number is three to the right of 72? How do you know? You are at 34, go right two steps and up three. Where are you now? You are at 68. How do you get to 75? Ask students to describe the jumps needed to calculate 24 + 39 and 83 – 47.

1000 Chart

Extend the previous activity by having students make up a 1000 chart with one to 100 along the top row, 101 to 200 on the second row and so on. Ask similar questions as students use the chart to work out and explain their jumps.

Leap Along a Number Line

Have students make jumps of one, ten or 100 on a number line to calculate 423 + □ = 632 or 891 – 674 = □. (See Key Understanding 2.)

Multiples of Ten

Invite students to build up their own rules for multiplying and dividing by multiples of ten, e.g. they could make up number trails for their partner, who can work backwards to check their answer.

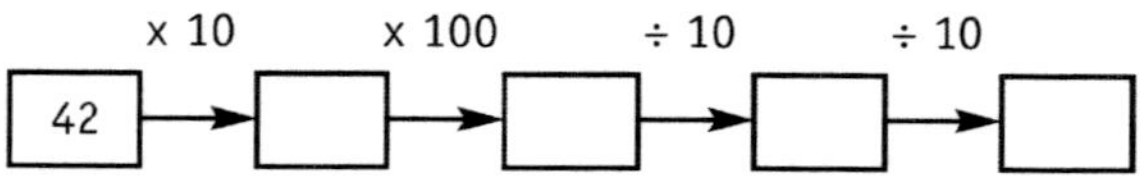

Sequences

Have students add on different sequences of ones, tens, 100s or 1000s to a starting number. For example: Write 38 on a card and line up MABs covered with a long card.

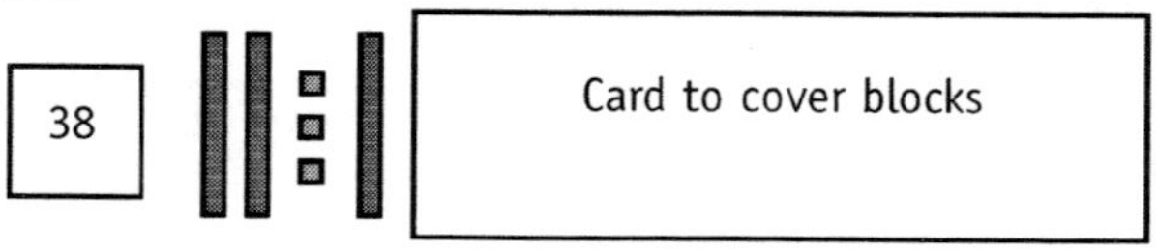

Students draw back the card to sequentially reveal the blocks as their partner counts on from the number: 48, 58, 61, 71. This can be extended by including hundreds (flats) or thousands (big cubes).

Decimals

Have students use a 2 mm grid with a 10 x 10 square representing one whole to calculate with decimals. For example: For 6 x 3.34 a student might draw around the squares showing six lots of 3.34 and show that 6 x 3 = 18 and write 18; 6 x three-tenths is one and eight-tenths, that's 1.8; 6 x four-hundredths is two-tenths and four-hundredths, that's 0.24. Add to reach a total. Discuss the different ways students used the grid to work it out.

Partitioning Numbers

Organise pairs of students to partition numbers to help do calculations. For example: For 99 x 27, they see 99 as 100 – 1, think *That's a hundred 27s less one 27*, and jot down: 2700 – 27

2600 + (100 – 27)

To calculate 4 x 27, they might think, *Four lots of 20 and four lots of seven*, and jot down the partial products on paper: 80 + 28

Later, for 34 x 27 they might think, *That's 30 27s, add four 27s*, leading to something like the standard algorithm. (Link to Key Understanding 6.)

Rewriting Number Sentences

Ask students to partition numbers and rewrite a number sentence in a variety of ways. For example: 73 – 38 can be written as 73 – 13 – 25; 73 – 21 – 17; (60 – 30) + (13 – 8); 73 – 30 – 8. Ask students to exchange number sentences with a partner who checks that the total has not changed. Ask: Which one of these ways would be most useful when calculating?

Rewriting Multiplication

Repeat the previous activity using a multiplication number sentence.
For example, 55 x 67 can be written as:

50 x 67 + 5 x 67; 100 x 67 ÷ 2 + 10 x 67 ÷ 2; 50 x 60 + 50 x 7 + 5 x 60 + 5 x 7.

Equivalent Number Sentences

Extend the previous activities by having students partition numbers and write equivalent number sentences that make calculating more difficult. Ask them to explain why it is more difficult in each case.

Division Number Sentences

Have students use place value and jottings to calculate division number sentences such as 272 ÷ 16. A student might jot down:

10 160
5 80
= 240, 32 left, that's another two 16s, so 17.

Ask students to share and try a different strategy. Ask: Which was easiest? Why?

KU 4

SAMPLE LESSON 1

Sample Learning Activity: Middle—'Grid Partitions', page 127

Key Understanding 2: We can think of a number as a sum or difference in different ways. We can rearrange the parts of an addition without changing the quantity.

Key Understanding 3: Place value and basic number facts together allow us to calculate with any whole or decimal numbers.

Working Towards: Levels 2 and 3

Teacher's Purpose

Students in my Year 3/4 class had used tiles and grid paper to explore partitioning.

18 is 6 columns of 3 = 3 columns of 3 + 3 columns of 3

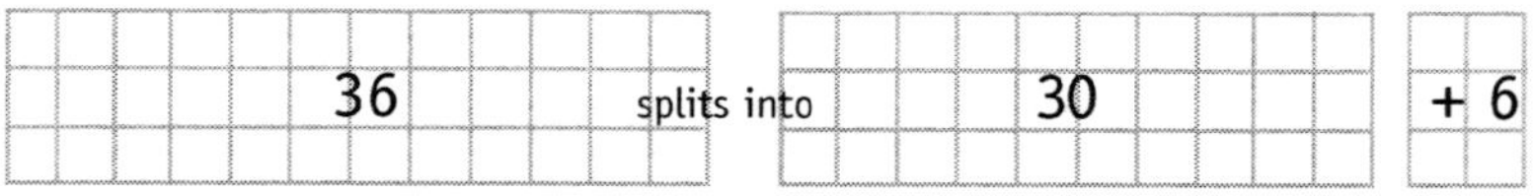

36 is 12 columns of 3 = 10 columns of 3 + 2 columns of 3

I wanted to introduce the idea that splitting quantities into tens often made calculating easier. I decided to give the students several problems over the next few weeks that would give me the opportunity to draw this out.

I asked students to plan how many sweets they needed to make sweet bags for a party. The numbers involved made it hard to count.

Action

Stacey used an array representation to help in the task. He was working out 12 bags with eight chocolate buttons in each bag. He drew eight dots in a row, then started to do another row of eight below it.

Stacey stopped, then continued down the page drawing the first dot only in a total of 12 rows. He explained that he didn't have to draw all the buttons, he could keep counting the first row over and over for all the rows. He wrote the total for each row as he went.

Connection and Challenge

I used the overhead projector to show Stacey's approach to the class. I thought he would be able to transfer his thinking to a grid array.

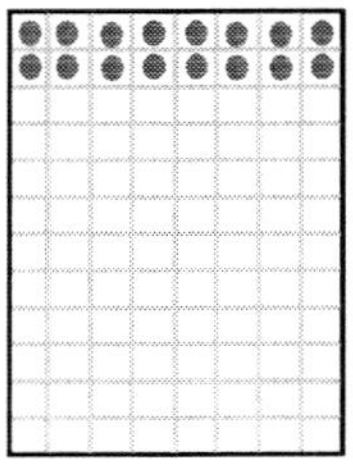

Stacey's rectangular array for 8 chocolate buttons in 12 bags.

I asked Stacey to draw the chocolate buttons from his first bag in a row, with one button in each grid square, and then the next bag in a row beneath that. I then challenged him: Without drawing any more sweets, make a rectangle around all the squares you'll need to finish drawing all your bags of chocolate buttons.

He drew a 12 x 8 rectangle and said: *It's got eight squares for eight sweets on that row, and that's one bag. Then I counted 12 rows down so there's 12 bags.*

I asked the class if Stacey needed to draw in all the buttons to find out how many. Everyone said no, he could just count the squares. I then asked them to show their sweets and bags on grid paper. All but one or two understood how the rows of squares showed how many sweets for each guest.

Drawing out the Mathematical Idea

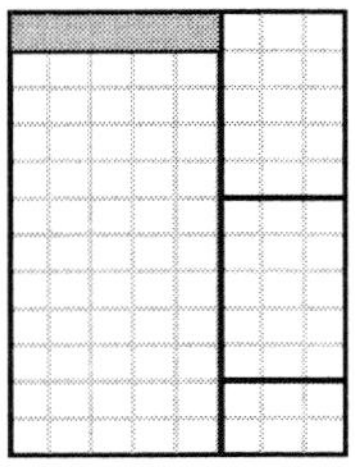

1. Stacey: *I did it in 5s, so you can do 5, 10, 15 ... 90 and then it's six more.*

We went back to Stacey's grid and talked about how his array could help him calculate how many chocolate buttons he needed.

Thus, I moved from Stacey's original array to partitioning in tens with its link to place value, which Su Li related to the work we had done with tiles.

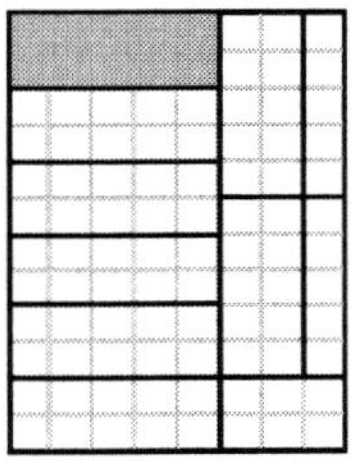

2. Teacher: *Great! That was easier than 1, 2, 3, ..., Is there a way to use 10s to do it?*

Stacey: you could put the 5s together like this and do 10, 20, 30 ..., 80, than 85, 90, and 6, 96, that's faster.

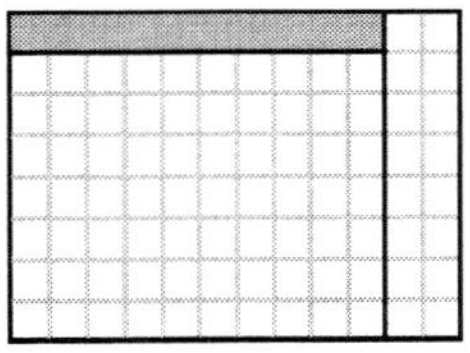

3. Teacher: *Yes! Now if we start again with it turned this way, can anyone find an even easier way to use 10s to help work it out?*

Su Li: (who also had 12 guests) *I'm thinking about the tiles and you could make 12 across into 10 and 2 then it's 8 rows of 10, that's 80 and 8 is 88 and another 8 ... that's 2 to make 90 and 6 left, 96.*

If students are to believe that counting the squares tells them how many chocolate buttons, a connection has to be made between the quantities shown on the grid and the quantities in the problem situation. This is not as obvious to students as we sometimes assume.

Opportunity to Learn

The students then returned to their own problems and showed the required quantities on an array while I worked with individuals.

Jason immediately split his 14 x 3 array into a ten by three and four by three. He then counted in tens, 10, 20, 30 and added on the 12 he knew to get 42.

Sandy was working with a much smaller multiplier (7 x 8) and she did not know the basic fact. Nevertheless, she used the idea of partitioning and first split her 7 x 8 array into two seven by fours, then each of those into two seven by twos. She wrote 14 + 14 + 14 + 14, then began doubling. 14 + 14 is 20, 24, 25, 26, 27, 28 (counting the last on four fingers). 28 + 28, oh, that's too hard. I helped her see how this calculation was represented on her array by the first split. We then drew a line to separate each 28 into 20 and eight and she immediately saw how to complete the calculation.

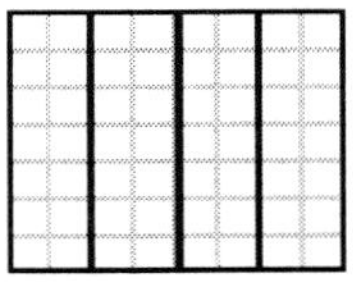

14 + 14 +14 + 14

28 + 28

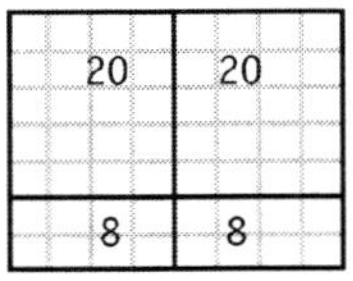

Sandy calculated by saying 20, 30, 40, 48 (then counted on by 2s, pointing at the squares) 50, 52, 54, 56.

Not all students yet saw why partitioning by tens was especially helpful, but all experimented with splitting their arrays in personally useful ways.

KEY UNDERSTANDING 5

There are strategies we can practise to help us do calculations in our head.

Students should learn to see mental arithmetic as the first resort when they need to calculate. Mental computation refers to doing calculations 'in your head' and involves much more than recall of basic facts. It is not necessarily quicker than written computation. Sometimes it will be slower. Its importance lies in its portability and flexibility. If students develop the idea that 'mental' should be quick or obvious, they may be reluctant to try to do calculations in their head.

Mental methods are usually different from written methods and students rarely get better at mental computation from practising written computation. The best mental methods help us to store the bits of the calculation in our heads as we go along. Thus, many people find it easier to do 37 + 26 mentally by adding the tens first (47, 57) and then the ones (and six more is) than to mentally add the ones, regroup and then add the tens as we do for the written algorithm. It helps to work from left to right so that the parts of the number are mentally stored in the order they are written and said—starting with the biggest part and progressively getting closer to the answer as you gather the bits: 37, 47, 57, 60, 63.

As they proceed through the primary years, students should develop an increasing repertoire of mental strategies to assist in calculating and estimating mentally—initially with whole numbers and later with money and simple fractions. A list of strategies for mental calculation is provided in the Background Notes (see page 194). Students should be encouraged to develop personal mental strategies, to experiment with and compare strategies used by others, and to choose strategies to suit their own strengths and the situation. This requires a *high* level of number sense based on a strong grasp of place value and of the relationships between operations. In general, mental methods backed up by informal written 'jottings' should receive more attention than standard written methods.

Students who have achieved Level 1 of the outcome mentally add and subtract small numbers generated from stories; that is, they work with small, easily visualised numbers that they count in their 'mind's eye'. At Level 2, they have begun to use some mental strategies to work out addition and subtraction facts that they do not know from those that they do know, and to make simple extensions. Students at Level 3 use mental strategies to work out basic multiplication facts that they do not yet remember. They have begun to build up a repertoire of strategies, such as compensation, which help them add and subtract 'easy' two-digit numbers mentally.

Those who have achieved Level 4 have considerably extended their repertoire of strategies for reducing memory load. They can mentally add and subtract two-digit numbers and mentally multiply and divide by single-digit numbers and multiples of ten for 'easy' numbers such as 4 x 32. Furthermore, they will try mental computation first for one-off calculations.

At Level 5, they are skilled in mental computation with whole numbers and money, and calculate mentally with easily visualised fractions.

SAMPLE LEARNING ACTIVITIES

Beginning ✓

Counting On

Have students say which number they are able to count on from when adding small collections, e.g. 3 + 2. Think of two, now count on three more. Think of three, now count on two more. Think of four and count on three more. Try thinking of five and counting on three more. Ask: What other numbers could you think of, then add three more on? Does it always give the same result as counting them all? (See Understanding Whole and Decimal Numbers, Key Understanding 2.)

Counting On and Back

When students have begun to use 'counting on', ask: Why did you start from three? Does it give you the same result as starting the counting at one? Compare 'counting the lot' with 'counting on' or 'back' when combining and separating small collections using materials and diagrams. Extend this later by asking: Does it give the same result when you count on from the bigger number when adding, say, eight and five? Does it help?

Adding Chunks

Begin a counting sequence at one. Have students take turns to count aloud the next ten, using their fingers to keep check. After several students have counted, ask students to predict where the next student will stop. Ask: Can you think of another way to find the next lot of ten without counting by ones? Repeat later with each student counting the next five.

More Chunks

Extend the previous activity by starting at any number to nine. For example: Start at three and use fingers to count aloud to 13 then move to another student to count ten more. After several students have counted, ask students to predict where the next student will stop. Ask: Can you think of another way to find the next lot of ten without counting by ones? Later, link to numbers in a column on a 100 chart and extend, adding into higher numbers.

Number Line

Have students use the class number line as an aid to hold numbers that are too large for them to keep in their head when mentally calculating. Ask them to think of the number line in their head and imagine counting on or back four from a given number to help them build a mental number line for themselves. For example: There are four students away today. Use your mental number line to count back to see how many are present.

Skip Counting

Vary the previous strategy to imagine skip counting up and down a number line. Teach someone else how you imagine it. (See Understanding Whole and Decimal Numbers, Key Understanding 1.)

Compatible Numbers

When adding a list of numbers, ask students to look for numbers they can combine more easily. Focus on adding the numbers that combine to make ten first, then go back to add others. For example:

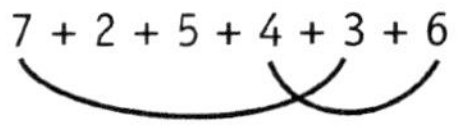

Ask: Which numbers add together to make ten? Is this way of adding a string of numbers more helpful than adding in the order they are written? Why? (See Key Understanding 6.)

Did You Know?

Place a scattered collection of ten or so 'number tiles' on the table in front of students and ask them to add to find the total score. Observe how they go about it.

Students in Years 2 to 4 were asked to do this. Many were able to add the numbers, using and building on basic facts. However, almost all added the numbers as they came to them. For example: 6 + 9 = 15 + 5 = 20 + 8 = 28 + 7 = 35 + 4, etc. Very few thought to use known combinations to ten to make the task easier.

Thus, although the students remembered basic facts and were quite good at adding on small numbers, they could not use them flexibly to make the task easier and probably more accurate. Indeed, in this case, they could have easily physically moved the tiles together to make combinations of ten, but rarely did.

It is important to encourage students to use their number knowledge in flexible ways to make calculation easier. This is an essential aspect of number sense.

SAMPLE LEARNING ACTIVITIES

Middle ✔✔

Compatible Numbers

Encourage students to develop a visual image of number partitions to 20 by using counters in one or two ten-frames as they are flashed on an overhead projector. Have students say how many counters and how many empty spaces they saw and record these combinations to 20. (See 'Ten-frames', page 111.)

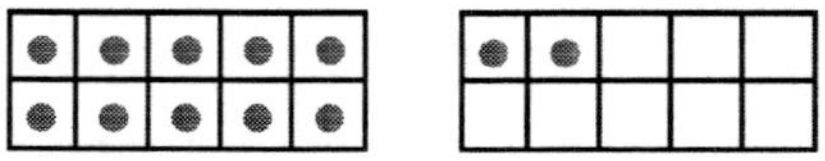

What Is the Question?

Give students a number (say, 36) and give them one minute to write as many questions as they can which have that number as the answer.

Choose the Operation (1)

Give each pair of students a die. Ask each student to write down 50, and take turns to throw the die and decide whether to add, subtract, multiply or divide the number on the die to his or her own score (starting with 50). The winner is the first to reach zero or 100.

Choose the Operation (2)

Extend the previous activity to include two dice and allow a combination of operations. Extend again to practise calculating with tens by labelling a die with ten through to 60. Start with 500 and have a goal of zero or 1000.

Target Practice

Make three dice with these numbers on their faces:

Die 1: 0, 1, 2, 3, 4, 5 Die 2: 6, 7, 8, 9, 1, 0 Die 3: 10, 10, 10, 1, 1, 1

One student in each group picks a target number less than 100 and throws the dice. Using the numbers showing on the dice, each group member writes a number sentence that gets as close as possible to the target. Any operations can be used. The winner is the one coming closest to target.

Roll the Dice

Use the dice from Target Practice. Break the class into two teams and roll the dice. Students in each team have three minutes to write as many correct number sentences (e.g. 2 x 8 + 10 = 26) as they can. When three minutes is up, members of one team read out their sentences. If both teams have the sentence, they both cross it off. Any sentence not crossed off is a point for that team. Continue until one team reaches a designated winning score.

Decade

Remove the picture cards from a deck of cards and let the ace be one. Have players choose a target decade, e.g. the thirties. Each player draws four cards and uses any operation to come up with a number sentence to make a number in the target decade. All four cards must be used. A point is scored for each correct sentence.

Wipe Out

Ask students to enter a two-digit number in their calculator. They then use addition to wipe out the first two digits from right to left to get 100. Do another, and another, and another. Ask: Can you do it in just one step? ('Wipe Out' means to replace with a zero.)

Doubling

Have students use doubling to add. For example: 39 + 47 could be changed to 30, add 40, add eight and eight. Give students a series of additions (e.g. 36 + 55, 18 + 49, 67 + 88) and ask: What double would be helpful for each?

Multiply the Parts

Ask students to investigate how numbers can be broken up to make multiplying easier. For example: 12 x 8 can be thought of as 10 x 8 add 2 x 8; 99 x 6 can be thought of as (100 x 6) – 6. Ask students to partition the numbers in a problem, solve it mentally and share how they stored it as they went along.

Compensation

Give students an example of another student's thinking to try. For example: Abbey did 58 + 37 by taking two from the 37 and adding it to 58 to make 60. Then she added 60 to 35 to get 95. Have students try Abbey's strategy of moving parts from one to another for: 19 + 21, 22 + 34, 39 +12. Ask: Why did you move that bit? What compatible numbers did you make?

Front-end Loading (1)

Have students visualise counting on and back on a number line or 100 chart to solve an addition or subtraction problem. For example: 24 + 37; start from the tens; repeat, starting from ones. Ask: What did you say to yourself when you started from the tens? What did you say when you started from the ones? Which way is easier to keep track of the answer? Draw out that it is easier to remember the bits in our head if we do the tens first because we keep saying the new number as we go, e.g. 37, 47, 57 and four more is 61.

Middle ✔✔

Front-end Loading (2)

Have students mentally calculate 42 + 37, then share what they said to themselves. Record their thoughts on the blackboard. Draw out the front-end strategies where:

- you start at the large number then bring in the tens then the ones of the other number, e.g. 42 add 30 that's 72, then add seven, that's 79
- you do the tens first then the ones, e.g. 40 add 30, that makes 70, add two, equals 72, add seven equals 79.

Have students use the front-end strategy to add and subtract. Later, extend to three-digit calculations such as 234 + 121 or 664 – 231. (See Understanding Whole and Decimal Numbers, Key Understanding 6.)

Front-end Loading 3

Repeat the previous activity to draw out subtraction strategies, e.g. for 66 – 28:

- 66 take 20 is 66, 56, 46, take eight, that's 46, take six (40) and take two (38)
- 60 take 20 that's 40 ,then add the six that's 46, take eight, that's 40, 38.

How Did You Do It?

Have students choose their own strategy for doing calculations in their head, then report on what they did and why they chose that approach. Draw out how certain approaches help you remember the bits (see Sample Lesson 2, page 142).

Constructing Arrays

Ask students to find factors by constructing all possible arrays for a given number using grid paper, geoboard or blocks. (See Key Understanding 3.) Write a list of factors for each number and use these to work out the more difficult basic multiplication facts. For example: To work out 7 x 8 you can say 7 x 4 x 2 or go further and say 7 x 2 x 2 x 2. Have students sort a range of multiplication facts according to whether using factors helps or not.

Factorising

Have students explore how factorising numbers in a multiplication number sentence can make mental calculations much easier. For example: 4 x 16 can be rewritten as (2 x 2) x 16, which is double 16, and double again. Ask students to solve similar calculations where using factors of two enables students to use the doubling strategy, e.g. 6 x 32, 8 x 21 and so on. Draw out the fact that you can hold the numbers in your head as you go so there is not as much to remember. (Link to Key Understanding 3.)

SAMPLE LEARNING ACTIVITIES

Later ✔✔✔

Compatible Numbers (1)

Have students practise recognising partitions of a 100 square at a glance. (See 'Grid Partitions', page 112.) Ask students to draw a line to partition a 100 square (on 2 mm squared paper) into two parts. Show your diagram to a partner and see how quickly they can recognise and name the two parts. Repeat the activity using ten adjacent 100 squares to partition 1000 into two parts.

Compatible Numbers (2)

Extend the previous activity by making the 100 square a unit of one. Have students name the two parts as compatible decimal or common fractions and percentages that add to make one, e.g. 0.3, $\frac{30}{100}$, 30% with 0.7, $\frac{70}{100}$ and 70%.

Target Practice

Play Target Practice (see 'Target Practice', page 136) and then extend to use more dice or to include fractions and decimals on the faces.

Choose the Operation

Play Choose the Operation (see 'Choose the Operation', page 136) and extend to practise calculating with tens by labelling a die ten through to 60. Start with 500 and have a goal of zero or 1000. Extend again by rolling the die ten times in front of whole class. Ask each student to decide whether to multiply by one, ten or 100 and record the result. After ten rolls they total their scores and the person closest to 1000 wins.

Compensate

Have students partition numbers in a calculation to make use of compatible numbers. For example: in 88 + 47 you can take 12 from 47, put it with the 88 to make 100 and you're left with 35, that's 135. 75 – 27 is 75 – 25 – 2, which is 48. Ask: How can you split the numbers in these calculations to use that strategy: 88 + 32, 25 + 78, 100 – 47.

Wipe Out

Play Wipe Out (see 'Wipe Out', page 137). Have students begin with a three-digit number and initially wipe out digits from right to left to get to 1000. Ask: Can you wipe out the three digits in fewer steps?

Number Sentences

Ask students to write number sentences that could be mentally solved using compatible numbers, e.g. 45 + □ = 100, 23 + 77, 1000 – 625. Swap with a partner to solve.

Later ✔✔✔

Front-end Loading (1)

Have students visualise a number line and make jumps of one, ten or 100 to solve problems such as 45 + □ = 107, 423 + □ = 632 or 891 – 674 = □. Ask students to say how they jumped to their goal number and kept track of the bits as they went. Ask: Is it easier to first add or subtract the ones, or the largest place in a number?

Front-end Loading (2)

Present what two students said when they were calculating 465 + 132: Ben said *465, 565, 595, 597*; Jeremy said *500, 590, 597*. Ask students to work out what they were thinking, describe the difference between the strategies and choose one to calculate these: 335 + 523, 464 – 212. Ask: Would you use the same approach to add 453 + 175 in your head?

Front-end Loading (3)

Ask students to use this approach to mentally solve a range of two-digit multiplications. For example: 34 x 12 could be thought of as 34 x 10 add 34 x 2. Ask: Are all two-digit multiplications made easy using this approach? Which ones were? Which ones weren't?

Factorising

Have students factorise numbers in a multiplication number sentence to calculate mentally. For example:

- 8 x 32 can be thought of as double, double, double 32
- 14 x 15 is jotted down as 7 x 2 x 3 x 5. That's ten times 21, which is 210.

Give students a range of multiplication calculations to solve by factorising.

Doubling

Invite students to look at a range of two-digit multiplications where factorising enables them to use a doubling strategy. For example: 19 x 4 can be done by saying double 19 is 38 and double again is 76. Ask: Would you be able to use doubling to solve 34 x 2, 45 x 4, 8 x 15 and 16 x 34? Why?

Factors of Two and Five

Repeat the previous activity, looking for the factors of two and five, which enable you to multiply by ten. For example: 15 x 18 is the same as 3 x 5 x 3 x 3 x 2, which is the same as 3 x 3 x 3 x 10, which is 270.

Renaming Fractions

Have students decide when it is useful to rename fractions as decimals (and vice-versa) to make calculation easier. Ask them to decide if renaming helps in the following examples if only an approximate answer is required: 20 600 000 x 0.52; 0.34 x 621; 824 x 0.26; 20% of $42. Students can write calculations with decimals where renaming would help, and share these with a partner.

Multiply the Parts

Present this approach for multiplying 99 x 6: 100 x 6 is 600, take away the extra six is 594. Have students use the same strategy to work out 99 x 4; 99 x 8; 7 x 99. Ask: Would this same strategy work with 19 x 3? How?

Shortcuts

Extend the previous activity by making a chart of other shortcuts using factors to mentally multiply. For example: To calculate 36 x 25 you can say 9 x 4 x 25, which is 9 x 100. Ask: What is it about the shortcuts that make it easier to do in your head?

Compensating with Fractions

Have students use the compensate strategy above when adding and subtracting fractions (e.g. fractional quantities in a recipe). To calculate $\frac{2}{3} + \frac{2}{3}$ you might say $\frac{2}{3}$ add $\frac{1}{3}$ is one. Add the other $\frac{1}{3}$ is $1\frac{1}{3}$. To calculate $3\frac{1}{3} - 1\frac{2}{3}$ you might say $3\frac{1}{3} - 1\frac{1}{3}$ is two, take the other $\frac{1}{3}$ leaves you with $1\frac{2}{3}$. Have students work out other similar examples using this strategy.

More Compensating with Fractions

Pose this problem: James rewrote the addition $\frac{3}{5} + \frac{4}{5}$ as $\frac{1}{5} + \frac{2}{5} + \frac{4}{5}$. Ask: Why would he do that? How does it make it easier to work out? Try this method on similar examples.

Partitioning with Fractions

Have students partition to solve problems involving fractions of whole amounts. For example:

- One-quarter of the 24 buttons were red. How many was that?
- Only three-quarters of the class of 32 remembered their bathers on the first day of swimming lessons. How many students was that?
- The sale is advertising 20% off all jeans. If the pair of jeans that James wants cost $50, what will the new price be?

Sale Time

Have students calculate the savings made during a '15% off' sale. Students can talk and write about what 15% actually means and then mentally calculate 15% of the cost of a backpack worth $35. Some students might think *15 cents for every dollar, so that's 15 x 35 cents*. Others may say *10% is $3.50, add half of that, which is $1.75, which gives you $5.25 off*. Students could use catalogues from supermarkets and other stores to mentally calculate common discounts such as 50%, 25% or 33% off.

Converting

Ask students to decide when it is useful to convert between fractions, decimals and percentages to make calculating easier. Ask: Does converting help in the following examples: 20 600 x 0.5; 0.5 x 620; 800 x 0.25; 20% of $40; 50% of 200.

SAMPLE LESSON 2

Sample Learning Activity: Middle—'How Did You Do It?', page 138

Key Understanding 5: There are strategies which we can practise to help us do calculations in our head.

Working Towards: Levels 2 and 3

Teacher's Purpose

I was working with my Year 4 class, over a number of weeks, identifying the range of strategies the students used to calculate mentally. I planned to heighten the students' awareness of how some mental strategies make it easier to store the bits as you go along, hence reducing memory load.

Action and Reflection

There is not one way of solving an example like this. Many different ways are possible. The idea is to encourage students to see the different ways and then to choose a method that best suits them. This lesson begins the journey towards understanding that there are many different ways of solving this sort of problem.

I wrote 38 + 27 across the board horizontally and asked the students to work out the answer in their head. After some thinking time, the majority of the students offered 65 as the answer and I wrote this on the board. I asked the students to tell each other what they had done.

Hayley said: *I did 30 add 20 that makes 50, and then I did 7 + 7, that makes 50 + 14, that's 64 and then one more, that's 65.*

I wrote on the board: 30 + 20 = 50; 7 + 7 = 14; 50 + 14= 64; 64 + 1 = 65

When I asked why she had done 30 + 20 first, Hayley said: *It makes it easier if I start from that side. I can remember where I'm up to.*

I asked: *So... Hayley says that by adding the tens first it's easier to keep track of where she is up to in her head, easier for her to remember. Did anyone else start from the tens first?*

Drawing Out the Mathematical Idea

Many of the students had started from the tens side. They agreed that it was easy to remember what they'd worked out this way, but I wanted them to think about this even further. I pointed to the initial number sentence 38 + 27 and asked them to say the first numbers aloud.

Me: *What part do you say first? They said: 30. I asked: So which number do you think about first?*

Students: *30.*

Me: *So what number do you think about first with 27?*

Students: *20, just like it is in reading it.*

James: *I tried to start with 38 but it was too hard so I changed it to 40. Then I could say 40 add 27. I can do it really quick. 40 add 27 makes 67.*

As he spoke, I wrote on the board: 40 + 27 = 67 to provide a focus for the students' thinking.

James: *I did 67 – 2, that makes 65.*

I wrote this up as 67 – 2 = 65 and then asked: *So who can tell us why James took the two away from the 67?*

Sacha: *Because he had added two to the 38 in the beginning.*

I emphasised this point: *Yes, so because he had changed the 38 to the 40 in the beginning by adding two, he had to keep this in his head and then remember to take away the two at the end.*

Hayley helped out at this point and told us that in the way she had worked hers out, she had to remember to add one at the end.

Hayley: *Because I couldn't do eight and seven, I did 7 + 7 because that's easy and then I had to remember to add the extra one afterwards. 7 + 7 is easy, it's a double like 5 + 5 and 6 + 6. You just know it, and then you don't have to stop and work it out like I have to do with 7 + 8.*

We went on to consider other ways people had begun with the tens. The lesson proceeded ...

Discussing several examples in detail is far more helpful in developing students' mental strategies than 20 examples worked alone with no discussion.

KEY UNDERSTANDING 6

There are some special calculating methods that we can use for calculations we find hard to do in our head.

Algorithms are step-by-step procedures for carrying out tasks. Most communities will expect students to be able to routinely, quickly and accurately add a column of several whole or decimal numbers, subtract one number from another, and multiply and divide at least by single-digit numbers or multiples of ten without the aid of a calculator. They may expect students to go beyond this minimum but perhaps not as quickly or automatically. Students may all have an efficient procedure but not all have the same (standard) routine. Whether or not *standard* algorithms are taught will be a decision for local school communities.

The development of any standard algorithms should *follow* the development of mental and informal written approaches and be introduced as an extension of students' existing strategies to enable them to deal with larger numbers easily. It is now understood that introducing standard written algorithms for simple numbers can be counter-productive. For example, emphasising addition of two-digit numbers in a standard column format where no trading is required, actually encourages students to focus on each column separately and to lose sight of the significance of the places. This can lead to many of the errors they later make when trading is needed. Also, we should be worried if students are using a vertical algorithm to calculate 10 000 – 9998, as it suggests that they are **not** thinking and have poor number sense. It is also important that students be expected to estimate the results of calculations prior to using any procedure.

To reiterate, students should use mostly mental approaches (see Key Understanding 5) supplemented by their own informal strategies (using diagrams or symbols) when they need the 'prop' of paper and pencil (see Key Understanding 4). *After* students are able to confidently carry out an operation using understood mental and informal paper-and-pencil strategies, it may be appropriate to help them develop standard written methods that will be efficient for more difficult calculations.

It should be made explicit to students that there are a range of standard methods that can assist accuracy and speed for more difficult calculations, but these do not replace other strategies. Students should choose the approach that suits the numbers, the context and their own preferences and skills.

Students should learn that there are a variety of alternative algorithms. They might, for example, compare some of their own strategies with the standard methods for ease, reliability and efficiency and reflect upon why we set certain algorithms out as we do, and the advantages and disadvantages of the setting out. They could also investigate and compare algorithms used in the past, and current algorithms in different countries, for example, inspecting textbooks from Australia, Japan and the Netherlands to see how they carry out subtractions or multiplications.

Students who have achieved Level 3 add and subtract whole numbers and amounts of money with ease and accuracy using efficient methods. These methods *may* be standard ones, but students do not have to learn standard methods in order to have achieved Level 3. At Level 4, they have similar facility with decimals and with multiplication and division by a single-digit number. At Level 5, they use a range of efficient, although not necessarily standard, written methods for adding, subtracting, multiplying and dividing whole numbers and common and decimal fractions.

SAMPLE LEARNING ACTIVITIES

Beginning ✓

Jottings

Ensure that students see you jot numbers down on scrap paper to use as a memory aid when calculating class numbers, times, etc. Encourage them to do the same, recording their numbers incidentally.

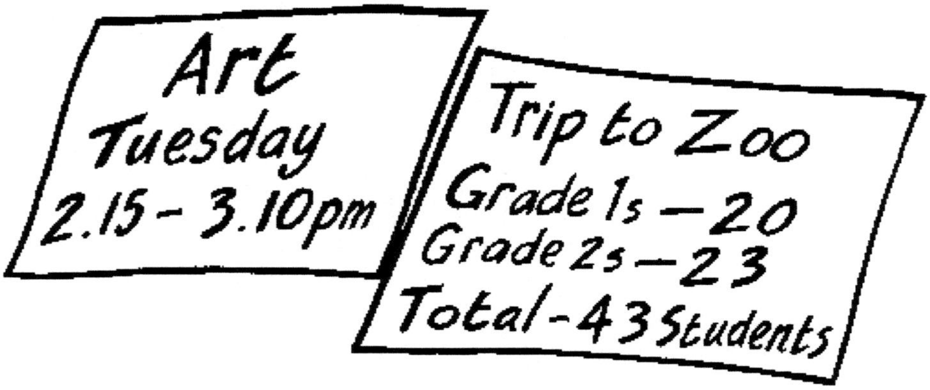

Describing

Have students describe their own methods for adding and subtracting. As the student speaks, set out the changes to the numbers as the description unfolds, e.g. *When I added 8 + 7 I took two from seven to make eight into ten.*

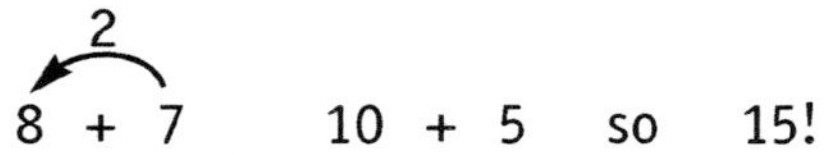

Set out students' different strategies and draw out the use of place value to make calculating easier.

Running Totals

Have students use running totals as a routine way to get totals when adding lists of numbers devised through everyday events and games, e.g. putting numbers on skittles, card games such as 21, dice games. Use dice with numbers instead of dots when playing the three-dice game (see 'Dice Games', page 100). Allocate values to letters when playing word games such as Boggle.

$$\begin{array}{r} 5 \\ +\ 6 \\ \hline 11 \\ +\ 4 \\ \hline 15 \\ +\ 1 \\ \hline 16 \end{array}$$

Informal Algorithms

When students are able to understand why 34 is 30 + 4, help them to see how expanding each number into standard place values partitions in their informal algorithms can make calculations easier.

34 is 30 + 4　　40 + 30
49 is 40 + 9　　40　　4 + 9
50　　13
60　　(10) + 3
70　　83
80

Extend to three and more addends, and later to three-digit numbers. Then have students use their own informal written strategies to solve subtraction problems. When they can confidently use their personal algorithms, encourage students to explore and share 'shortcuts'.

SAMPLE LEARNING ACTIVITIES

Middle ✓✓

Trading

When students are fluent with bundling and trading games, show them how to record the numbers and operation set-out the same way as the groups of tens and ones. For example: 36 + 46

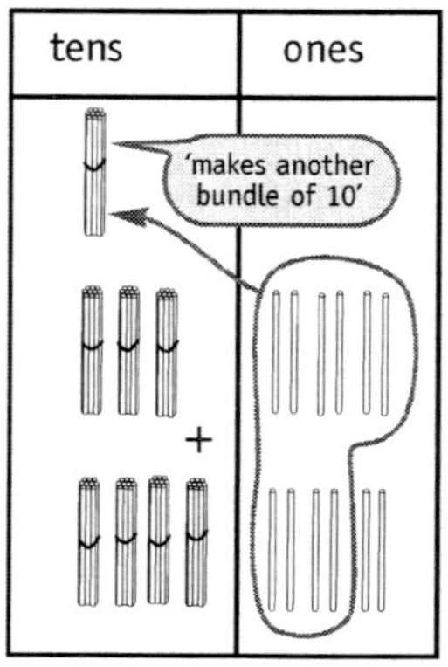

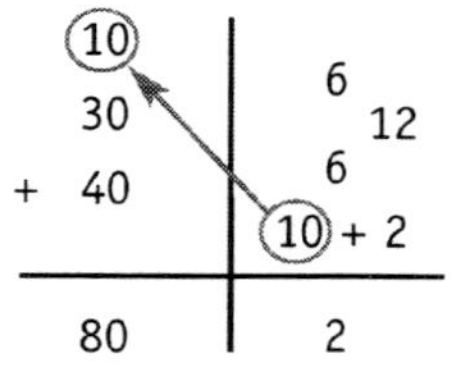

Focus students on the value of the numbers, e.g. 6, 30. Extend into the hundreds column when students need to trade into the hundreds. (See Understanding Whole and Decimal Numbers, Key Understanding 6.)

Junk Mail

Using junk mail, have students choose three prices to add and describe the different ways they have written down their numbers. Invite students to compare and debate the value of vertical and horizontal setting-out and consider whether it is easier to add the tens or the ones first. (See 'Informal Algorithms', page 147.)

Shopping

Similar to the previous activity, have students find a way of writing their numbers down to help work out how much money they have left after buying their items. Ask: How does it help to write the numbers one above the other? When dealing with large numbers, is it easier to start subtracting from the tens or ones? Why?

Try Another Way

Extend the previous activity by giving students an example of another student's thinking for them to try. For example:

56	*First I did 50 – 20 and that is 30.*
– 29	*Then I did 6 – 9 and that is – 3.*
30 – 3	*So then I did 30 – 3 and that made 27.*

Ask students to try this for several subtraction examples and say why it works.

Other Methods

Ask students to interview their parents and grandparents (or people from other cultures) to find out how they were taught to do calculations. Ask students to present to the class a method for each operation. Ask them to compare the different methods and say why each works. Students can then select a method and use it to solve similar problems.

Everyday Problems

Have students ask their parents how they solve most addition/subtraction problems in their daily lives. Ask them to compare these methods with the written methods discovered above and say why they are different.

Making It Easier

After students solve a problem using their own informal written methods, discuss how their methods are the same/different from the methods they discovered their parents use (see previous activity). Ask students when they might use their own methods and when their parents' might be more useful. (See Sample Lesson 3, page 152.)

Multiplication Grids

Have students use grid paper to represent multiplication situations. (See Key Understanding 4, 'Grid Partitions', page 127.) For example, Mum bought five T-shirts for her nieces for Christmas. Each cost $17. How much did they cost altogether? Help students see how five rows of 17 squares can represent five lots of $17, and that partitioning the rows into tens and sevens can give two easier multiplications.

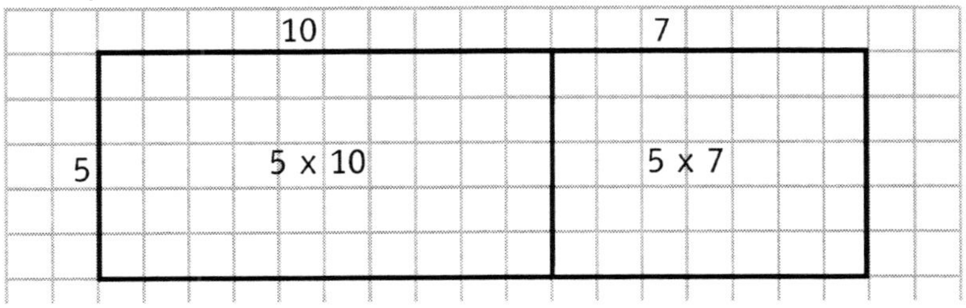

Ask students to record the separate calculations required to solve the problem. Later encourage them to use informal written strategies from the number alone.

Class Routines

Have students develop routines as a class for commonly occurring calculations. For example, adding consecutive numbers is a calculation required to solve many problems. Ask students to work out a method that is easy and reliable. Encourage students to convince others of the merits of their routine. Make a chart of the method that has been arrived at by class consensus.

SAMPLE LEARNING ACTIVITIES

Later ✓✓✓

Comparing Strategies

Invite students to compare mental and written strategies for speed and ease in different cases, some which are difficult to solve mentally and others which are easier. Model the steps in a range of standard algorithms to show how to find a solution. Ask: Is that how you would find the solution? Why?

Family Strategies

Have students ask their families to show them how to set out and carry out calculations like 554 – 376. Share these with the class and make a chart of the different ways. Ask: Did your parents do the calculation the same way as your grandparents? How are they different? Why does the 'borrow and pay back' method work?

Total Scores

Ask students to work out the total scores for each of the contestants in a gymnastics competition. For example: Dale received 7.60 in round one, 8.35 in round two, 8.80 in round three; Robin received 8.15 in round one, 8.45 in round two, 9.00 in round three. Ask students to find a way of adding the scores that is easy for them. Share the methods of adding with the class. Ask: Why do you think the routine of using columns was developed? Why do you think the routine of adding from the right column was developed?

Rules Rule!

To illustrate how rules can be misapplied, present scenarios such as: Marcy said, *Right is right! You always line up the numbers on the right, get your answer then put in the decimal point*. Ask students to explain why Marcy's rule does not work for this calculation. (Hiebert and Wearne, 1994)

$$\begin{array}{r} 3.5 \\ +\ 0.62 \\ \hline 0.97 \end{array}$$

Multiplication Grids

Extend 'Multiplication Grids' (page 149) and have students use 2 mm grid paper to represent and solve multiplication calculations with larger numbers. For example: 24 x 56. Ask: Which part of the grid shows 4 x 6, 20 x 6, etc.? Later, have students use 1 mm grid paper and place value partitioning to multiply numbers like 78 by 157.

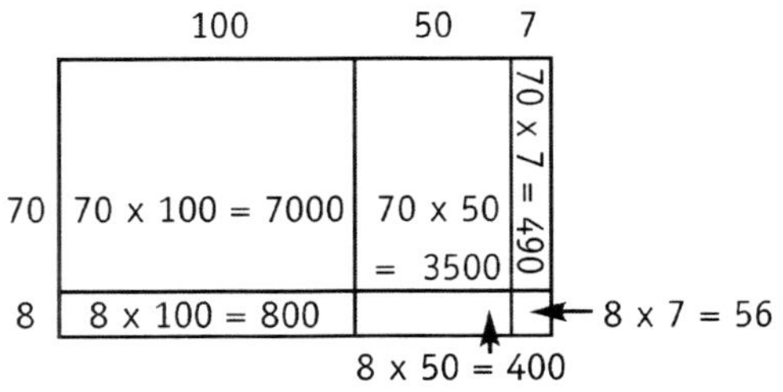

78 x 157 = 7000 + 3500 + 490 + 800 + 400 + 56

Grids and MAB Blocks

Extend the above activity by having students use MAB blocks to represent the quantities in the different sections of the multiplication grid. Ask them to relate these quantities to the various calculations in a standard written procedure for the same multiplication. Ask, for example: where is 70 x 50 represented in the written algorithm? Try re-calculating the algorithm with 157 written beneath 78 (instead of the other way round). How does this relate to the grid and the MAB blocks?

Which Is Easier?

Have students compare their own setting-out to that of standard methods such as a short division algorithm. For example: To calculate 495 ÷ 5, Sharie did

90 x 5 = 450, 45 left,

8 x 5 = 40, 5 left

1 x 5 = 5, 0 left, so A = 99

and compared this to $\begin{array}{r} 9\ 9 \\ 5\overline{)49^{4}5} \end{array}$

Ask: Which is easier for you and why? Which method would you use to compute 495 ÷ 15?

Historical Calculations

Ask students to research different methods of calculation used in earlier times. The Russian Peasant Method, the Venetian Grid Method and Napier's Rods are some historical multiplication methods. Have students try each method and discover why they work.

SAMPLE LESSON 3

Sample Learning Activity: Middle—'Making It Easier', page 149

Key Understanding 6: There are some special calculating methods that we can use for calculations we find hard to do in our head.

Working Towards: Levels 2 and 3

Teacher's Purpose

Our school had decided that being able to add a column of four or five numbers or amounts of money easily without a calculator was a useful adult skill (e.g. for checking the bill in a restaurant). We felt we should help students develop an efficient approach to column addition, although we did not expect them all to use the same method.

My Year 4 class had a lot of experience in adding two two-digit numbers. Students used a variety of mental and paper strategies including jumping along number lines, and partitioning numbers in various ways. Many could also do some simple additions involving hundreds (e.g. 132 + 27). I thought they had the understanding needed to develop an efficient written method, but wasn't sure how to 'motivate' it since, in most circumstances, a calculator would be readily available for the more difficult calculations.

Motivation and Purpose

The students were doing a science project to investigate camouflage in nature. The activity involved them in scattering a large but equal number of four different coloured small snips of paper on the oval. Each student then picked up as many pieces of paper as they could in a fixed time. The idea was that students would find fewer pieces of the colours that are harder to see against the grass.

I asked each group of four students to work out their total for each colour. They first counted their collections but then had difficulty adding to find the total for each colour.

The students were able to get started but they found adding four numbers a bit of a struggle. Almost all of them added two of the numbers, then added in the third, then the fourth and this was quite time-consuming with a lot of room for mistakes.

Many groups found that the two pairs got different answers the first time and had to check to see who was right. The students found this tedious. The purpose of this particular lesson was science, but I had set it up so that it provided me with the opportunity to introduce the idea of there being some efficient ways of adding 'lots of numbers' or 'bigger numbers'.

Connection and Challenge

Later, I reminded the students of the difficulty they had had. They agreed that usually a calculator would be available and sensible for such situations, but it is handy to have an easy way to deal with the other times. Several students commented about how their parents did 'sums'. I suggested that the easy methods for adding lots of numbers or big numbers were quite similar to methods many of the students already used for adding two numbers and it wouldn't be much of a shift for them to learn these techniques. I wrote 35 + 47 on the board and asked the students to do it however they usually would.

After the students had all had a go, I asked for volunteers to explain what they had done. Craig reported using a roughly sketched number line to work out 35 + 47 and said: *I jumped along 40 to get 75 then I had seven to go so I went five more to 80 and two more to get to 82.*

Craig
35
+ 40
75
+ 5
80
+ 2
82

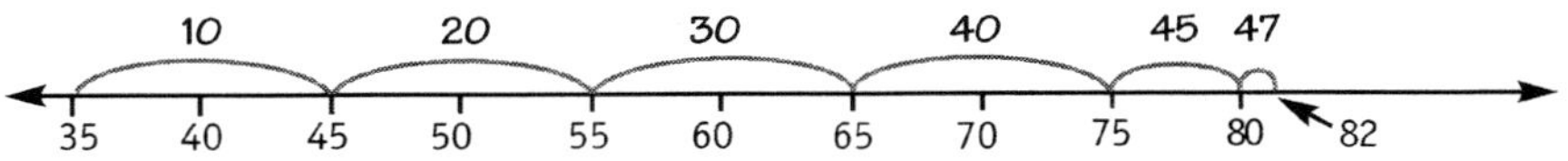

Without comment, I recorded the calculation vertically as Craig spoke (see right).

Danni said: *I added the tens and got 30 and 40 is 70, then I added five and seven which is 12, and 70 + 12 is 80 then two more is 82.*

Danni
35
+ 40
70
+ 12
80
+ 2
82

Again, without comment, I wrote it vertically (see right).

I wrote up three more students' approaches, although they looked quite similar to Craig's and Danni's. I drew attention to the fact that each approach involved thinking about tens separately from ones. As they talked, I wrote notes to the side of each of the examples on the board.

Craig	Thinking	Danni	Thinking
35	35	35	30 + 5
+ 47	+ 40 + 7	+ 47	40 + 7
75	75	70	70
+ 5	+ 7	+ 12	+ 12
80	80	80	80
+ 2	+ 2	+ 2	+ 2
82	82	82	82

Drawing Out the Mathematical Idea

I focused on Danni's approach, saying: *A lot of you have used something like Danni's methods. It is quite close to the special method for adding lots of numbers, so I want to make sure that you all understand how to do it.* I then wrote an addition on the board, 28 + 36, in vertical format and had a volunteer, Lynley, say what Danni's thinking would be: *Do the tens first so 20 + 30 is 50. Do the ones next, so 8 + 6 is 14. Shift 10 from 14 to the 50 makes 60 plus four makes 64.*

Write	Think
28	20 + 8
+ 36	+30 + 6
50	50
+ 14	+ 14
60	60
+ 4	+ 4
64	64

I had written the 14 under the 50 and, when Lynley said to shift the ten from the 14 to the 50, I remarked casually that it was like going back and doing the tens again. I then asked students to make up one for themselves, set it out vertically, do it, check their working with their partner, and then to practise on several more. As I moved around, I reassured myself that all but one or two students (to whom I returned later) were confident—for many it was close to what they had been doing, even if they had not set it out so systematically.

16
18
37
+ 22
70
+ 23
90
+ 3
93

I decided to move on to adding several numbers and wrote 16 + 18 + 37 + 22 on the board, choosing an example with a sum under 100. The students all wrote the numbers down in a column, and they talked though the process: *Do the tens first, then do the ones, then shift any extra tens across ...* They proceeded happily with this, and did not appear to notice that they were shifting 20 across to the tens rather than the ten they had dealt with so far. I gave them another to try. Several students asked if they could skip the last bit and go from 70 + 23 directly to 93. I asked the opinion of the class, and all agreed it seemed sensible.

I had decided that they had done enough for one day, when the decision was taken out of my hands. Chris said that his parents said you were supposed to do the ones first! I then asked the students to talk in their group about why they thought Chris's parents had learned to do the ones first and which way was better.

Somewhat to my surprise, several groups suggested that when you were writing them down you could save a line if you did the ones first because you could add in the 20 right away! I asked other students their view, and several agreed that if you were writing it down, doing the ones first saved a line. I suggested that they all try doing the ones first, but that those who preferred to set it out in full should, and those who preferred to shorten it should.

In full	**Shortened**
16	16
18	18
37	37
+ 22	+ 22
23	23
+ 70	93
93	

KEY UNDERSTANDING 7

We can calculate with fractions. Sometimes renaming fractions is helpful for this.

Adding and subtracting fractions should follow naturally from understanding what fractions mean, visualising fractional parts and counting backwards and forwards in fractional amounts. Students should represent fractional amounts in materials and pictures and, for example, count forward: one-fifth, two-fifths, three-fifths, four-fifths, one, one and one-fifth, etc. (See Understand Fractional Numbers, Key Understandings 3 and 7.) This leads quite naturally to the idea that 'two-fifths add one-fifth is three-fifths'. Students initially work in words, both oral and written, and use abbreviations such as 2 fifths + 1 fifth = 3 fifths to record the results of their thinking. When they are confident with the ideas, the conventional recording (i.e. $\frac{1}{5} + \frac{2}{5} = \frac{3}{5}$) can be used.

Adding three-fifths and four-fifths could be seen in the same way, by imagining or drawing a diagram or 'counting forward' to get seven-fifths or one and two-fifths. Alternatively, as suggested for Key Understandings 2 and 5, students might imagine partitioning the four-fifths into two lots of two-fifths, combine one lot with the three-fifths to make the whole, and hence get one and two-fifths.

Learning a procedure such as 'add the numerators and leave the denominators unchanged' is initially unhelpful since it focuses upon the two separate parts of the fraction and encourages students to think of fractions such as $\frac{2}{5}$ as two numbers rather than one. This often results in students producing answers such as $\frac{1}{2} + \frac{1}{2} = \frac{2}{4} = \frac{1}{2}$, which suggest that they have not thought of the fractions each as a number in itself, but rather have focused on the numerator and denominator separately.

For fractions with unlike denominators, students need to build upon their understanding that the same fractional amount can be written in different ways, so that, for example, one-half is the same amount as two-fourths (see Understand Fractional Numbers, Key Understanding 4). Given extensive experience with partitioning and equivalence, adding and subtracting unlike fractions follows naturally, so long as the relationship between the denominators is easy to see. That is, the partitioning and equivalence knowledge required to work out sums and differences like $\frac{1}{2} + \frac{1}{4}$ and $2\frac{3}{4} - \frac{1}{2}$ is reasonably intuitive because the $\frac{1}{4}$ is contained in the half and students generally can readily visualise $\frac{1}{2}$ as two-fourths. When students first begin to add and subtract fractions, the emphasis should be on visualising each fraction as an entity and the fractions involved should be those which are relatively easy to imagine or draw in simple diagrams. To add $\frac{1}{3}$ and $\frac{1}{4}$ is much more difficult, since a common unit that is not instantly recognisable needs to be found. This work should build on the partitioning of Key Understanding 3 in Calculate, Key Understanding 2 in Understand Fractional Numbers and Key Understanding 5 in Understand Operations. Students will need considerable experience in choosing how many parts they need to partition wholes into so that both fractions can be represented. It is not obvious to students and cannot be rushed.

Finding a fraction of a number (e.g. $\frac{1}{3}$ of 27 or $\frac{1}{3}$ of 28 or $\frac{1}{3}$ of 28.2) involves partitioning the number into equal parts and taking the appropriate number of those parts (in these cases, taking one part of three). Often factors are useful for this (see Key Understanding 3). Again the emphasis should be on the partitioning of collections and wholes into easily visualised or drawn parts.

Students will need developmental activities for several years in order to develop computational flexibility with fractions. Students who have achieved Level 3 can count forward and back orally in unit fractions (one-sixth, two-sixths, three-sixths) and write these in words. They are therefore able to add and subtract simple fractions presented in words, although they may not be able to add or subtract the same fractions presented in conventional symbolic forms. Students who have achieved Level 4 will be able to carry out such computations, even when presented symbolically, but they will use mostly mental methods based on counting forwards and backwards in fractions. Students who have achieved Level 5 can mentally add and subtract fractions that are easily visualised or drawn or involve well-known equivalences, and can record the stages in adding and subtracting fractions that they cannot complete mentally. They can find unit fractions of whole numbers mentally and find proper fractions of quantities either mentally or with written support.

SAMPLE LEARNING ACTIVITIES

Middle ✔

Sharing Pizzas

Have small groups of students share equally a number of paper circles that represent pizzas to say what fraction of a circle each will get. For example: four students share three pizzas, using diagrams to plan how they could divide the paper pizzas. Ask students to cut the circles into parts and combine them to make their share, then record the answer in shorthand.

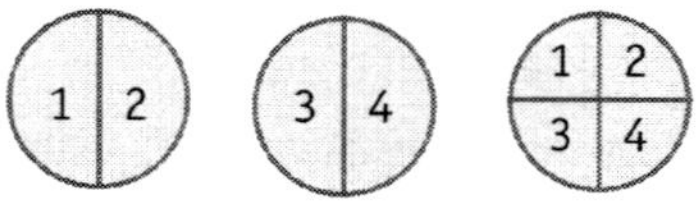

So each person gets half + quarter or three-quarters of a pizza.

Partitioning Collections

Ask students to partition and combine collections of material and solve simple number problems. For example: Partition 16 chocolate buttons into eighths then show three-eighths. Ask: How many eighths will be left if you give away three-eighths? Ask students to say the answer: *If you take away three-eighths of the chocolate buttons, five-eighths are left.* Help students record in symbols, drawing out that the collection of chocolate buttons is the whole or 'one' ($1 - \frac{3}{8} = \frac{5}{8}$). Ask: If I ate four-eighths and then one-eighth, how many eighths have I eaten? Write in shorthand (e.g. 4 eighths + 1 eighth = 5 eighths). Record in symbols.

Practical Fractions

Invite students to use materials to solve simple practical problems involving fractions. For example: If all 32 of us use half a piece of paper each, how many whole pieces of paper will that be? Ask students to reflect on what they did and record it as a number sentence. Ask: How can you write a sentence to show you needed a half, 32 times? (Link to Understand Operations, Key Understanding 3.)

Partitioning Circles

Have students partition circles into halves and/or quarters to work out examples such as, $1\frac{1}{2} + 1\frac{1}{2}$ or $2 - \frac{3}{4}$. Encourage students to compare their approaches.

Arrays

Using a 10 x 10 array, ask students to colour in ten squares on the first line, nine on the next, eight on the next and so on. Use this to find the difference between fractions, e.g. $\frac{10}{10}$ and $\frac{4}{10}$, $\frac{7}{10}$ and $\frac{2}{10}$. Have students write a number sentence to record their findings, e.g. $\frac{7}{10} - \frac{2}{10} = \frac{5}{10}$. Ask them to write their own rule for subtracting fractions with like denominators. Extend to other denominators.

Number Line

Have students use a number line to combine fractions. For example: Show $1\frac{1}{2} + 1\frac{1}{2}$ by first finding $1\frac{1}{2}$ and then counting on to find the position of $1\frac{1}{2}$ more.

Making a Whole

Ask students to find the different fractions that can be put together to make a whole during area activities. For example: When finding the area of a leaf, *That is about $\frac{3}{4}$ of a square and that one is about $\frac{1}{4}$ so we could count the two together as one.*

Double the Quantity

Have students decide how to double quantities in cooking, for example, $\frac{3}{4}$ of a cup of sugar. Ask them to talk about the ways of finding out the answer. For example: $\frac{3}{4}$ could be seen as $\frac{1}{2}$ and $\frac{1}{4}$ so when doubling, the $\frac{1}{2}$ and $\frac{1}{2}$ could be put together and then the $\frac{1}{4}$ and $\frac{1}{4}$ to make $1\frac{1}{2}$.

Pattern Blocks

Ask students to use Pattern Blocks to find fraction combinations that add to one. For example: If the hexagon is used as the whole, then one blue rhombus and four triangles equals one. Have students write this, $\frac{1}{3} + \frac{4}{6} = 1$, and say how it is possible to add thirds and sixths by comparing the size of the rhombus to the size of the triangles, or vice-versa.

Equivalent Fractions

Ask students to investigate equivalent fractions with pattern blocks. For example: If we make a shape with a blue rhombus and a triangle, how much of a hexagon do we have? What fraction of the hexagon does the triangle show? The rhombus? Have students write an addition sentence to show their equivalent fractions, e.g. $\frac{1}{6} + \frac{1}{3} = \frac{1}{2}$ or $\frac{1}{6} + \frac{2}{6} = \frac{1}{2}$. They then say how much of the hexagon is not covered and write a sentence, e.g. $1 - \frac{1}{2} = \frac{1}{2}$.

Passing Time

Have students use a clock with movable hands to find out how much time has passed. For example: Spelling took a quarter of an hour and printing took a quarter of an hour. How much time did we use? Ask: How many minutes in a quarter of an hour? Does it help to add minutes instead of quarter hours?

SAMPLE LEARNING ACTIVITIES

Later ✔✔✔

Check for Sense

Have students focus on the meaning of fractional quantities to check that their calculations make sense. For example: Connie wrote $\frac{3}{4} + \frac{1}{2} = \frac{4}{6}$, saying this was how long she'd watched TV. One show was $\frac{3}{4}$ hour and the other $\frac{1}{2}$ hour. Show why Connie's result does not make sense.

Dividing Whole Numbers by Fractions

Ask students to divide whole numbers by fractional quantities using linear representations such as string and number lines in situations such as: We need $\frac{3}{4}$ m lengths of ribbon. How many can we cut from 5 m?

Leftovers

Have students relate division to the fraction notation where the quantities to be shared are not whole amounts. For example: three-quarters of a pie was left in the fridge. Three students were to share the piece. What fraction of the leftover piece of pie will they each get? ($\frac{1}{3}$) What fraction of the *whole* pie will they get? ($\frac{1}{4}$) Draw out that $\frac{3}{4} \div 3$ is the same as one-third of $\frac{3}{4}$, which is $\frac{1}{4}$. Have students solve similar problems where a fractional part needs to be shared.

Area Problems

Use an array representation to solve fraction area problems. For example: What is the area of a rectangle that measures $\frac{1}{3}$ km by $\frac{1}{4}$ km? Draw a diagram to show the calculation. Ask students to explain why the result is less than one.

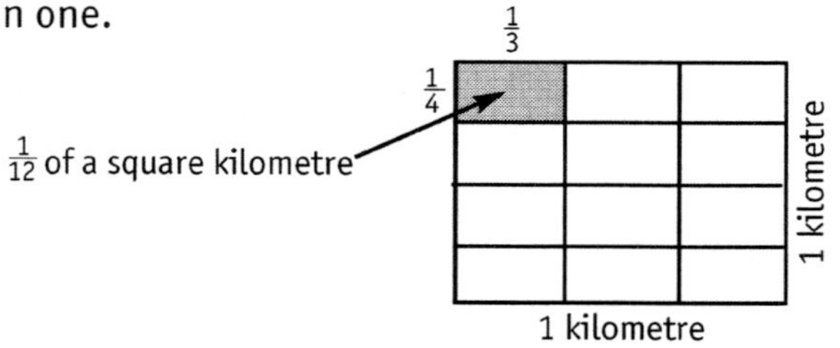

Pizzas and Pies

Have students use their own methods to solve problems involving fractions and 'share and compare' strategies.

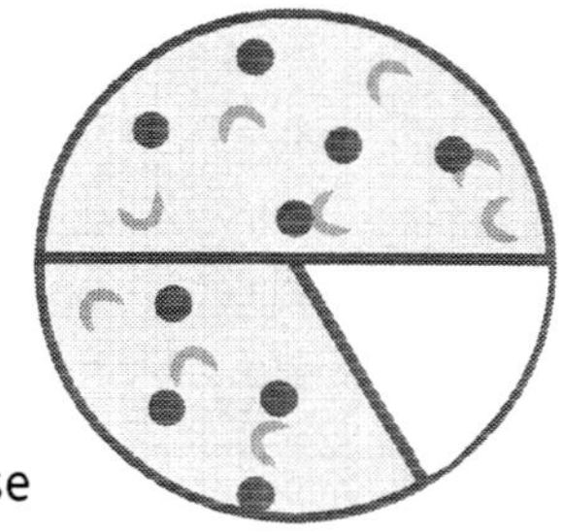

- *The pizza problem.* Show students a diagram of two pieces of pizza on a plate: a half and a third. Say: The whole pizza was the same size as the plate. Point to each piece and ask: What fraction of the whole pizza is this? What fraction of the whole pizza are these two pieces together?

- *Three-quarters of a pie.* Three-quarters of a pie was left in the fridge. Six students have to share the piece of pie. Ask: What fraction of the whole pie is each share? ($\frac{1}{8}$) What fraction of the three-quarters piece of pie is each share? ($\frac{1}{6}$)

Pattern Blocks (1)

Have students add fractions with Pattern Blocks, using two yellow hexagons taped together as the whole. They check which pieces can be used to show fractional parts (green triangle = $\frac{1}{12}$, blue rhombus = $\frac{1}{6}$), list ways in which two different coloured pieces can make one whole, and write as a sum, e.g. $\frac{2}{6} + \frac{8}{12} = 1$. A partner checks by covering the whole with the appropriate pieces.

Patterns Blocks (2)

Use the blocks as in the previous activity to add and subtract simple fractions, e.g. $\frac{1}{2} + \frac{1}{4}$, $\frac{1}{4} + \frac{2}{6}$, $\frac{1}{4} + \frac{5}{6} + \frac{1}{12}$, $\frac{1}{2} - \frac{2}{6}$, $\frac{1}{4} - \frac{1}{12}$. Ask: How did renaming or trading the pieces help you find the solutions?

Finding Fractions

Ask students to find fractions of whole numbers. For example: Find $\frac{3}{4}$ of 24 biscuits and use materials or diagrams to explain the process you used.

Multiple Slices

Have students decide how many partitions are needed to be able to easily take two different fractions of the same thing. For example: How many slices could I cut the cake into so it is easy to take a third? (3, 6, 9, 12, ...) To take a quarter? (4, 8, 12, 16, ...) Ask: How many so it is easy to take a third and a quarter? Draw out that the number of pieces has to be a multiple of each number. Build on this and extend to find the fraction of the slice that is gone if we eat $\frac{1}{3} + \frac{1}{4}$. (See 'Multiple Slices', page 120.)

Calculator Addition

Invite students to use calculators such as the Texas Maths Explorer to add fractions. For example: For $\frac{3}{4} + 1\frac{2}{3}$, enter 3 / 4 + 1 unit 2 / 3 = . Ask: Why do you think the calculator display would read 1u$\frac{17}{12}$? Which keys change that to a simpler fraction? Try this method on other scientific calculators. Do they operate the same way? Experiment by carrying out other operations on simple fractions. Check the answers by using diagrams or materials.

Equivalent Forms

Have students use diagrams, number lines, counters or arrays to show that fraction number sentences can be written in equivalent forms without changing the quantity. For example: Jim said, 'I have to calculate what $\frac{1}{3} + \frac{1}{4}$ is, so I'm going to change it to $\frac{3}{12} + \frac{4}{12}$ to make it easier to work out.' Ask students to show why he can do this. Rename fractions in other calculations, such as $\frac{3}{4} - \frac{1}{3}$, to make them easier to work out.

KEY UNDERSTANDING 8

Rounding, imagining a number line, and using properties of numbers and operations help us to estimate calculations.

Good estimation and approximation skills enhance our ability to deal with everyday quantitative situations. Students should be provided with ample opportunity to decide whether an estimate of the result of a calculation is sufficient and, if so, how close the estimate needs to be and of what form. As described in Key Understanding 10, they should also learn to use estimation routinely to judge whether the results of more accurate calculations are reasonable and to determine the order of magnitude of a result.

Approximate calculations are accurate calculations based on simplified numbers. They often involve rounding and single-digit mental arithmetic and powers of ten. Thus, to approximate 27 x 16 we could round to the nearest ten in either direction and say that the result is between 20 x 10 = 200 and 30 x 20 = 600. Alternatively, we might get a bit closer by saying it is a bit more than 25 x 16 = 25 x 4 x 4 = 400. To check decimal places for 25.14 x 3.5, we might think 'it'll be between three 25s and four 25s, which is between 75 and 100'. To estimate the gate-takings each day, we might take the number who came through the turnstile today (343) and round it to 340, saying the gate-takings should be about 340 times the cost of admission, $8.

Whether we round to the nearest one, or five, or ten, or 100, or half depends upon the context. For estimating 0.61 x 558, a sensible strategy might be to find half of 600, yet some students will round the 0.61 to one and 558 to 600 and draw the inappropriate conclusion that the approximate answer is 600. Often, rounding is not the best strategy for approximating answers. For example: For 79 ÷ 9 we might choose 'nice numbers' and say it is a bit less than 81 ÷ 9. We might also compensate, e.g. 43 x 51 is about 40 x 50 = 2000 and three more 50s, so 2150 is closer.

Whether we round 'up', 'down' or 'to the middle' also depends upon the context. To ensure you have enough money for a series of purchases, you will probably round up rather than to the middle. Repetitive exercises in rounding numbers out of context are likely to lead students to think that there is a single right way to round. They may also see rounding as just another meaningless mathematical exercise, rather than a practical tool for everyday estimation.

Experiences should also be provided to enable students to judge about how much an answer will be without calculating. For example, after sketching a number line (say from zero to ten) and marking 2.6 on it approximately, students could judge three lots of the distance from zero to 2.6, or one-third of the distance. This will give an estimate of 3 x 2.6 and $\frac{1}{3}$ x 2.6. With experience it is possible to estimate in the 'mind's eye' with sufficient accuracy for many purposes.

Students should also learn to use their knowledge of properties of numbers and operations to judge the size of an answer. For example, they should be able to say that 0.2 x 0.3 must be smaller than 0.2 (since it is multiplied by a number smaller than one) thus it cannot be 0.6 (a common error). There is a close link with Key Understanding 6 in Understand Operations and many activities are suggested there.

Students at Level 2 estimate in simple ways to check two-digit additions and subtractions, e.g. saying that 16 + 19 cannot be 25 because it has to be more than 30. At Level 3, they estimate both sums and products by rounding to single-digit numbers or simple multiples of ten and by visualising on a number line, although they may need prompting and support. At Level 4, students do this without structured help. They will, for example, say that 47 + 49 will be more than twice 45 (90) and less than twice 50 (100). They will also say that 16 x 9 is more than 90 (10 x 9) and less than 160 (16 x 10).

SAMPLE LEARNING ACTIVITIES

Beginning ✔

Estimating Collections

Invite students to look at a collection of things and estimate if there will be more than, less than or enough for everyone in a small group to have one each. For example: Spread seven pea seeds in front of a group of three students. Ask students to say whether there will be too many or not enough.

Benchmarks

Have students use small numbers such as two as benchmarks on a number line and say where other numbers would be.

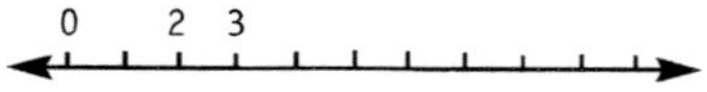

Pegs

Ask students to partition and round up amounts to tens to estimate how many packs will be enough when things come in packs of ten. For example: Everyone needs a peg each and the pegs come in packs of ten. Ask students to suggest ways to work this out mentally. Draw out partitioning into decades and ones, e.g. 32 = 30 + 2. Three tens and two ones. Then focus on rounding up. Ask: How many packs must we buy? Will three be enough? Why? Why not? Ask students to justify their estimates, using diagrams to support their idea. (Link to Understand Whole and Decimal Numbers, Key Understanding 6.)

Bulbs

Have students use partitioning into fives or tens and rounding down to decide how many, e.g. when needing to make equal groups. For example: Mark's granddad gave him 28 tiny bulbs and five pots. He thinks that will be about six bulbs in each pot. Ask: What do you think? How could you check? Are there any more ways we haven't thought of?

Number Scrolls

When skip counting with a calculator, ask students to record the numbers on paper strips and say what number will come next and what number they might reach at the end of the strip. Ask: How did you decide? (See Understanding Whole and Decimal Numbers, Key Understanding 4.)

Money

Have students estimate using doubling and rounding. For example: Collect catalogues and rewrite the prices for items in multiples of ten cents or dollars, e.g. 40 cents, 50 cents, 90 cents, $1.10. Ask students to select an item and say whether $2 will buy two of them. Focus on doubling and rounding. Extend by having the students choose several items and then either $1, $2 or $5 to cover the cost. (Link to Key Understandings 1 and 4.)

SAMPLE LEARNING ACTIVITIES

Middle ✔✔

Number Lines

Ask students to imagine numbers on a number line or 100 chart to decide whether to round up or down to the nearest ten and then to use this to help estimate answers to problems. Ask: When should you round up/down?

Calculator Test

Have students use the calculator to test which way of rounding will give the best estimate. For example: For 268 + 425, try 200 + 400, 300 + 400, 300 + 500 and 200 + 500.

Shopping Estimates

Given a shopping context and real prices, have students round to decide if they have enough money for specified items. Ask them to share their estimations and tell whether they overestimated or underestimated. Discuss the situations where we would want to overestimate and underestimate and our strategies for doing this.

Multiplying by 26

Have students use a calculator to find a number that can be multiplied by 26 to give an answer between 100 and 150. Ask: Which number did you start with? Why? Did you then choose a bigger or smaller number? Why?

Guess the Answer

Ask students to say what the answer to a calculation should be between. For example: Five packets of biscuits at $2.20 should cost between $10 and $15. Ask: Can we say that it will definitely be more than $11, or less than $14? Try to get the range as small as possible to make a close estimate.

Supermarket Receipts

Have students estimate to match supermarket receipts with the totals that have been cut off. As a class, consider which strategies were commonly used to estimate and why. Repeat the activity using a different strategy from the one first used. Ask: Do supermarkets round up or down? Why?

Middle ✔✔

Working with Wood

Have students decide how close their estimate needs to be when working out how much wood they will need to make a picture frame for their artwork. Ask: Should the answer be within 10 m, 1 m, 50 cm, 10 cm or 1 cm? Why?

Place Value

Ask students to say which answer must be right using estimation based on place value. For example: 5 x 15 = 7.5, 75 or 750; 24 x 61 = 1464, 126, 1224 or 142; 39 x 0.5 = 195, 155, 19.5 or 1595.

When to Estimate?

Have students brainstorm to create a list of situations where they have used estimation instead of a precise calculation. Ask them to interview parents to add to the list. Ask: How close did the estimate have to be to the exact answer? Why?

Does It Make Sense?

Without actually doing the calculation, involve students in thinking, talking and writing about whether an answer makes sense. Explain why. For example: 304 x 2 = 600; 3 x 345 = 1050; 66 ÷ 7 = 10 r 4; 238 x 5 is greater than 1000.

Estimating Collections

Invite students to estimate how many there are in a collection, using either pictures of large amounts of things, or visual images. For example:

- How many parents came to the special assembly?
- How many sheep in a paddock?
- How many trees around the school oval?
- How many people on a page of *Where's Wally*?

Compare estimations and reasons for the amounts decided. For example: At assembly, I know that about 20 people can stand across the back and there were some people behind, so that makes about 40.

SAMPLE LEARNING ACTIVITIES

Later ✔✔

Exact or Approximate?

Have students decide whether exact or approximate calculations are appropriate. For example:

- You know that a can of paint covers 16 square metres and you want to paint your bedroom.
- The pears cost $1.45 kg. Jane had $2\frac{1}{2}$ kg in the scales. Would the $4 she had be enough to pay for it?
- Check that $87 collected from 58 students paying $1.50 each for swimming lessons is correct.

Ask: What calculation will you use for each? Will you round, or use an upper limit or a lower limit to approximate the result? Why?

Bigger or Smaller

Have students judge the effect of operations on numbers to say whether the answer will be bigger or smaller than the first number, and explain why in each case. For example: 26 x 2, 23 x 0.95, 24 ÷ 2, 24 ÷ 48, 24 ÷ 0.5, 24 + 2, 24 + 0.45, 24 – 2, 24 – 0.2. Ask: Do any answers seem surprising? Why?

Estimating Fractions

Have students choose a unit (say, a decimetre) and use it to make fraction tapes of six units (say, six decimetres), marked to show quarters in one colour and thirds in another colour. They then cut a number of paper strips of different lengths (but shorter than their fraction tape measure) and fold to find one-third of each strip. They then place their paper strips alongside their fraction tape measure and say how long their strip is and how much a third of the strip is, e.g. the first strip is $2\frac{1}{4}$ long and one-third of that is about $\frac{3}{4}$; the second strip is $3\frac{2}{3}$ long and one-third of that is between $2\frac{1}{4}$ and $2\frac{1}{3}$. (See Sample Lesson 4, page 169.)

Estimating Thirds

Ask students to estimate one-third of different amounts by judging directly on the fraction tapes made in the previous activity. For example: Judge 'by eye' one-third of $4\frac{1}{4}$. Check by folding. Continue until they can confidently estimate one-third, then estimate two-thirds (one-third from the opposite end). Repeat for other unit fractions. Draw from a class discussion that estimating the size of the fraction can help us estimate and check multiplication and division. (See Sample Lesson 4, page 169.)

Later ✓✓

Fraction Tapes

Design number lines of the same length, which extend from zero to about ten. One number line can show the halves, e.g. 0, $\frac{1}{2}$, 1, $1\frac{1}{2}$, 2 … , another the thirds, others quarters and fifths. Have students look at their 'half' number lines and estimate where $\frac{1}{2} \times 4\frac{1}{2}$ would be. Ask: How did you think about that? Repeat with their thirds number line and visualise where $\frac{3}{4} \times 2\frac{1}{3}$, $\frac{1}{2} \times 4\frac{2}{3}$ and so on would be. Repeat with similar questions using the other fraction tapes. (See Sample Lesson 4, page 169.)

Adding Fractions

Using the tapes made in the previous activity, students can cut a paper strip to match the 'length' of each fraction. They then stick the two together and use the fraction tapes to find their best estimate of the total. Do this for several and then challenge students to do the same thing in their 'mind's eye', estimating the lengths.

Other Strategies

Ask students to use their fraction tapes to find other strategies for estimating the addition of two fractions. For example: For $3\frac{1}{2} + 2\frac{3}{4}$, begin at $3\frac{1}{2}$, jump along two and then another quarter.

Is It Reasonable?

Have students decide whether situations are reasonable. For example:

- When eight people won a million dollars on Lotto they got $12 500 each.
- Enough cans of cool drink for the class would cost about $30.

Best Estimates

Ask students to write calculations that will give the best estimate. For example: 9572 + 6956; $\frac{9}{31} + \frac{4}{9}$; 537.05 – 38.45; 297 x 378; 2.123 x 4.89; 165 ÷ 9. Ask students to describe how they simplified the numbers.

Upper and Lower Limits

Have students identify the upper and lower limits for a calculation. For example: Start with visual situations such as estimating the number of 2 mm squares on a page, the number of books on a shelf, or the number of 100s and 1000s on a piece of bread. Ask students to show how they worked out what the lower limit and the upper limit is for each. Extend to actual calculations such as 125 x 42.

Posting Calculations

Extend the previous idea to 'Posting Calculations'. Label three or four boxes with a range of limits for the solutions to calculations. For example: 1–99, 100–199, 200–299. Have students write number sentences on cards for others to 'post' into an appropriate box. Extend to include number sentences using decimals and common fractions. Change the limits to match.

SAMPLE LESSON 4

Sample Learning Activity: Later—'Fraction Tapes', page 167

Key Understanding 8: Rounding, imagining a number line, and using properties of numbers and operations help us estimate calculations.

Working Towards: Levels 4 and 5

Teacher's Purpose

During an activity where my class of 11- and 12-year-olds needed to scale down quantities of ingredients in a recipe, I noticed many had difficulty finding a fraction of the quantities. While they could easily calculate one-third of three tablespoons of margarine, they couldn't find one-third of quantities like two teaspoons of salt or $2\frac{1}{2}$ kg of cheese. When they tried to use numbers to make the calculations, they came up with quite improbable results without noticing something must be wrong. I decided to help them estimate the results of such calculations using a 'tape measure' representation for fractions.

The students had previously built up fraction number lines using paper tape. Each was five units long, the unit being a decimetre. One tape was labelled halves, quarters and eighths, and another thirds and sixths.

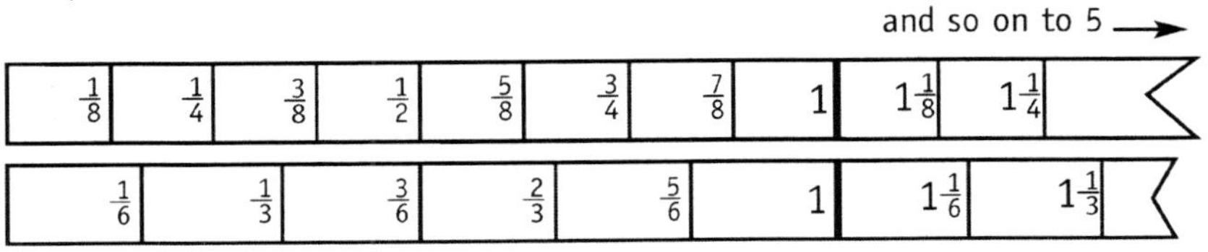

I decided to use these as the basis for some work on estimating fractions, to try to build students' number sense about the results of calculations.

Students commonly visualise fractions as 'slices' of shapes like cakes or pies, which makes the result of calculations like $\frac{1}{2}$ of $2\frac{1}{2}$ very difficult to think about. How do you visualise $2\frac{1}{2}$ pies in three equal parts? On the other hand, a 'tape measure' representation enables students to see $2\frac{1}{2}$ as a single continuous quantity, a whole that can easily be visualised in three equal parts. At the same time, the 'tape measure' mental image for fractions more closely matches the abstract idea of a number line, giving fractions meaning within the whole number system.

Connection and Challenge

I began by asking each student to cut a length of paper less than half a metre long. I then asked them to use their fraction number lines to find the length of their paper strip in decimetres and to record this on the end of the strip. Since few paper strips exactly matched one of the fraction marks on the number line, this required estimation. Students compared their strips to both number lines to decide whether 'eighths' or 'sixths' worked better and then worked in small groups to check each other's estimates. As I moved around the room, I saw the students understood the task and were able to use the number lines to estimate the length of their strips in decimetres.

I then asked students to look at one strip and, without folding, mark where they thought one-third of it was. Each strip was then passed around the group so that every group member could mark their estimate of a third on it. Once the strip had been around the group, it was folded to check where one-third actually was. This was compared to students' estimates, talking about how they mentally made their estimates just by looking at the strip. They then repeated the process for the next group member's strip, trying to improve their 'eye' for one-third.

Once each group had their estimates and the actual third marked on their strips, I pinned two of the fraction number lines on the board and asked for someone to bring their strip to the front. Terri volunteered and I asked her to tell everyone the length of her strip and show where a third of it was. I then asked her to use the number lines I'd pinned on the board to find the length of the third of her strip in decimetres. Since the third did not exactly match a fraction mark on the number line, this required another estimate.

The total length of Terri's strip was a little less than $2\frac{3}{4}$ decimetres, and she now estimated her one-third to be between $\frac{5}{6}$ and one, but closer to $\frac{5}{6}$. *So what have we discovered?* I asked. After a bit of a struggle Terri said doubtfully, *A third of the strip*. I asked: *And how long was the strip?* Still somewhat hesitantly she said: *Nearly $2\frac{3}{4}$*. I wrote with a flourish on the board: So $\frac{1}{3}$ of nearly $2\frac{3}{4}$ = a bit more than $\frac{5}{6}$.

I then called on another volunteer and we repeated this with a new length. The rest of the students then used the process on their own strips, writing down their results as number sentences. I then wrote a range of fractions on the board, and challenged them to use whatever strategy they wished to estimate a third of the various numbers. Some cut a length of tape to match the number and folded it carefully to make thirds, while others judged directly from the fraction number lines—some folded the actual number lines and other 'just looked'. I encouraged them to try to judge first, even if they then folded, since the whole point of the activity was to improve their confidence in their capacity to judge a given fraction of any length.

After they'd found a third of several different numbers, I asked the students to each write down a fraction between one and five and ask their partner to mark the number on a number line and estimate a third of it, without cutting and folding strips. This they did with ease. We then talked over the strategy they used and Allen suggested: *It's like you had to forget about the $2\frac{1}{2}$ and think of it as a whole strip that you make into thirds like it's a licorice shared in three pieces, then you can think about where that comes to on the fraction strip.*

Opportunity to Practise

Students continued to practise the process, challenging themselves to see how well they could visualise and estimate a third of different numbers between zero and five just by looking at their fraction number lines. They then folded and measured to see how reasonable their estimates were.

I extended the opportunity for estimating with fractions by suggesting they do the same thing for finding one-quarter. I hinted that they might want to begin by practising finding one-quarter 'by eye' on blank strips of tape. The students used language like *in between..., a bit more than..., close to...* to identify their results. Some even began to use their knowledge of fractions to estimate twelfths and sixteenths by halving the spaces. For example, Kate said: It looks about halfway between $\frac{5}{6}$ and one, so it must be about $\frac{11}{12}$, because twelfths are halfway between sixths. Over the next several days and weeks I often asked students to estimate a fraction of another fraction, to provide practice using the strategies they had developed.

***Future Directions:* Students made good use of their fraction strips in future lessons involving operations and calculations with fractions. We used them as practical tools to add and subtract fractions with unlike denominators, compare multiplication situations like $5 \times \frac{1}{4}$ to $\frac{1}{4}$ of five, and divide by fractions, e.g. how many $\frac{3}{4}$ in four? All of which continued to support the development of their ability to estimate and make sense of calculations involving fractional numbers.**

KEY UNDERSTANDING 9

To use a calculator well we need to enter and interpret the information correctly and know about its functions.

Students should have ready access to calculators from the earliest years of schooling. Calculators help students to develop many mathematical concepts earlier and more thoroughly than they can if they don't have them, to work on more realistic applications, and to develop calculator skills that they will use in their everyday life. For laborious or repetitive computations, calculators are the sensible choice. The regular use of calculators is assumed throughout the curriculum. This Key Understanding, however, is about the conceptual and technical knowledge needed to use them to calculate efficiently and correctly.

At the simplest level, students need to learn through exploration that digits are entered from left to right as you read them, thus 24 is entered [2] then [4]. Entering 3 + 7 is intuitive on most calculators if the equal sign is remembered: [3] [+] [7] [=]. Entering 16 + 7 x 3 may be more difficult, depending upon the type of calculator used. According to the rule of order, multiplications and divisions are completed before additions and subtractions so 16 + 7 x 3 means 16 + (7 x 3). Simple four-function calculators usually carry out calculations in the order in which they are entered, so if 16 + 7 x 3 was entered as in the order shown, the 16 + 7 would be calculated first, giving the wrong answer. Students should learn how their calculator works and enter calculations in the appropriate order. Older students should realise that calculators differ and develop the habit of checking how the calculator they are using operates.

Students may experience entry difficulties even with simple computations. Some will enter [3] [÷] [15] [=] for $3\overline{)15}$. Others will always enter the larger number first in a subtraction or division, believing that you cannot 'take a bigger from a smaller' or 'divide a smaller by a bigger'. Some who know that there are two 50 cents in a dollar and hence sixteen 50 cents in $8, will enter the calculation as 8 ÷ 50 or even 50 ÷ 8. Thus, using a calculator often helps to expose conceptual misunderstandings. The cognitive conflict caused when the calculator answer does not fit their common sense can provide a helpful stimulus for students to overcome misconceptions and inconsistencies in their thinking.

Students should learn to use the various features of their calculators effectively: repeated operations (e.g. using the constant function on many calculators—to count by threes you press 3 + = = = ...), memory and bracket facilities, change of sign, and so on. Interpreting the results of computations (e.g. 1.5 as $1.50, a negative answer when finding a difference, remainders from a division) can be conceptually demanding and requires special attention. As indicated in Key Understanding 8, students should also learn to use estimation for effective calculator use, providing a way of checking that a problem has been correctly formulated for the calculator, and the keystrokes have been executed correctly.

SAMPLE LEARNING ACTIVITIES

Beginning ✓✓

Exploring Calculators

Have students use calculators to explore, press keys and discover what happens. Focus students on watching the display to notice what happens each time they press a number key. Have them take turns to read out the digits on the display for others to make the same numbers.

Clearing

Encourage students to become familiar with the function of particular keys, e.g. C/CE. After a student discovers how to clear numbers, ask them to show all students the steps. To practise, they key in 1, press the clear key to clear it back to zero. Continue in order through the numbers to 12. Later as they enter calculations, e.g. 24 + 36, show them how pressing this key once clears the 36 and pressing it twice clears all back to zero. Practise this through games such as 'Simon Says'.

Explaining to Others

When students find something that always happens on the calculator, have them explain it step-by-step to others. For example: When you have a sequence of numbers and press C/CE, it changes the numbers to zero.

Correct Terms

Ask students to use common correct terms to describe what they do on the calculator, and see what happens, e.g. press, key in, display, clear. At first students will use their natural language to describe the function keys that are beyond their everyday use, e.g. for the square root sign they might say 'the squiggly thing'. Over time, support them to rename terms.

Recording Device

Have students use the calculator as an informal recording device to enter multi-digit numbers such as telephone numbers, dates, game scores, to read and for others to copy. Ask: Which number (digit) did you put in first? Why?

Counting Device

Ask students to use the calculator as a counting device. For example, use the constant function as shown on page 180 (Sample Lesson 5) to:

- Count collections of things by ones or in groups, e.g. count ants on an ant trail by ones or another class entering a room by twos.
- Discover and explore negative numbers by counting backwards from a given number.

Constant Function

Have students watch numbers increasing into the hundreds using the constant function to skip count.

- Number scrolls: students record the numbers vertically on long strips of paper. Interrupt the count at times for students to predict the next number. (See Key Understanding 8 for estimation focus, and Understanding Whole and Decimal Numbers, Key Understanding 7, for place value focus.)
- Develop 'number lines', e.g. lily pads for a frog to jump along.

Computational Tool

Use the calculator as a computational tool. Have students choose which operation key to use when numbers are too large to solve mentally. Students may begin to use the ÷ key for sharing, e.g. eight bears need to share 74 cakes. How many cakes will each bear get? Share 74 cakes among eight bears.

SAMPLE LEARNING ACTIVITIES

Middle ✔✔

Prior Knowledge

Have students in small groups write down what they know about the calculator and how it works. Share this information with the whole class, and make a chart of the results. Add to this throughout the year as the students extend their knowledge.

Count Forwards and Backwards

Invite students to explore the use of the constant function in counting forwards and backwards. Ask them to create patterns for others to solve, e.g. 112, 117, 122, 127 ... Ask: What is being added each time? When they are adding tens, relate this to counting on or back by tens to solve addition and subtraction problems.

Big Numbers

Have students work with a partner to put the biggest number they can into the calculator. Ask them to read out their numbers and say which digit they entered first. Ask: Can you make a bigger number by starting with a different digit?

Really Big Numbers

Ask students to write down and then read out a 'really big number' (or later, a decimal) for their partner to enter into the calculator. Check the screen with the written version of the number and say why they might not be the same. (Link to Understand Whole and Decimal Numbers, Key Understanding 5.)

Memory

Have students use the memory button to keep a progressive score for a school version of darts, particularly when working out doubles and triples. For example: 12 add double 18, key in 12, M+, 18 x 2 , M+, RCM.

Rule of Order

Have students explore the 'rule of order' in doing a series of operations. Start by finding an easy way to get the answer to practical questions such as: (7 x $4) + (2 x $6). Have students share and compare methods and then try doing the same example with a calculator. Ask: Is the answer the same for some people and different for others? Why? How can you use the memory button to store the first result while working out the second part?

Experimenting

Ask students to experiment with the CE, C, +/–, ÷ and % buttons and say what effect each has on the numbers.

Calculator Division

Have students compare the results of calculator division with results found through sharing materials. For example: Share ten felt pens between four students. The calculator says 2.5 and the sharing says two each and two left over to share. Ask: How are these the same? What does .5 show half of? Compare other division examples, such as: Three children in a family shared $37. Kate used her calculator and entered 37 ÷ 3. Ask: Can you help her explain what her answer of 12.333333 means? How much will each child get? Why?

SAMPLE LEARNING ACTIVITIES

Later ✓✓

Interpreting Displays

Have students interpret calculator displays to answer problems. Present these problems, calculations and calculator displays of the answer. Have students work out what the answers must be in each case.

- 1 kg of ham costs $8.75. How much will 2.25 kilograms cost? 8.75 x 2.25. The display reads 19.6875.
- How many 1.5 m lengths of plastic rope can be cut from a total length of 32 m? 32 ÷ 1.5. The display reads 21.333333.

Memory Functions

Have students use the **M+**, **M–** and **RM** functions. For example: Use an electrical goods catalogue to spend $5000. Start by keying in **5000** into the **M+**. As the items are 'purchased', key the amount into the **M–**. (To buy two CD players at $129 each, key in **2** **x** **129**.) See how much is left by pressing **RM**. Have students think of other situations where this function would be useful.

Constant Function

Ask students to investigate how the constant function works for different operations. For example: Key in **6** **x** **4** **=** **=** **=**. The numbers 24, 144 and 864 appear in the display. Ask: Is the calculator constantly multiplying the four or the six? Now enter **6** **+** **4** **=** **=** **=**. Ask: Is the calculator constantly adding four or six? Now try 12 – 2 and 12 ÷ 2. Ask: Which part of the number sentence is constant? How can you check? How would this information be useful if you wanted to practise your eight times table or make your calculator count by 0.4?

Complex Calculations (1)

Ask students to work out the correct order to enter complex calculations. For example: Calculate the cost of a list of items like 16 large pieces of card at $1.36 each, 8 m of laminating at $3.50/m and $2.50 for binding. Ask one group of students to key in the calculation as they say it: 16 x $1.36 + 8 x $3.50 + $2.50. Another group records the answer to each bit: 16 x $1.36, 8 x $3.50 and then adds the bits. Ask: Which answer is correct? How can using the memory function be useful in this situation? Does this occur with all the calculators you use?

Complex Calculations (2)

Extend the previous activity by presenting scenarios like: Jamie recorded his number sentence on paper as (4 x $1.20) + (3 x $2.35). His calculator does not have the 'rule of order' function. What would he have to enter into the calculator to get the correct answer? Show Jamie how this is done.

Change of Sign

Have students use calculators with a change of sign function (+/–) to calculate with positive and negative numbers. For example: Pairs of students take turns to throw a ten-sided die four times and record the numbers in a 2 x 2 array. Subtract the second number from the first in each row and then add the two results with the calculator to get your score. The lowest score wins. For instance, if the result from the top row was –3 and the result from the bottom row was seven, you would need to key in 3 then +/– then + 7 followed by =. Ask students to check their answers on a number line.

5	8	-3
10	3	7

Compare Answers

Encourage students to compare calculator answers to answers from pen-and-paper or mental strategies when multiplying large numbers. For example: The calculator answer to 40 000 000 x 4 is E 1.6000000; the actual answer is 160 000 000. Ask students to find other examples. Ask: What do you have to do to the E number to get the correct answer? Why do you think this happens? Does this occur with other calculators?

Rounding

Have students investigate how the calculator rounds numbers. Ask them to find the decimal for one-third by dividing 1 ÷ 3. Then reverse the operation and multiply the result by three. Ask: Why is the answer not one? Try 2 ÷ 3. Ask: Why is the answer .6666666 for some and .6666667 for others? Multiply by three—why is the answer not two? Does this happen with other divisions? Why? Does it happen with decimals?

SAMPLE LESSON 5

Sample Learning Activity: Beginning—'Counting Device', page 175

Key Understanding 9: To use a calculator well we need to enter and interpret the information correctly and know about its functions.

Working Towards: Levels 1 and 2

Action and Reflection

It was Term 1 and I wanted my Year 1 students to begin to learn about calculator functions. Ashana gave me the opportunity I'd been looking out for. She came rushing to me exclaiming excitedly, saying *Look! Look! The numbers keep changing. I pressed three, then I pressed this big one (+), and then this one (=) and look! It goes 3, 6, 9, 12 ... I think it's counting!* The rest of the students all wanted to know what she'd done so I used Ashana's directions to draw the appropriate calculator key sequence on the board:

3 + = = = = =

There was great excitement as the students followed this sequence to make their calculator 'count' for them as well. Peter was particularly excited and told the class that the equals button was called the 'channel changer' because *you keep getting a different picture on the screen*. I realised that I had been able to introduce the constant function to the students by building on their own discoveries.

When the effects of the constant key had been referred to as 'counting' by Ashana and the rest of the class, I did not immediately notice that students understood 'counting' in different ways.

The question 'Will it work for fives too?' created an opportunity for everyone to experiment with different numbers. *Look how far I can count!* said Luke, who was counting by tens and had reached 50. When I asked him how far he thought he could go, Luke ventured: *A hundred?* His incredulous tone implied that he had made a most improbable suggestion. He later returned and reported that: *Getting to 100 was easy ... a cinch! Now I can count by 100s ... 100, 200, 300, 400 ...*

One group of students found that by entering 1 + then = = = = they produced a sequence that was the same as for 'real' counting, i.e. *one, two,* three, *four* ... There was the sudden realisation for these students that this was indeed 'counting' and that the calculator really could be used to find out how many just by entering 1 +, and then = as they pointed at each object they counted.

I began to see the different ways students used the word 'count'. For some 'counting' meant making sequences of increasingly larger numbers; others recognised it as 'counting by' particular numbers, or 'skip counting'. I soon realised that few saw any connection between the counting sequence they saw on the display and the process of counting to find out how many.

I realised I would need to help many of the students make the connection between the number sequences created by using the constant function, and the process of finding out 'how many' in collections. As I continued to focus students on learning to use the constant key efficiently, I frequently drew attention to this important understanding.

Opportunity to Learn

By the next day many of these young students had forgotten how to 'make the calculator count'. I realised they would require practice if they were to use this important feature of the calculator effectively. Over the next few weeks I developed language patterns associated with using this function by repeatedly talking the students through the sequence in the following way:

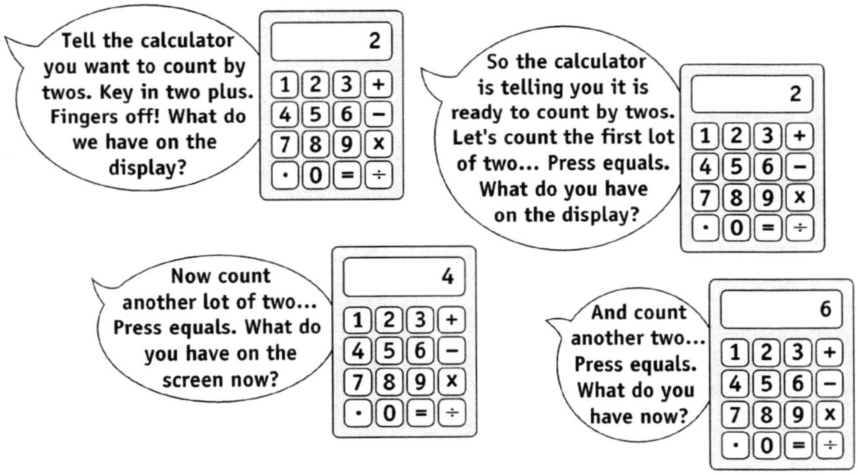

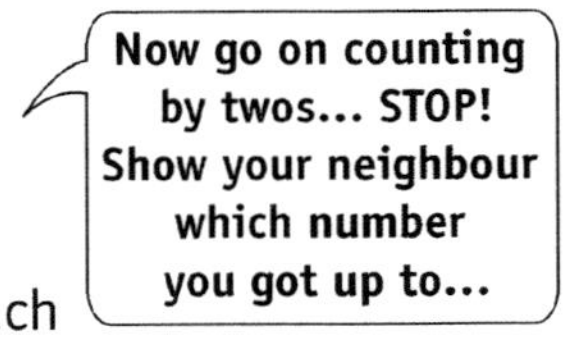

The students devised a number of strategies to make sure they counted each object or group of objects once only. Some pointed their calculator at each one as they pressed the = key; others nodded their heads at the items as they carried out their counts.

Drawing Out the Mathematical Idea

While the students were working, I constantly emphasised the connection between using this function and counting to find 'how many'. Therefore, I was surprised to hear Tiasa exclaim loudly, *Oh, I see! It's counting!* after she finished 'counting' the glue bottles on the shelf using the function. On several previous occasions I saw her 'count' other things with her calculator and assumed she already understood the process. Clearly, just showing her what to do was not enough—she needed the opportunity, time and experiences to make the connections for herself.

KEY UNDERSTANDING 10

Thinking about what makes sense helps us to check and interpret the results of calculations.

Students should be expected routinely to check that their answers are reasonable. Above all, they should develop the expectation that the answers produced by their computation should make sense, and that if they don't, some correction is likely to be needed. This is closely linked to the Apply and Verify outcome in Working Mathematically.

Checking Calculations

The first aspect of 'making sense' involves checking on the likely correctness of any calculations undertaken. Computational errors are common and forgivable, but sticking with answers that *cannot* be right should be considered much more worrying. Students should learn to check their answers using both their mathematical knowledge and their contextual knowledge.

Contextual Checks on Accuracy

Compare answers to what common sense suggests they should be. For example, students should notice that their answer cannot be right if the average height they have worked out is greater than that of anybody in the group.

Mathematical Checks on Accuracy

- ***Do the calculation a different way.*** Although we can check answers by going through the calculation a second time or re-entering the data into the calculator, we often reproduce the same error. Doing a calculation in a different order (adding up the column instead of down) or using a different mental strategy will be more likely to pick up a mistake.

- ***Estimate and approximate answers (see Key Understanding 8).*** Students should notice, for example, that their answer cannot be right if they have added three-quarters and two-thirds and get an answer less than one (such as five-sevenths), since both numbers are bigger than one-half.
- ***Think about the effect of particular types of operations (see Understand Operations, Key Understanding 7).*** Students should notice, for example, that their answer cannot be right if they have multiplied by a number bigger than one and got a smaller answer, or multiplied by six and got an odd number.

Interpreting Results of Calculations

The second aspect of 'making sense' involves interpreting the results of calculations in sensible ways and deciding whether answers need to be rounded or adjusted in some way. For example, how we interpret remainders in division depends on the situation. It is more sensible to say that each student got seven chocolate buttons and there was one over, than it is to say that each student got 7.2 chocolate buttons. Similarly, 90 eggs is 7.5 dozen or seven dozen and six left over. But the answer to the question 'How many cartons are needed to hold all the eggs?' is eight, whereas the answer to the question 'How many cartons can we fill?' is seven. For money, 4.5 on a calculator is read as $4.50 and $4.128 is rounded to $4.13 or possibly $4.15 or $4.10, depending on the context. Finally, it is generally not sensible to give answers that are more accurate than the data that produced them. Thus, if students' heights were found to the nearest centimetre, then finding an average more accurate than a centimetre usually wouldn't be sensible.

SAMPLE LEARNING ACTIVITIES

Beginning ✔

Numbers in Literature

Have students think about the numbers in literature and say if they make sense. At times change the numbers to focus them on the reasonableness of the numbers. For example:

- Read *Is It True Grandfather?* (Lohse and Sands, 1993) to the class. Change the text to say the oldest was five and the youngest was eight.
- Have students make a sequel to *Counting On Frank* (Clement, 1990), using similar situations, e.g. Frank said, I accidentally knocked ten peas on the floor every day for a week so now there are hundreds of peas down there. Ask: Could this be right? Why? Why not?

Could It Be Right?

Invite students to imagine sharing out a quantity of things, or skip count, to select an answer that they think could be right. For example: Tell them that three students want to share 12 biscuits. Jim thinks they will get six each. Sharon thinks three and Hank isn't sure but he thinks they will get at least two each. Ask: What do you think?

Sensible Answers

Decide whether answers need to be rounded or adjusted in some way to make sensible solutions. For example:

- Dad needs half an apple to make muffins. How many apples does he need to buy? ('Half an apple' is not sensible.)
- Two families are going on a trip in two cars. There are four adults and five children. How many children in each car? ('2.5 children' is not sensible.)
- A bus can carry 20 children. How many buses will be needed for 30 children? ('$1\frac{1}{2}$ buses' is not sensible.)

SAMPLE LEARNING ACTIVITIES

Middle ✔✔

Problems in Context

Have students interpret answers given on the calculator within the context of the problem and write a description of what the result really means. For example: Dad gave me $45 to pay for lunch and buses for me and my five friends. How much is that each? Ask students to calculate 45 ÷ 6 to get 7.5. Ask: How much is that? How many dollars and how many cents? Vary to produce different numbers of decimal places.

Place Value

Ask students to use place value to think about the reasonableness of calculations. For example: Would five bags of sweets be enough for our class of 27 and the 30 students next door? How would thinking about the number of students as 'tens' and 'ones' help?

Realistic Remainders

Encourage students to investigate ways of dealing with remainders in realistic situations. For example:

- Share seven litres of juice between three large containers for the class picnic.
- Five students share 18 marbles.
- Fourteen students need a ride to the tee-ball game—how many cars will be needed if four can go in each car?

Discuss the sensible way to deal with the remainder in each situation.

Check the Answer

Have students check results of calculations carried out on calculators by checking the hundreds, tens and ones. For example: 420 + 346 = 866; 420 + 346 = 786; 420 + 346 = 760.

Sensible Answers

Invite students to choose a sensible answer to a problem, given a variety of answers. For example: If an experienced painter took three hours to paint a wall and the apprentice took seven hours, how long would they take to do the job together—21 hours, ten hours, four hours, three hours, two hours or half an hour? Ask: Which answer is the most sensible and why?

Middle ✔✔

Rounding

Have students round to make sense of calculator results. For example: How many rows of chairs will we need if we can fit 26 chairs across the assembly area and we want to seat 175 parents? Ask students to draw a diagram to represent the chairs and then write a division number sentence to use on the calculator to check their working out. Ask: What does the result of 6.7307692 tell us about the number of rows? How can you have .7307692 of a row? If we round this to 0.75, how much of a row should this be? Does your diagram show this exactly? (Link to Key Understanding 8.)

Age Estimates

Ask students to estimate how old they are in months, in weeks and then in days and then say which answer should be the biggest and by how much. Ask: How much bigger should the number of weeks be than the number of months? Does your estimate show this? Ask students to then use their calculator to find exact answers and compare their results with their estimates. Where there is a big difference, ask: Which answer is likely to be right? Why?

Bigger or Smaller

Have students anticipate whether the answers to problems are sensible. For example: Using a seating plan of a bus, ask students to find the total number of adults allowed to travel on the bus if there are two adults to each seat and six along the back. Then ask them to work out how many students can be seated if three students can take the place of two adults but, before they do, ask: Should the answer be bigger or smaller than the number of adults? Can the answer include fractions? Why not?

SAMPLE LEARNING ACTIVITIES

Later ✔✔

Problems in Context

Have students interpret calculator answers within the context of the problem and where necessary write a more appropriate answer. Present a series of problems and the calculator answer. For example: 1 kg of apples cost $1.99; how much will 2.5 kilograms cost? 1.99 x 2.5 = 4.975. Ask: Is the answer in kilograms or dollars? How many dollars and how many cents? If anyone suggests $13.75, ask: How do you know this answer is too big? What does the .975 mean? Draw out that it is .975 of a dollar, it is not the number of cents. Provide examples involving money, where the answers on the calculator may be, for example, 3.7 or 21.333333. Ask: How should we read these?

Spot the Mistakes

Without doing the calculation, have students explain why answers such as those below cannot be true, and what mistake the person might have made:

- Why can't 2.5 + 1.5 make 3.10?
- Why can't 0.5 x 0.5 make 2.5?
- Why can't 2.25 + 3.2 make 257?
- Why can't 4.5 x 100 make 4.500?

Real-life Remainders

Ask students to deal sensibly with remainders in real-life situations.
For example:

- Lengths of ribbons measuring 80 cm are needed to hold each medal for the sports winners. How many lengths can be cut from a 25 m roll of ribbon?
- A large 25 L container of punch is to be shared among the six groups in the class. How much does each group get?
- A farmer has 1324 sheep to transport. A sheep truck holds 235 sheep. How many trucks will he need?

Sensible Answers

Have students interpret and label answers to calculations so that the problem can be answered in a way that makes sense. Present students with the problems, the calculation and the answer. For example:

- If I travel at 95 km/h, how long will it take me to drive 250 km? 250 ÷ 95 = 2.63.
- I had my school photo enlarged. It was originally 120 cm long. Now it is 360 cm long. By how many times has it been enlarged? 360 ÷ 120 = 3.
- How many different outfits can I wear if I have three t-shirts and four pairs of shorts? 4 x 3 = 12.

Ask students to label the answer in each case so that it makes sense.

Reasonable Answers

Without doing the calculations, have students say whether answers are reasonable or not. For example: Students mark the calculations done by a hypothetical student and say why some answers cannot be correct and explain what he or she has done wrong. Include whole number and decimal fraction examples:

238 + 26 + 412 = 910

$\frac{1}{2} + \frac{2}{3} = \frac{3}{5}$

475 ÷ 5 = 905

97 x 2.4 = 23.28

2.5 x 5.3 = 132.5

0.5 + 0.2 + 0.3 = 0.10

Making Problems

Ask students to think of problems that require the same calculation but have different interpretations of the remainder. For example: 500 ÷ 45 can result in the answers 11.1111 or 11 remainder 5 or approximately 11. Ask students to invent number stories that would make each of these answers sensible.

Inaccuracies

A calculation gives an exact answer that may not always occur in real life. For example: An employee being paid at a rate of $15.20 an hour will receive $60.80 after four hours' work. However, sawing off four lengths of wood measuring exactly 15.2 cm each will require more than 60.8 cm of wood because the saw cuts use up some wood. Ask students to brainstorm other measurement calculations where inaccuracies may occur in real life.

BACKGROUND NOTES

Learning their Basic Facts

Students should not be expected to try to memorise facts they do not understand. Equally, however, understanding where the basic facts come from and having worked them out for themselves is NOT enough to enable students to remember them. Students usually do need some drill with number facts if they are to be able to readily recall them. What is needed is a rational rather than a rote approach to learning the basic facts.

Addition Facts

Students might first discover and record the addition combinations to ten, convincing themselves that particular number facts 'always work' (see Key Understanding 1). They can often do some of these by counting in their mind's eye (e.g. three and two more) and/or quickly checking using their fingers, as well as by using materials. They should develop organised lists showing the numbers that fit together (part-part-whole) to make five or eight or ten. Once there is a meaningful basis for these 'facts', students need focused practice on remembering them— small amounts at frequent intervals.

Meanwhile, many of the combinations to 20 should be being established using materials and diagrams. Students should be using mental arithmetic to extend the facts they already know and remember (e.g. *I don't know 7 + 5 but it is* 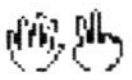 +  *, which is two more than 5 + 5 so it must be 12; 8 + 6 is like two sevens so it must be 14).*

Once the combinations to 20 have been discovered and recorded, students should be introduced to the use of a two-way table to record the facts.

Addition Facts

10	11	12	13	14	15	16	17	18	19	20
9	10	11	12	13	14	15	16	17	18	19
8	9	10	11	12	13	14	15	16	17	18
7	8	9	10	11	12	13	14	15	16	17
6	7	8	9	10	11	12	13	14	15	16
5	6	7	8	9	10	11	12	13	14	15
4	5	6	7	8	9	10	11	12	13	14
3	4	5	6	7	8	9	10	11	12	13
2	3	4	5	6	7	8	9	10	11	12
1	2	3	4	5	6	7	8	9	10	11
+	**1**	**2**	**3**	**4**	**5**	**6**	**7**	**8**	**9**	**10**

Students will need to learn how to read the table and should investigate patterns in it. They should note the sums on either side of the diagonal are in a sense 'the same' and that the number of facts to be remembered is almost halved when we use the commutative property of addition (55 instead of 100). The 'double numbers' on the diagonal (2, 4, 6, 8, 10, ...) are helpful in a lot of contexts and students' attention should be drawn particularly to this sequence of numbers.

Multiplication Facts

The usual approach to learning multiplication facts is to learn to chant through the multiplication facts in order. Students learn the two times 'table', the three times 'table', then the four times 'table', then the fives, etc. While students do need to memorise the basic multiplication facts, learning them by chanting tables is not a particularly helpful approach, for the following reasons.

- Firstly, many students who have learned their 'tables' in this way have difficulty remembering the facts without chanting through the table. Hence, it hinders the development of instant recall rather than helping it.
- Secondly, setting out the multiplication facts in columns and learning each set of tables separately masks the commutative property. Therefore, many students who *do* know, say, six fives, do not relate it to five sixes and have to remember almost twice as many facts as they need to.
- Thirdly, other patterns, such as that six times is double three times, are masked, which also increases the memory load for students.

It is likely to be much easier for students to remember basic facts if they practise them in clusters that help work them out. A possible sequence could be as follows:

Build up the facts to 5 x 5

Start with the twos (doubles), fours (double doubles), fives (because of the easy patterns and the links to our fingers) and then the threes. Put these in a two-way table. Commutativity reduces the 25 facts to be remembered to only 15, and if we remove the ones, there are only ten to remember. Use the five by five table to show students that by learning just ten facts they 'get' 25! Consolidate these facts and build up speed of recall with frequent short periods of practice.

5					25
4				16	20
3			9	12	15
2		4	6	8	10
1	1	2	3	4	5
×	**1**	**2**	**3**	**4**	**5**

Note that students may, at the same time, be able to skip count in twos, threes, fours and fives well beyond these facts. However, this requires them to work their way through the skips. This is not the same as being able to immediately recall 4 x 3, which is what focused drill should help them to do.

The ones and twos

At this stage, students could focus on the notion of 'doubling' and build their capacity to readily find 'double a number'. (This should be linked to the diagonal of the addition table and to the notion of even and odd numbers in order to help students make connections between related mathematical ideas.)

The tens

Focus on groups of ten and counting in tens. Help students become convinced about why three tens are the same as ten threes and practise these together. There will be ten facts to remember, but the pattern makes them easy and students will readily recall them.

The squares

Many teachers also find that explorations of patterns of squares help students learn the squares: 1, 4, 9, 16, 25, 36, 49, 64, 81, 100. It seems students 'like' the square numbers and learn them fairly readily. Thus, facts such as 7 x 7 may be learned earlier than other related facts. Students should develop instant recall of these facts.

Students have now developed the facts from 1 x 1 to 5 x 5 and the facts involving one, two and ten and the squares. Help them make a two-way table in which they record the multiplication facts they now know.

Multiplication Facts

10	10	20	30	40	50	60	70	80	90	100
9	9	18							81	90
8	8	16						64		80
7	7	14					49			70
6	6	12				36				60
5	5	10	15	20	25					50
4	4	8	12	16	20					40
3	3	6	9	12	15					30
2	2	4	6	8	10	12	14	16	18	20
1	1	2	3	4	5	6	7	8	9	10
×	**1**	**2**	**3**	**4**	**5**	**6**	**7**	**8**	**9**	**10**

There are various orders in which the remaining 'facts' can be developed. Some teachers find it most helpful to move out in an ever-increasing square, so that the next cluster of facts is those to fill in the square to 6 x 6. This requires the addition of three new facts (6 x 3, 6 x 4, 6 x 5) and their 'partner' facts (3 x 6, 4 x 6, 5 x 6). Then move out to 7 x 7 and so on.

An alternative sequence could be as follows.

The five facts

Build up the five facts to 5 x 10, noting the relationship to the ten facts (e.g. five eights is half of ten eights; half of eight tens is four tens or 40; so 5 x 8 is 40) and the pattern in the units digits. Add to the table and memorise.

The four facts and eight facts to 8 x 8

First build on the 'doubles' or twos (2 x 1 to 2 x 10) to get the 'double doubles' or fours (to 4 x 10). Add these to the table. Double the four facts to produce the eights up to 8 x 5 (if you know 4 x 3, you can double to get 8 x 3). Add these to the table. Use commutativity to work out the additional facts (if you know 8 x 3 you also know 3 x 8). When first practising these facts, give students plenty of time to work them out mentally using the doubling strategy or some other method they prefer. Gradually build up speed to get 'instant recall'. Use various doubling and other patterns to build up the extra eight facts (8 x 6 to 8 x 8). Practise to memorise.

The three facts and six facts

Build up the three additional three facts (3 x 6, 3 x 7, 3 x 9) and add to the table. Double these to get the sixes or use other known facts (e.g. six fours is five fours and four more). Five new facts to learn and their partners give you ten more.

The nine facts

Build on the threes and the sixes using number partitions to add the additional two nine facts and their partners. Although most are known, revisit the nines to link them to 10 – 1 so that students see that 9 x 7 is ten sevens take seven. Initially, allow students time to do the calculation using mental arithmetic strategies and gradually help them memorise for speedy recall.

The seven facts

The seven facts are all known!

This is not the only possible sequence. The important thing is to assist students to use rational thought processes rather than rote memory to learn the facts.

Reducing the Stress

If students have reached the upper primary years and are struggling to remember the multiplication facts, they may have built up some anxiety about them. Often it is worth spending time explaining how to read a 10 x 10 multiplication table and then having them systematically work through the table, crossing out those they know.

Everyone can draw a line through the 'one times' and the 'times one'. Most know the doubles and the fives and tens. Quite a lot will know the squares. Spend some time on the commutative property. Students do not need to remember the word, but they should be able to say and understand why: *If I know 8 x 5 then I also know 5 x 8*. Show students how this reduces the number of facts to be remembered.

Remarkably, after removing the ones, twos, fives and tens and the squares, only 15 of the 100 facts remain. Emphasise that they are almost there! Most students will be able to cross off at least some of these 15.

Students can then make personal 'prompt' cards for their remaining unknown facts. Have them set a personal target of, say, three to learn this week. During the week, help students work out how their three target facts relate to other facts they know. Periodically through the week, their partner should test them on the facts. When they have correctly recalled a fact, say, ten times, they cross it off their multiplication table list and store the card for later re-testing. Over the next several weeks their partner should test them on previous weeks' facts, as well as their targeted three for this week.

Techniques for Mental Calculation

Students need practice with a wide range of strategies for calculating mentally. Mental arithmetic is flexible and only occasionally unthinking and so it cannot be made routine. For example, to add 99 to 125, a sensible strategy would be to add 100 and subtract one; to add 64 to 125, you might add 60 and then four; to add 64 to 96, you might add the four and then the 60.

The fact that the calculation is done mentally does not mean that the presentation is always oral. Often we add a string of numbers that we can see, e.g. when playing Scrabble. When we add the digits in each column for column addition, the sums often go well beyond the basic facts and so mental arithmetic is needed. In some cases, students (like adults) will use some informal jottings on paper to help keep track of their thinking. Jotting partial answers down is widely used by adults and should not be discouraged. The choice is not between fully mental approaches and standard written approaches. The goal is flexibility and efficiency rather than standardisation.

Students should use place value to extend the range of calculations they carry out mentally. For example:

- count backwards and forwards in tens: 10, 20, 30, 40, ...
- count in tens from any starting point: 14, 24, 34, 44, ... and 53, 43, 33, ...
- add in tens, twenties and thirties, hundreds, etc., from any starting point: 23, 43, 63, ...
- generalise basic facts, e.g. 8 + 7 = 15 so 18 + 7 = 25, 28 + 7 = 35; 6 x 7 = 42 so 60 x 7 = 420.

The properties of the operations (e.g. when multiplying several numbers, the order does not matter), the relationships between them (e.g. division is the inverse of multiplication), number partitions and place value form the basis of the following mental calculation strategies.

Use relationships (commutativity and inverses)

- Adding: the order doesn't matter. **4 + 27** is 27 + 4, so 28, 29, 30, 31.
- Multiplying: the order doesn't matter. **24** twos is **2** twenty-fours, so 48.
- Subtracting: thinking of an addition might help. **13 – 8**, think 'eight add what is 13?'
- Dividing: thinking of a multiplication might help. **63 ÷ 9**, think 'how many nines make 63?'

Compensate (partition and rearrange)

- Add: take some from one number to give to the other. **8 + 7** is 10 + 5; **68 + 37** is 70 + 35

- Multiply: take out a factor from one to give to the other. **15 x 6** is 15 times 2 times 3, so 30 times 3, so 90.
- Subtract: change the numbers by adding or subtracting the same amount. **62 – 37** is 65 – 40.
- Divide: change the numbers by multiplying or dividing by the same amount. **29 ÷ 5** is 58 ÷ 10.

Use compatible numbers and bridge

- Making change: **100 – 68**. I am thinking 100, what fits with 68? OR It cost 68 cents, what's the change from $1?
- Rearrange the order: **8 + 7 + 2** is 8 and 2 is 10 plus another 7 is 17; **68 + 27 + 12** is 68 and 12 is 80 plus 20 is 100 plus seven, so 107.
- Bridging: **9 + 4** is 9 + 1 + 3 = 10 + 3 = 13; **68 + 47** is 68 and 32 will make 100 and 15 left, so 115.

Front load (start with the biggest place)

- Bring on the tens and then the ones: **28 + 37** is 38, 48, 58 and 7 more, so 60, 65.
- Do both tens and then both ones: **68 + 37** is 90 + 15, so 100 and 5 more, so 105.

Imagine a number line

- Jump along or back: **364 – 198**: starting at 198, it takes 2 to get to 200 and another 164 to get to 364, so 166; OR starting at 364 go back 64 to 300, 100 more to 200 (so that's 164) and back 2 more to 198, so 166.

Multiply in parts (partition and multiply the parts)

- Round a number and adjust: **7 x 9** is 7 tens take 7 ones, so 70 – 7, so 63; **99 x 6** is 600 take six.
- Use place value partitions: **6 x 25** is 6 x 20 add 6 x 5, so 120 add 30.

Use factors

- Double, double, double: **4 x 14** is double double 14, so double 28, so 56.
- Change to a multiplication you know: **3 x 18** is 3 times 3 times 6, so 9 times 6, so 54.
- Multiply by five—**5 x 8** is 8 fives, which is 4 lots of 2 fives, 4 tens so 40.
- Multiply by fifty: **50 x 72**; 50 is half of a hundred, so half of 72 hundred, so 36 hundred or 3600.
- Multiply by twenty-five: **36 x 25**; I saw the 25 and looked for 4 to make 100, so 9 x 4 x 25 or 900.
- Doubling and halving: **45 x 14** is the same as 90 x 7, so 630.

CHAPTER 5

Reason About Number Patterns

This chapter will support teachers in developing curricula that relate to this outcome in Number:

Investigate, generalise and reason about patterns in number, explaining and justifying conclusions reached.

Overall Description

Students observe regularities and differences and describe them mathematically. By identifying common features in mathematical situations, they are able to make generalisations about numbers, space and data. Thus they may observe that every time they combine three things with nine things and count, they get 12 things, and make the generalisation that three add nine is always 12.

They know that there may be many patterns in the one situation, and generate and investigate a number of different conjectures about it. Students understand that a mathematical generalisation must be true *always* rather than *mostly*, and that one exception invalidates it. They attempt to confirm or refute their own and others' generalisations and prepare arguments to convince themselves and others that a generalisation *must* hold in every case and not only for all the cases tried.

They write (and speak) mathematics clearly and precisely, expressing and explaining their generalisations verbally and with standard algebraic conventions.

<table>
<tr><th>Levels of Achievement</th><th>Pointers
Progress will be evident when students:</th></tr>
<tr><td>Students have achieved Level 1 when they copy, continue and make repeating and counting patterns and use numbers to represent their patterns.</td><td><ul><li>copy and continue in materials the pattern of the counting numbers or 'skip counting' in twos or threes, e.g. make and continue a staircase that starts one cube, two stacked cubes, three stacked cubes; copy by threading two red onto the first rod, two red and two green onto the next, two red, two green and two yellow on the next, and continue the pattern in their own choice of colours</li><li>copy and continue repeating patterns, e.g. a necklace beginning: two gum leaves, three gumnuts, one shell, two gum leaves, three gumnuts, one shell</li><li>repeat a pattern in a different medium, e.g. show the necklace pattern in sounds or the xylophone pattern in colours</li><li>use simple language such as 'pattern', 'over and over', 'repeat' and 'again' to describe patterns</li><li>use a sequence of numbers to represent a repeating pattern, e.g. write 2, 3, 1, 2, 3, 1, 2, ... as another way to show their leaves, nuts and shell pattern</li></ul></td></tr>
<tr><td>Students have achieved Level 2 when they recognise, continue, represent and describe patterns involving counting, grouping, and constant addition or subtraction of whole numbers.</td><td><ul><li>represent simple adding and subtracting patterns visually, choosing materials to help make the pattern obvious, e.g. represent 21, 31, 41, 51, ... by grouping materials to show the tens in some way</li><li>write a pattern of numbers to fit a toothpick pattern and use it to predict the toothpicks needed for later terms</li><li>identify 'one-stage' rules such as 'add three', 'subtract five' or 'double' when playing 'guess my rule'-type games</li><li>describe a rule that could have been used to generate an adding or subtracting sequence and test, e.g. say: To make that sequence you could start with 50 and take three each time; use the constant function on a calculator to reproduce and extend the pattern</li><li>order sets of related additions or subtractions to generate additional 'facts' based on patterns, e.g. use 1 + 14, 2 + 13, 3 + 12 to conjecture other sums to 15</li></ul></td></tr>
<tr><td>Students have achieved Level 3 when they recognise, describe and use patterns involving operations on whole numbers, and follow and describe rules for how terms in a sequence can be linked by multiplication or an addition- or subtraction-based strategy.</td><td><ul><li>build sequences of simple shapes such as triangles, squares, 'L' or 'T' shapes, which increase in size systematically and write the equivalent number pattern</li><li>describe and continue number sequences based on addition or subtraction but involving more than adding or subtracting a constant amount, e.g. say: For the sequence 100, 99, 97, 94, ... a rule that fits is start with 100 and take one, then take two, then take three, so the next one would be take four</li><li>identify the starting number and the constant multiplier needed to generate a number sequence, e.g. 6, 12, 24, 48, ... could have the rule 'start with six and keep doubling'</li><li>follow a rule to generate a number sequence based on an addition or subtraction strategy, e.g. follow the rule 'start with one, two, then each time add the two previous numbers'</li><li>fill in number sequences involving addition or subtraction by a constant amount, e.g. fill in 6, 11, ..., 21, 26, ..., ... to make a pattern</li><li>use patterns in sequences of related additions or subtractions to generate new equations, e.g. fill in the missing numbers in 19 – 14 = 5, 29 – 14 = 15, 39 – 14 = 25, ? – 14 = 35, 59 – ? =</li></ul></td></tr>
<tr><td>Students have achieved Level 4 when they recognise, describe and use patterns involving operations on whole and fractional numbers, and follow and describe rules for how successive terms in a sequence or paired quantities can be linked by a single operation.</td><td><ul><li>fill in number sequences involving constant multiplication or division, e.g. 2, 6, ..., 54, 162, ...; 128, 64, ..., 16, ..., 4</li><li>follow a rule based on multiplication, division or simple fractions to generate a sequence, e.g. start with 81 and find one-third each time</li><li>represent constant addition or multiplication sequences of decimal fractions with materials or diagrams, e.g. show 0.3, 0.6, 0.9, ... by jumping along a number line; represent 3, 0.3, 0.03, .003 with materials</li><li>describe a sequence sufficiently for a peer to reproduce it, e.g. for 3, 7, 11, ... it is insufficient simply to say a rule that works is add four—it is also necessary to indicate the starting point, e.g. a rule that works is begin with three and add four each time</li><li>identify, describe and continue patterns linking pairs of numbers on a coordinate grid or in a table by a single operation, e.g.<table><tr><td>1</td><td>2</td><td>3</td><td>4</td><td>5</td></tr><tr><td>7</td><td>14</td><td>21</td><td></td><td></td></tr></table><table><tr><td>1</td><td>2</td><td>3</td><td>4</td><td>6</td><td>8</td><td></td><td>24</td></tr><tr><td>24</td><td>12</td><td>8</td><td>6</td><td>4</td><td></td><td>2</td><td></td></tr></table></li></ul></td></tr>
<tr><td>Students have achieved Level 5 when they recognise, describe and use number patterns involving one or two operations, and follow, compare and explain rules for how successive terms in a sequence or paired quantities can be linked using one or two operations.</td><td><ul><li>identify the pattern in a sequence involving two operations and describe how each term in the sequence is related to the previous term, e.g. say the rule is start with $100 and add 50% each year; identify the pattern in 2, 5, 11, 23, 47, ... by noting that the differences between successive terms form a doubling pattern beginning with three</li><li>follow general one- and two-stage rules, e.g. write the sequence of numbers for 'the nth term is three times the number take away one'</li><li>identify patterns in the results of sets of related computations involving more than one operation (e.g. 1 x 9 + 2 =; 12 x 9 + 3 =; 123 x 9 + 4 =) and use to predict other results</li><li>find a general rule to relate each element of a sequence to its position where one or two operations are involved and hence find any term, e.g. say: The first number was three times one add one, the second number was three times two add one, the third number ... Each number is three times its position add one, so the 20th number would be three times 20 add one, which is 61</li><li>identify the rule connecting the pairs on a graph</li></ul></td></tr>
</table>

Key Understandings

Teachers will need to plan learning experiences that focus on the following Key Understandings (KU). These Key Understandings underpin achievement of the outcome. The learning experiences should connect to students' current knowledge and understanding rather than to their year level.

Key Understanding	Stage of Primary Schooling—Major Emphasis	KU Description	Sample Learning Activities
KU1 We use regularity or pattern to infer one thing from another thing and to make predictions.	Beginning ✔✔✔ Middle ✔✔ Later ✔✔	page 200	Beginning, page 202 Middle, page 204 Later, page 206
KU2 Representing aspects of a situation with numbers can make it easier to see patterns in the situation.	Beginning ✔✔ Middle ✔✔✔ Later ✔✔✔	page 212	Beginning, page 214 Middle, page 216 Later, page 218
KU3 To describe a number pattern means to provide a precise rule that produces the pattern.	Beginning ✔ Middle ✔✔ Later ✔✔✔	page 224	Beginning, page 226 Middle, page 228 Later, page 230
KU4 There are strategies that help us become better at recognising common types of patterns.	Beginning ✔ Middle ✔✔✔ Later ✔✔✔	page 234	Beginning, page 235 Middle, page 237 Later, page 239
KU5 Our numeration system has a lot of specially built-in patterns that make working with numbers easier.	Beginning ✔✔ Middle ✔✔✔ Later ✔✔✔	page 242	Beginning, page 244 Middle, page 246 Later, page 248
KU6 Some numbers have interesting or useful properties. Investigating the patterns in these special numbers can help us to understand them better.	Beginning ✔ Middle ✔✔ Later ✔✔	page 250	Beginning, page 252 Middle, page 254 Later, page 256

Key

✔✔✔ The development of this Key Understanding is a major focus of planned activities.

✔✔ The development of this Key Understanding is an important focus of planned activities.

✔ Some activities may be planned to introduce this Key Understanding, to consolidate it, or to extend its application. The idea may also arise incidentally in conversations and routines that occur in the classroom.

KEY UNDERSTANDING 1

We use regularity or pattern to infer one thing from another thing and to make predictions.

Students are most likely to recognise the significance of pattern when their attention is regularly drawn to it in the context of other work across the curriculum, in all strands of mathematics and in conjunction with the other Key Understandings for Reason about Number Patterns. As students note and use familiar patterns in their everyday lives and the more structured patterns of the classroom, their attention should be repeatedly drawn to the following two aspects to this Key Understanding.

Firstly, in a mathematical context, we use the word 'pattern' to refer to the underlying regularity or ongoing repetition in a situation. For example, in a fabric design made by turning and sliding a motif, it is not the motif or the overall design that is the 'pattern', rather the pattern is the regularity of the turning and sliding. To describe the pattern means to describe *how to get* the design or overall picture. To copy a pattern means to reproduce the regularity.

Secondly, the main reason we focus upon pattern is that patterns enable us to predict, expect and plan. Mostly, we respond to patterns without noticing that we have. Thus, even though the details of each day are different, the underlying regularity or pattern in our days enables us to infer the time from signs around us (e.g. the car noises and voices outside school signal that the school day is almost over). Pattern also helps us to predict and hence plan, such as when buses are scheduled to fit typical days.

Students who have achieved Level 1 of this outcome use obvious patterns to make copying arrangements and sequences easier; that is, they no longer reproduce simply by matching each component one at a time. They are able to talk about the regularity in the events of their own daily life using simple language such as 'pattern', 'over and over', 'repeat' and 'again', and are beginning to understand that it is the regularities in everyday life that enable them to 'know what to do' at various times and to say what is likely to happen in the future. This Key Understanding underpins the outcome at all levels, although students who have achieved higher levels will have an increasing awareness and capacity to explain what we mean by 'a pattern' and how patterns help us. They will apply their understanding to an increasing repertoire of patterns and make increasingly sophisticated predictions and inferences, as indicated in Key Understandings 3 to 5.

SAMPLE LEARNING ACTIVITIES

Beginning ✓✓✓

Incidental Activities

For example:

- ***Learning a song.*** Ask: How did you manage to learn the words so quickly? What is the pattern? How did it help?
- ***School's out.*** Say: Some of you are getting ready to go. How come? Why do you think it is time?
- ***Stories.*** When telling and retelling stories with repetitive features, stop and ask students to predict what comes next. Ask: How did you guess/remember so well?

Daily Activities

Encourage students to look for the repeating events in daily routines such as arriving at or leaving school. Ask them to draw the separate events. Make copies of the drawings for them to set out showing the events over several days. Encourage students to say what happens over and over again, e.g. come, go, come, go OR come, put bag away, set up, bell goes, come, put bag away, set up, bell goes.

Sound and Movement

Have students follow sequences of movements and sounds, comparing those that are patterned with those that are not. For example: Ask them to first copy and join in with a 'clap clap, turn around' repeated sequence and say what they think comes next. Then copy and join in. Where the sequence has no obvious repetition, stop the sequence and ask: What comes next? (They can't tell.) Which was easiest to follow—the first lot of movements or the last one? Why?

Lining Up

Invite students to use the repeating pattern in the actions of a line of students to predict what comes next and what they will have to do. For example: Ask students to form a line around the room. Walk along the line and as you tap each student on the shoulder tell them to 'stand, stand, sit, sit, sit, sit, stand, stand, sit, sit, sit, sit', and so on. Say it as a chant and have students join in as you go. Once the rhythm is established, stop and ask: What will Kia (next student) be doing? Repeat. Extend this to predicting several ahead. Ask: How do you know? (Because the teacher is not just making it up as she or he goes along—there is a pattern.) Stop giving the instructions and ask the rest of the students, one at a time, to sit or stand according to the pattern.

Watching the Line-up

Have students look at a line of students pre-arranged in a repeating pattern such as in the previous activity. Ask them to decide what the pattern is and what the next several students will need to do to continue the pattern. Focus on the repeating parts.

Necklaces

Ask students to reproduce a string of beads that shows a repeating pattern such as blue, blue, red, blue, blue, red. Draw out the 'pattern' by having students chant aloud the sequence of colours. If necessary, model the rhythm. Ask students to make their string longer than the original. Ask: How do you know what comes next? Repeat for a variety of repeating patterns and extend to three colours.

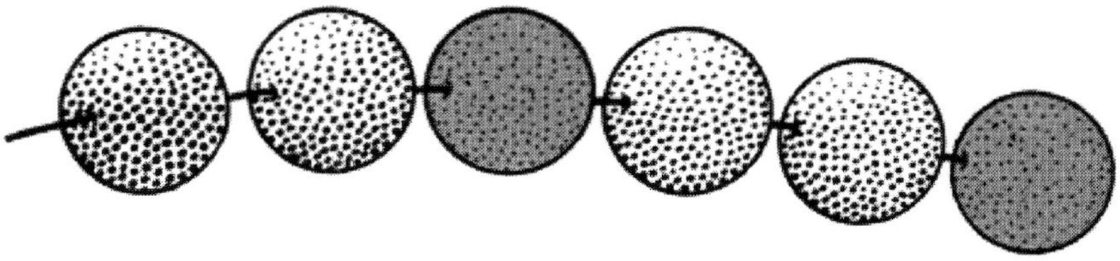

Varied Objects

Have students repeat the previous activity, but include several types of objects or beads where the only repetition is in the colour. For example: The repeating pattern might be blue, blue, red, blue, blue, red ... but the actual objects quite varied. Draw out that this pattern is in the colour. Other things could be different. Repeat with a line of students: girl, girl, boy ... Each student is different but there is a pattern in the gender. Repeat for eye colour, ignoring other variations.

Decades

Count in rhythm with students as they go up, over and through the decade numbers. Use variations in pitch and volume of voice to emphasise one to nine repeating within each decade, and the decades (tens) also following this pattern. Stop periodically and ask: How do you know what comes next? What is the pattern? How does it help?

SAMPLE LEARNING ACTIVITIES

Middle ✔✔

Incidental Activities

See also 'Incidental Activities', page 202.

- ***Learning a dance.*** Ask: What makes remembering the steps easier? How does the pattern help?
- ***Checking work.*** Ask: How could you tell you must have made a mistake? How did the pattern help you decide where you had gone wrong? (See Sample Lesson 1, page 208.)

Dance Patterns

Have students learn the steps to a simple dance such as the heel-toe polka, and then identify and write down the series of steps that makes the basic repeating unit of the dance. Ask students to then make their own dance by changing this basic repeating unit in some way, and teach it to other students. (Link to Key Understanding 2.)

Daily Activities

Have students record their own daily events on a 24-hour timeline for five to ten weekdays. Ask them to line up their timelines and look for regularities. Ask: Do you have a regular time for getting up? For going to bed? What else can you say about a typical day? What might cause a change in the pattern of your days? Have students write a letter to an e-mail pal from another country, describing what their own typical school day is like. Compare these with similar responses from e-mail pals.

Families

Extend the previous activity by having students compare each other's days. Ask: What is the same? What is different? Which parts of the day are most alike? Is there a pattern that fits most students? Draw out that even though each day is different and each family is different, there are patterns in our days that result from natural (e.g. dark and light) and designed (e.g. school timetable) processes, which make generalising possible and sensible.

Shadows

Have students graph the length and direction of the shadow of a plant at different parts of the day over a number of days. They can then use this to predict which part of the playground will be the shadiest during recess and lunchtime. Ask: Is there likely to be more shade at recess or lunchtime tomorrow? Will this be the same every day? How do you know?

What Time Is It?

Pose simple problems involving time. For example: It is 9 o'clock now, what time will it be in two hours? In three hours? In four hours? Why not 13 o'clock? How do you know? (The hours of the day have a repeating pattern: 1, 2, 3, 4 ... 12, over and over.) Challenge students further. For example: If the bus leaves at 9.30 and the trip takes two hours, what time will we arrive? What if the bus breaks down and the trip takes three hours? We can predict because of the patterns built into our system for describing the time of day (which match the natural cycle of day and night).

More Time

Extend the previous activity to the repeating or cyclic patterns within each hour: the quarter hours (o'clock, quarter past, half past, quarter to) and the minutes (cycles through 60 minutes, for each hour).

The Answer Is ...

Ask students to make up an addition that has a specified answer, e.g. 24. Ask them to make up another, and another—as many as they can. Encourage them to put their sums in order and fill in any gaps. Ask: Can you use patterns in the numbers to make sure you have all the pairs of whole numbers that add to 24?

$1 + 23 = 24$

$2 + 22 = 24$

$3 + 21 = 24$

Ask: What happens to the second number as the first goes up by ones? Have students explain to partner. Challenge them: I worked out that 237 + 492 = 729. Can you find some other pairs that must add to 729 (without doing the calculation)? If I increase the 237 to 238, what do I need to do to the 492? (See Sample Lesson 1, page 208, and Calculate, Key Understanding 2.)

More Answers

Repeat the previous activity, but using subtractions rather than additions to give a specified number. (See Sample Lesson 1, page 208, and Calculate, Key Understanding 2.)

Bus Times

Have students investigate the times on bus timetables to work out the regularity. Ask: How often do buses go on weekdays? How often on weekends? If you miss the bus, how long will you have to wait until the next bus arrives on a weekday? On a weekend?

SAMPLE LEARNING ACTIVITIES

Later ✔✔

Incidental Activities

See also 'Incidental Activities', pages 202 and 204.

- Students making a wall chart to show π (pi) to 30 places find it hard to quickly copy it accurately. Compare with copying a recurring decimal such as 0.231231 ... Ask: Why is this? (See also 'Copying Decimals' page 207.)

How Hungry?

Have students record and then graph their hunger level every half hour through a typical day. Ask: How does your graph compare to others? When does hunger suddenly drop? How long does it take to drop? When is it least? Highest? How long does it take to rise to its highest? Does your graph show what happens? Discuss whether the differences between students' graphs reflect real differences in their days (e.g. how regularly they eat and when they eat). Have students re-draft graphs to better show the typical hunger pattern in their own days.

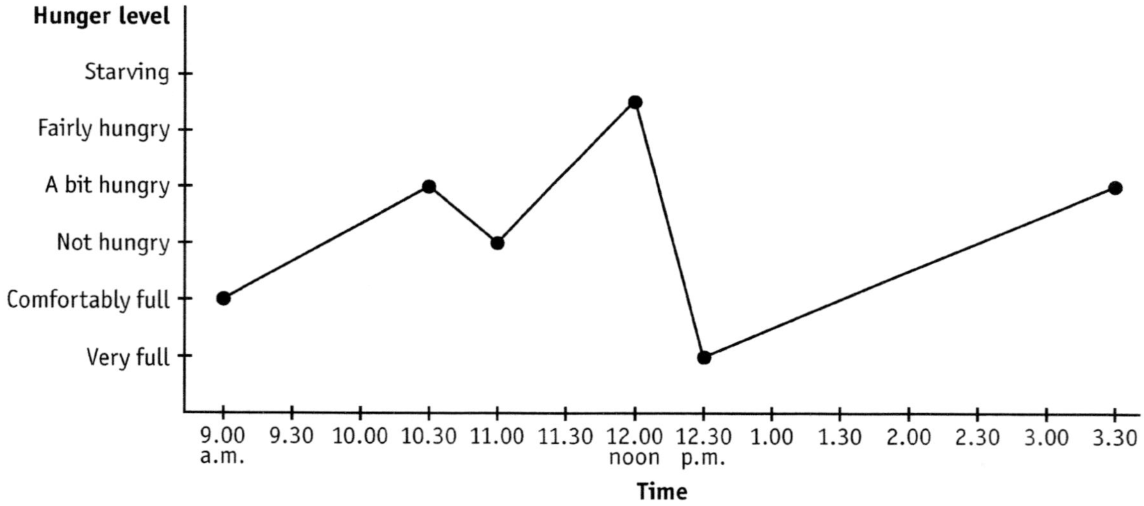

Other Features

Repeat the previous activity for other variable features of students' days, such as how temperature varies, how active they are, or how tired they are feeling through the day.

Holidays

Ask students to compare weather patterns in different locations to predict what weather will be like and to plan a trip. For example: Compare weather data for Broome, Perth and Albany and consider questions such as: At what time of year would you most like to go to Broome? Albany? Perth? If you go to Broome in July, what sorts of clothes should you take? What if you go to Albany? Draw out that even though each day/year is different, the general weather pattern enables you to plan with some confidence. Extend this to investigate how weather patterns affect crops, sea life, population (related to tourism) and special events.

Investigating Primes

Give students a three- or four-digit number that you know is a multiple of seven, e.g. 2247. Ask them to decide whether or not it is. After they have confirmed it is, ask: What is the next multiple of seven? And the next? How do you know? Then give students a number you know to be prime (e.g. 2331) and challenge them to decide whether or not it is. After they have confirmed it is, ask: What is the next prime? What is the problem? (No pattern, can't predict.) (Link to Understand Operations, Key Understanding 5.)

Copying Decimals

Write on the board two lists of ten numbers, each with, say, 12 decimal places:

- On List 1, include only numbers in which the digits are obviously patterned, e.g. 3.454545454545.
- On List 2, include only numbers in which digits are not obviously patterned, e.g. 3.414283371429.

Ask one student in each pair to copy List 1 as quickly (but correctly) as they can, and the other to copy List 2, and to record which partner finishes first. Collect data as a class. It is likely that more students copying List 1 will finish first. Discuss why this might be. Ask: How did the pattern help? Link to what sorts of phone numbers are easiest to remember. (This could precede work on recurring decimals.) (Link to Key Understanding 5.)

Calculating with Patterns

Have students use patterns to make calculating easier. Present this scenario: Sam was doing homework. He drew diagrams to work out $\frac{1}{4} \times \frac{1}{2}$, $\frac{1}{3} \times \frac{1}{5}$ and so on. He thought $\frac{3}{4} \times \frac{6}{7}$, $\frac{2}{3} \times \frac{5}{8}$ and $\frac{5}{6} \times \frac{1}{4}$ were too hard. He had a calculator that could calculate fractions so he decided to use that. He worked out that $\frac{3}{4} \times \frac{6}{7} = \frac{18}{20}$, $\frac{2}{3} \times \frac{5}{8} = \frac{10}{24}$. Ask: Can you see a pattern that would help Sam work out similar examples without using his calculator? (Link to Calculate, Key Understanding 7.)

SAMPLE LESSON 1

Sample Learning Activity: Middle—'The Answer Is ...', page 205

Key Understanding 1: We use regularity or pattern to infer one thing from another thing and to make predictions.

Working Towards: Levels 2 and 3

Background to the Sample Lesson

As I walked past a class, I heard a boy say '18'. The teacher said, 'That's right!' What question could the teacher have asked? Write down as many as you like.

I originally set the students in my Year 3 class a task designed to help me understand what they knew about numbers and number patterns. (The task is shown at the left of the page.) The students had constant access to calculators and were encouraged to use them as a matter of course.

Some students produced a quite varied list of examples, others lists of related examples. Some also experimented with their calculators to produce expressions that were well beyond what one would normally expect of students in Year 3. Almost all produced many more calculations and questions than I would have set them! Over the next few weeks I returned regularly to selected work samples as a starting point for different activities.

Several students relied heavily on patterns to generate a large number of related calculations. I took the opportunity to use these to develop the key understanding that we can use pattern to infer one thing from another thing and to make predictions.

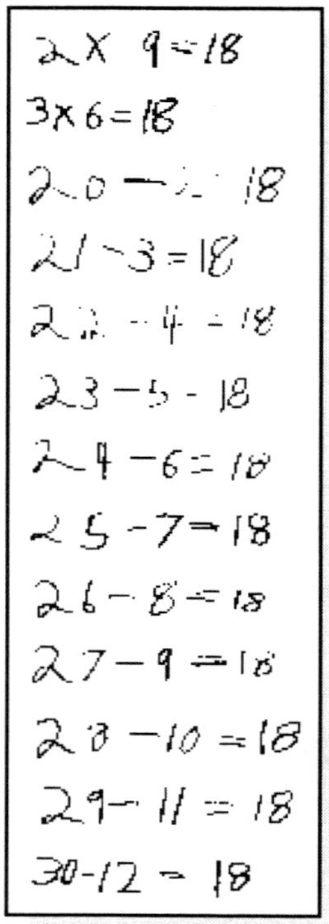
2X 9=18
3x6=18
20-2=18
21-3=18
22-4=18
23-5=18
24-6=18
25-7=18
26-8=18
27-9=18
28-10=18
29-11=18
30-12=18

Setting Up the Situation

I made an overhead of Maria's work and showed it to the whole class. I asked Maria to explain what she had done. She immediately stated that she could see she would get the same answer for 22 – 4 as for 21 – 3 and for 20 – 2, and so she was able to make up a lot of examples very quickly by adding one to each number.

I then asked all the students to think about what Maria had done, to talk it over with their partner and decide whether it would always work. I called on several students to say whether they would be prepared to rely on the pattern Maria had used and why. Because all of Maria's examples worked, the students said they would accept it. I then asked them how far they would be prepared to go. Would they go to higher numbers? Would they add 100 to each number? I wanted to force them to be explicit about what rule they were using.

Drawing Out the Mathematical Idea

I then returned to the key point I wanted to draw out by removing Maria's overhead and asking students to check whether the following six calculations had an answer of 18.

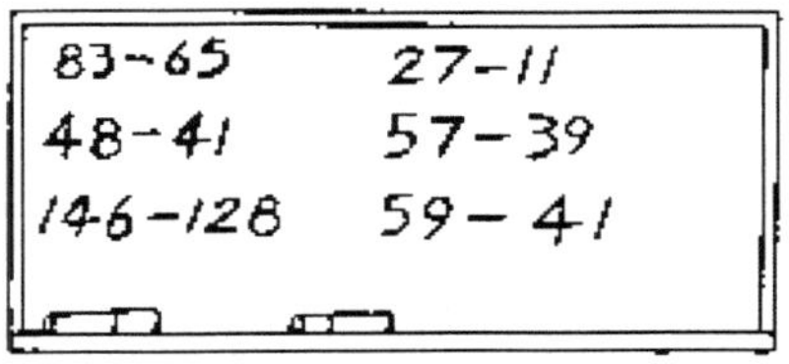

They were to put the pens/calculators down and sit up straight once they had decided. I didn't immediately review their decisions but rather noted with simulated surprise that it had taken them quite a while to decide, and yet Maria had produced lots of calculation more quickly. How come?

Maria was bursting to explain that, once she began to use the pattern, she didn't need to check each one. I asked her what was different in her list and the list above that made it easier for her. After a pause, she (and others) said that her list was in order and so she could just go up one at a time. She could decide that a calculation would have to give 18 without having to work each one out. Although she did not use the word, she was saying that she could use one difference to infer a lot of others.

Other students generally agreed that she hadn't needed to check each one, although a few seemed to think that relying on the pattern somehow minimised her achievement. I didn't overtly challenge this view that 'harder is better', but instead made a big point of saying how in mathematics we always try to find the easiest way to solve problems; that the reason we look for patterns in maths is so we don't have to do each problem as though it were new. We can use what we learn in one problem to do others more easily.

Extending the Mathematical Idea

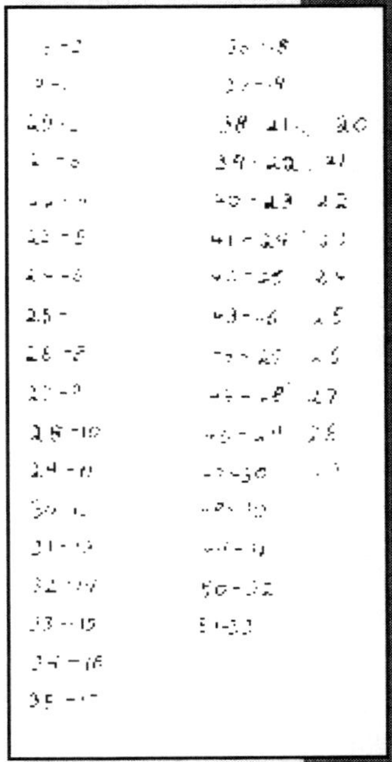

To my delight, one of the students then asked: *What if you make a mistake in one? Wouldn't all the rest be wrong?* Had he not asked this I was prepared to bring it up myself. I turned to Andre and said: *Andre can tell you about that, can't you?* I pulled out the worksheet he had produced and Andre explained that he had used a pattern to produce his list of calculations but suddenly realised when he got to 47 – 30 that it couldn't be right. He said: *I knew I must have made a mistake so I just went back up the list until I found where I went wrong.*

I asked: *How did you do that? Did you work out every one?*

No, he said. *I looked at the pattern and could see that the first number changed by one each time but the second number changed by two here* (pointing to where the error occurred).

So what is the lesson here? I asked.

In the brief discussion that followed, I was able to draw from the students that we can make mistakes even when using a pattern. Therefore, we need to check every now and again that we haven't gone wrong—preferably, as Andre did, with examples that are easy to check. However, organising the examples in a list so that the pattern in the numbers was obvious helped Andre to notice and find his mistake.

The Next Phase

I then moved on to develop two other Key Understandings:

- Firstly, our numeration system has a lot of specially built-in patterns that make working with numbers easier (Key Understanding 5).
- Secondly, there are strategies we can practise to help us do calculations in our head (Calculate, Key Understanding 5).

Thus, students learned to use related calculations such as: 56 – 37 is the same as 59 – 40, which is much easier.

Did You Know?

It is important to check that students actually do recognise and respond to familiar or readily observed regularities in mathematical situations. Sometimes we think they are copying a pattern, when they have not even noticed it.

For example, students might be asked to copy the pattern in a necklace of threaded shapes: ●●▲●●▲●●▲●●▲. If students copy the necklace by carefully matching each shape one at a time, they have either not noticed the pattern or are not seeing its relevance to the task. Either way, they have not copied the **pattern**. For these students, the order of shapes may as well have been random.

When students recognise the pattern, they can use it when copying the necklace, perhaps muttering 'circle, circle, triangle' over and over again. They can reproduce the sequence without looking back constantly and they notice errors and can self-correct the copy. Also, once they see the pattern, they will be able to continue it beyond the items provided to extend the necklace.

Many students will do this quite naturally, but some will not. They can be helped by the teacher modelling, through voice and actions, the rhythm of the pattern.

KEY UNDERSTANDING 2

Representing aspects of a situation with numbers can make it easier to see patterns in the situation.

Students should learn that representing aspects of a situation with numbers and then looking for patterns in the numbers can help us understand the situation better, often making patterns more obvious and predictions easier. For example, young students observing a necklace that shows repetitions of 'bead, leaf, leaf, shell, shell, shell, shell' might chant the numbers *1, 2, 4, 1, 2, 4, 1, 2, 4, 1,* ... and then say *It goes 1, 2, 4 over and over,* or *It goes one bead, two leaves, four shells over and over*. From the number pattern, students could ask and answer questions such as: *If I keep making the necklace bigger will I need more beads, more leaves or more shells? If I use 16 shells, how many leaves will I need?*

In the middle years students might be asked to build a sequence of L shapes with squares starting with the one shown below, so that the arm lengths increase by one each time.

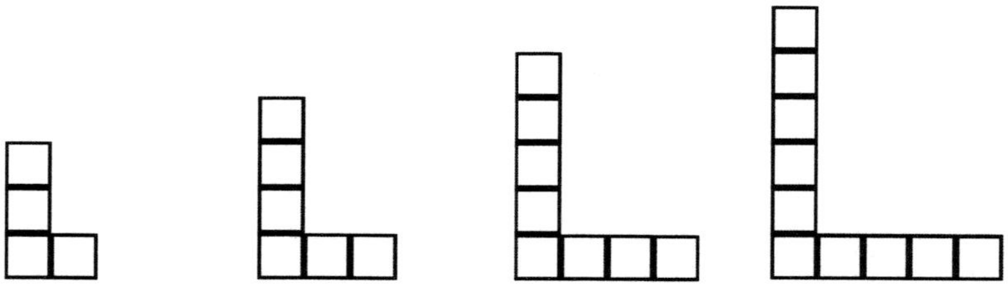

They could represent the pattern made by the number of squares needed as: 4, 6, 8, 10, ... and use this to predict how many squares they will need for the next L and the next. Using the constant addition function on their calculator, they might predict how many squares it would take to make the tenth or the 20th 'L'.

In the later years, students could generalise further and find a way to say how many for the 100th L, without having to count through the whole 100 terms. They could also work out whether you could build an L with 127 squares. This is not obvious just by looking at the Ls. All the early numbers, however, are even and each new L involves adding two, so 127 cannot work.

Students should also learn that the same number pattern can be present in many different situations. For example, the repeating pattern 1, 2, 4, 1, 2, 4, ... in the necklace above is the same as in 'one squat, two jumps and four claps' repeated over and over. This is useful because it means that the questions we have answered about the necklace have also been answered about the matching body actions.

Students who have achieved Level 1 can represent a simple repeating or counting pattern using numbers, and use the numbers to help them continue the pattern. Prompted, they will show the same repeating or counting number pattern in different forms and media. At Level 2, they can represent a variety of patterns using numbers, and will find ways to represent number sequences in materials in ways that help to expose the pattern.

Those who have achieved Level 3 build sequences of simple shapes (squares, triangles, Ls) that change systematically, and write a matching number sequence. Those who have achieved Level 4 understand that, for example, the same sequence of shapes could be represented with different number sequences, depending on which aspect of the sequence of shapes was focused on.

SAMPLE LEARNING ACTIVITIES

Beginning ✔✔

Necklaces

Ask students to thread two colours of beads on string in a repeating pattern such as 'blue, blue, red, blue, blue, red' and record as a number sequence: 2, 1, 2, 1, 2, 1, ... Later, extend to more than two parts repeating.

Isolating the Pattern

Have students isolate the repeating section of a sequence. For example: Draw boxes around two blue, one red in the previous activity. Ask: What is the shortest way to say the pattern? What is the smallest part that is repeated?

Lining Up

Extend 'Lining Up' (page 202). Have students use numbers to describe the repeating pattern in the line of students. Model the process, e.g. it was 'stand, stand, sit, sit, sit, sit, repeated over and over' so that is two stands, four sits, over and over, or 2, 4, 2, 4, 2, 4, 2, 4, 2, ... Ask students to use the same pattern to make other arrangements such as 'two twirl and four stamps' repeatedly.

Stairs

Have students make a staircase out of coloured paper, felt or magnetic squares in response to hearing stories about stairs. Ask them to record the number pattern for their staircase, e.g. 1, 2, 3, 4, 5 or 3, 6, 9.

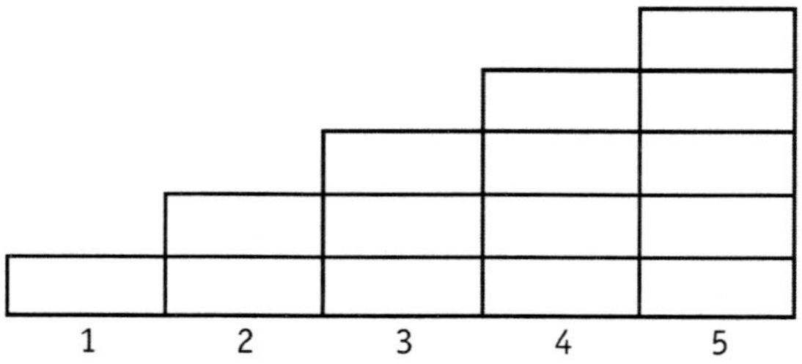

Print-making

Focus on the number pattern in students' sequences. For example, when print-making, a student may make ●●●●🍎🍎●●●●🍎🍎. They could name it as a 4, 2, 4, 2, 4, 2 pattern and look for 4, 2 ,4, 2 patterns made by others. Focus on the idea that they are the same pattern.

Matching Patterns

Play games involving matching number patterns to cards with object patterns. Make several object pattern cards for each number pattern. Ask students to find several object patterns for the same number pattern, e.g. 4, 2, 4, 2, 4, 2 would match the pattern of wheels of a car, bike, car, bike, etc. or the legs on dog, hen, dog, hen. Ask: Why can there be many sets of picture patterns for each number pattern?

Sound and Action

Invite students to create sound or action patterns for others to follow, based on a single number pattern. For example: Make instructions for a line dance using four stamps, eight claps, four kicks, eight skips. Copy and continue the pattern, then create other steps in a 4, 8, 4, 8 pattern. Students say whether each sound or action pattern follows the given number pattern.

Reference Chart

Make a chart of the number patterns generated during activities for students to refer to when using patterns to create art or dances.

How Many?

Ask students to use a number pattern to plan how many objects they will need to make a given number of repeats. Ask them to choose a number pattern from the class chart made previously, e.g. 1, 4, 2, and choose from three containers where there are twice as many shells as nuts and straws to make a pattern. Help them plan how many of each object they will need if they make three repeats.

SAMPLE LEARNING ACTIVITIES

Middle ✓✓✓

Material Patterns

Ask students to choose materials to create a sequence that 'shows' a provided number sequence such as 3, 4, 3, 3, 4, 3, 3, 4, 3, ... (e.g. □□□❀❀❀❀❍❍❍□□□❀❀❀❀❍❍❍...). Compare displays and draw out that all the displays share the same pattern. Have students then work in groups to use the pattern in other 'creative' ways, e.g. body actions and poses, music, dance steps, people.

Pasta Patterns

Have students plan a pattern using three types of pasta, e.g. three spiral, two bow and one shell. After constructing the pattern, ask students to identify and group similar patterns and write the number sequence for each group. Ask: Does a 1, 4, 1 pattern look different from a 1, 1, 4 pattern? Why or why not?

Tricycles

Pose the following scenario: You need to help a tricycle manufacturer work out how many parts are needed for different-sized orders. Begin with wheels. How many wheels will be needed for an order of one tricycle, two tricycles, three tricycles? How many wheels will be needed for nine tricycles? Ask students to write a number pattern to help find the answer. Extend this to produce a table showing the number of parts for different numbers of tricycles.

Number of tricycles:	1	2	3	4
Number of wheels:	3	6	9	12
Number of seats	1	2	3	4
Number of hand grips:	2	4	6	8
Number of tyres:	3	6	9	12

Draw out that the same number pattern may apply to different parts so, for example, if you know how many wheels you also know how many tyres. (Link to Key Understanding 5 and to Understand Operations, Key Understandings 3, 4 and 5.)

Letter Grid

Have students write their name, with one letter per square, into a grid. They can choose the size of the grid, between 4 x 4 and 8 x 8. At the end of each line the letters are continued onto the next line until the whole grid is filled. Ask students to find others with the same pattern and try to decide why their patterns are the same. Is it the number of letters or the number of letters and the number of squares in the grid that is the same?

They then write a number pattern to explain their pattern. For example: For the name Kaye in a 5 x 5 grid, the pattern would be 4, 1; 3, 2; 2, 3; 1, 4. (Link to Calculate, Key Understanding 2.)

K	A	Y	E	K
A	Y	E	K	A
Y	E	K	A	Y
E	K	A	Y	E
K	A	Y	E	K

Triangular Numbers

Investigate different arrangements for the sequence of triangular numbers: 1, 3, 6, 10. For example: How many line segments are needed to join 2 dots, 3 dots, 4 dots, 5 dots ...? How many blocks are needed to make a staircase 1 block high, 2 blocks high, 3 blocks high ...? How many triangles can be found in a triangle with a fold from 1 of its vertices, 2 folds, 3 folds ...? Ask: How are all of these patterns the same? Why do you think this sequence is called triangular numbers?

What's Next?

Have pairs of students make a model of the sequence 1, 2, 3, 5, 8, ... e.g. with popsticks, and then say what the next three numbers might be. Ask students to use their model to explain to others how they decided what the numbers should be. Ask: How did you know to put 13 popsticks next?

Area Problems

When studying area, have students find the possible dimensions for a rectangular paddock of 24 squares. Order the results to confirm that all possibilities have been discovered. Ask: Is there a pattern in the numbers for length and width? (Link to Calculate, Key Understanding 3.) What is the longest and shortest perimeter possible for this shape? Have students use the number pattern to help find the longest and shortest perimeters of other sized paddocks, without having to make the model.

Puppies

Have students look for adding and subtracting patterns to make predictions about situations. For example: Johnny and Su Lin were trying to figure out how much each of their puppies would weigh at ten months.

Johnny's Jack Russell								
Month	3	4	5	6	7	8	9	10
Weight	14	20	25	29				

Su Lin's Great Dane									
Month	2	3	4	5	6	7	8	9	10
Weight	10	18	26	32	38	42			

Ask students to work it out using the tables. Ask: How did you decide how heavy each dog would be? How did the weights change for each dog? (See Key Understanding 4.)

SAMPLE LEARNING ACTIVITIES

Later ✓✓✓

Picture Frames

Have students build a sequence of squares with a white border and black central tiles, and represent different variables in numbers.

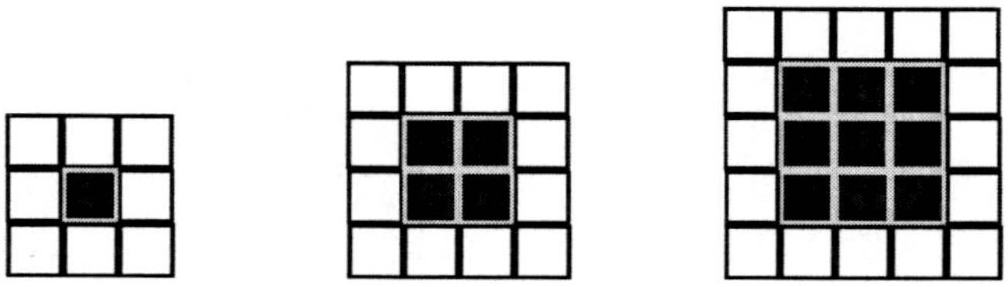

Position in the sequence:	1	2	3	4
Length of the black square:	1	2	3	4
Number of black squares used:	1	4	9	16
Perimeter of black squares:	4	8	12	16
Number of border squares:	8	12	16	20
Perimeter of border:	12	16	20	24

Draw out that different aspects of the situation can be represented with numbers depending upon the question to be answered. Different aspects (variables) have different patterns.

River Crossing

See Sample Lesson 2 (page 221). Have students act out, draw diagrams or use other methods to solve the problem when there are eight adults and two students. Ask: How can you represent that situation with numbers? Why is this helpful?

Triangle Toothpick Design

Extend the 'Picture Frames' activity above. Have students copy this design with toothpicks:

Ask them to write number sequences that would be needed to answer the following questions: How many triangles in each shape? What is the number of toothpicks needed to make each shape? How many diagonals in each shape? What question could have been asked to get a number pattern like 1, 1, 2, 2, 3, 3, ... from the design?

Folding Paper

Have students represent situations that grow rapidly. For example: Record the number of regions created by successive folds of a sheet of paper. Record how the number of regions grows, e.g. after one fold there are two regions, after two folds there are four regions. Fold to see how many regions for four folds. Predict how many regions there will be for five and six folds.

Rumour Mill

Invite students to investigate different situations that can be represented with the same number sequence. After the previous paper folding activity, present this scenario: A rumour started at school with one student telling two others that there was to be a pupil-free day on 10 June. The two students were told that next day they must each repeat the rumour to two more students. Each of these new students was to repeat the rumour the next day, to two more students. If the rumour started on 1 June, how many students would have heard it by 10 June? How do you know? How is this problem similar to the paper-folding problem? Draw out that representing the situations with numbers enables them to see that the same pattern exists for both.

Painted Cubes

Have students solve problems by representing them with a number sequence.

- The letters A to M are being painted on wooden cubes. A is painted on one cube, B is painted on two cubes, C is painted on three cubes and so on. How many blocks are painted altogether?
- Investigate the number of handshakes there would be in a group of people. How many for two people? How many for three people? And so on.
- Investigate joining dots on a circle. How many lines for two dots, three dots, four dots and so on?
- The T-ball committee is planning to have each of the six teams play each other once. How many games is that? What about for any number of teams?

Ask: What do you notice about the number sequences for the different situations? What is the pattern? Draw out that different situations can be represented by the same pattern.

Fibonacci

Ask students to follow rules to produce the Fibonacci sequence. Use 1 cm squared paper. Draw a 1 cm square near the centre of the page. Draw another square above that. See the two squares as a rectangle and draw a square onto the right of this rectangle. Draw a new square onto the long side of the rectangle. Keep drawing new squares onto the longest side of the rectangle.

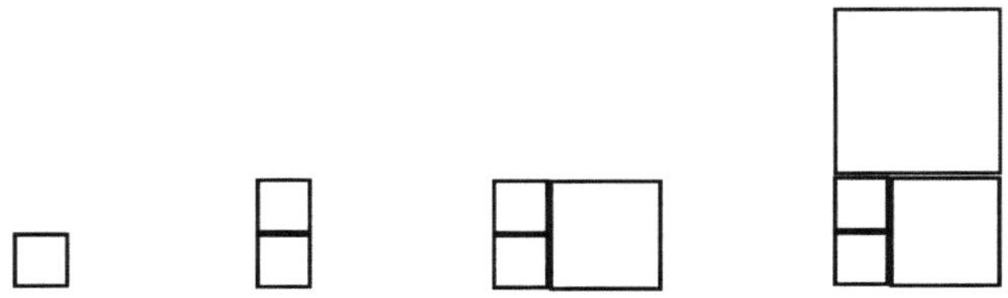

Ask students to record the length of the sides of each new square as a number sequence. Ask: Can you see a pattern? Use the pattern to predict the lengths of the squares beyond those that you have already drawn. (The sequence will be 1, 1, 2, 3, 5, 8, ... which is the Fibonacci sequence.)

Recreate the Rectangle

Have students recreate a similar sequence to the previous activity from the different available sizes of the A4 series of paper. Start by folding and cutting a half piece of A4 paper into two postcard pieces (size 105 mm x 148 mm). Use the same building-up process as in the previous activity.

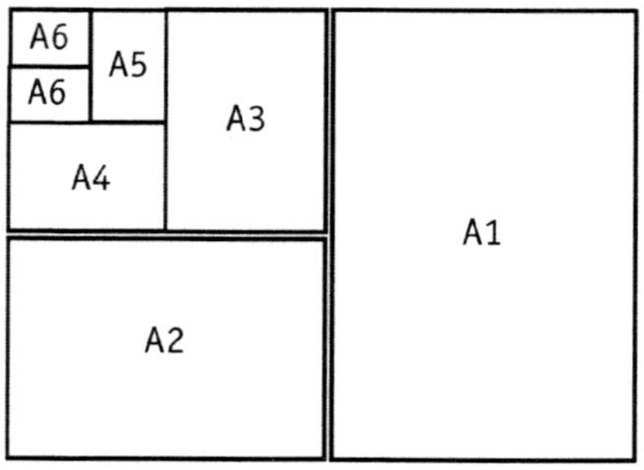

That is, place two postcard sizes (A6) one above the other. Place the half A4 (A5) size next to that. Place the A4 underneath those. Use the pattern of moves to sketch in the position and the approximate size of the A2 and finally the A1 sheet. Have students record the dimensions of the sizes A6 through to A3. Ask: Can you see a pattern? Ask students to predict the dimensions of the A2 and the A1 sheet of paper. Ask: Is there any paper in your artroom that matches the A1 size?

Money Patterns

Encourage students to look for common number sequences in the problems they solve. For example: You have $1 and $2 stamps that you stick in a line onto parcels to make up certain prices. Draw diagrams to show the different arrangements of stamps to make up totals of $1, $2, $3, $4 and so on. (Reflections are included.) Draw and record the number of arrangements for each price. For example: There is only one way to make $1. That is a $1 stamp. For $2 you can have two arrangements: two $1 stamps or a $2 stamp. For $3 there are three possible arrangements: three $1; a $2 and a $1; or a $1 and a $2. For $4 you could have:

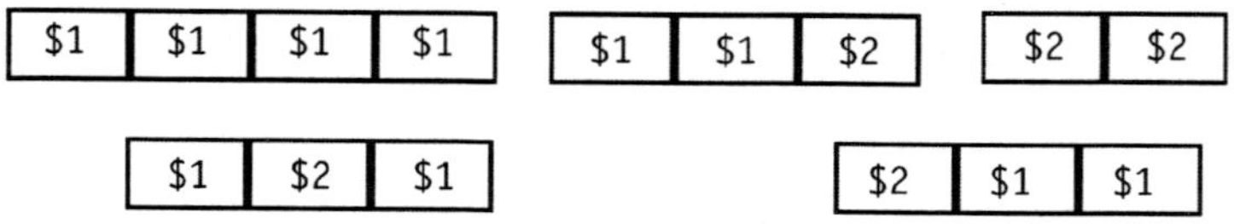

Ask: What kind of number sequence is this? Look out for other problems that have this sequence.

SAMPLE LESSON 2

Sample Learning Activity: Later—'River Crossing', page 218

Key Understanding 2: Representing aspects of a situation with numbers can make it easier to see patterns in the situation.

Working Towards: Levels 4 and 5

Background to the Task

I had presented my class of eleven- and twelve-year-olds the problem at the right to solve. Some groaned when they saw the problem, commenting that it was 'old hat'. Many started to move popsticks and counters across an imaginary river and others drew diagrams to represent the trips and crossings.

A group of eight adults and two children want to cross a river. Their boat can hold just one adult or up to two children, but not an adult and a child together. Everyone can row the boat. What is the minimum number of one-way trips needed for all to cross the river?

There was some discussion about how to minimise the number of trips. Christian said: *You have to send two children to start with, because if you only send one child or one adult they just have to come back to get another child, so it's a waste of a trip.* Eventually they all agreed that the minimum number of trips suggested by the majority of students (i.e. 33 trips) was correct.

CHALLENGE to Current Way of Thinking

Most thought their task was complete and were surprised when I asked: *What if there were different numbers of adults? What is the minimum number of trips for six adults and two children to cross, or 15 adults and two children, or 100 adults and two children?*

Initially many worked through the additional problems in the same way they had worked out the first problem. However, several began to anticipate the tediousness of working through the 100-adult example, and groaned in an exaggerated way.

I used this as the excuse I needed to suggest if they looked for some kind of pattern in the river crossings, they might find an easier way to solve the problem for 100 adults. We had spent a fair bit of class time on 'being systematic' when looking for patterns or winning strategies for games, so the students had some previous experience in recording the steps in a problem solution. They began to focus on recording their actions, rather than just the results of the actions. Many drew pictures or diagrams; others used a tally.

Tara and Michelle demonstrated a pattern they'd found with counters. *First you send two children over, next you bring one child back, then you send an adult over, and the other child brings the boat back. It doesn't matter how many adults you have, you just need two children.* Andreas said: *Look, I can do it over and over the same way—two children cross, one child back; one adult cross, second child back; two children cross, one child back and so on.* He drew a line under the second child back to show where the pattern started again. Sarah commented: *Every four trips were the same—you just do it over and over and they all get across.*

Number of Adults	Number of Trips Needed
6	25
8	33
12	49
15	61

Eventually, most students could see and explain the repetitive pattern in the minimum strategy for getting across the river. However, few were able to use this to work out the minimum number of trips. At best they could say things like, *It helps because you know it's the same pattern over and over no matter how many adults there are,* or *You just have to keep track so you know when to stop repeating it.* Sarah's comment came closest, but even she was unable to see how to use her generalisation to say how many trips it would take to move 100 adults.

Number of Adults	Number of Trips Needed
1	5
2	9
3	13
4	17
5	21
6	25
8	33
10	41
12	49
15	61

I wasn't surprised by this—even seeing how the crossings should be made doesn't make a general rule 'pop out'. This is a good example of a problem where the number pattern is easier to deal with than the actual situation, which was why I had chosen it.

So I decided to intervene, saying briskly: *Why don't we get systematic and put the information we have in a table?* I quickly drew a table on the board and put in the data we had, commenting that it often helps to organise the information in order. Some students had tried different numbers than those I suggested and we put those in. I then suggested that we try to fill in some gaps. *Where will we begin? With the easy numbers or the hard ones?* We then assigned the numbers below six with several students doing each number (as a check) and filled in the information.

Immediately the pattern jumped out at them. *Every extra adult takes four more trips,* said one. *That's what I said before,* said Sarah.

I asked: *How many for one adult?* They all said: *Five.*

How many for ten adults? I asked. A couple of students started to blurt out, 50, but stopped almost immediately, laughing sheepishly. *Yes, how do we know it can't be 50?* I asked. After a pause, looking at the table on the blackboard, Tao told us that it would be between 33 and 49: *It would be more than for eight adults and less than for 12 adults.* After another short pause, several students volunteered that it would be 41. One said it would be two more fours after eight adults.

So how many for 100 adults? I asked. Pause. *Don't all shout it out at once,* I said laughingly, *talk it over with your partner and when you agree, write it down*. Within a few minutes, most of the students had decided it was 401. A couple initially said 410, but were dissuaded by others. A few began by counting forward on their calculator in fours. Most either began by jumping 40 for each additional ten adults, or followed the lead of those who had. However, there were a small number who gave an answer almost immediately, having multiplied 100 by four and added one.

At this stage, I decided to draw out the key understanding that representing a situation with numbers can make it easier to see the patterns. I pointed out that they had all done an excellent job of working out the minimum strategy and could see the pattern in the trips themselves, and some had even noted that four was significant. However, turning it into an easy rule to decide how many trips for any number of adults proved quite hard. Letting them struggle with the diagrams for a while was part of my strategy for emphasising how the pattern of the numbers helped. *In this case,* I said, *you knew how to do the trips in the minimum way and so had a strategy for doing it for 100 adults, but it was only when you looked for a pattern in the numbers that you were able to quickly say how many trips it would take.*

KEY UNDERSTANDING 3

To describe a number pattern means to provide a precise rule that produces the pattern.

Within a mathematical context, to describe a number pattern means to provide an unambiguous rule or relationship that produces it. Students should be able to follow rules provided by others, create rules for themselves and produce rules that fit the information provided. There is advice on this in the Background Notes (page 258). There are some conventional mathematical types of rules that students should begin to use in the primary years. For example:

- Sequences of numbers can be described by giving a rule that says where to start and how to get from any number in the sequence to the next one. For example: Start with seven. Each number after that is five more than the one before (7, 12, 17, 22, ...).
- Sequences of numbers can also be described by giving a general rule that says how to work out any number in the sequence by knowing what its position in the sequence is. For example: Each number in the sequence is two added to five times its position (7, 12, 17, 22, ...).
- Other patterns can be described by rules that say what the general relationship is between two quantities. For example: The area of a square is the square of the length of its side.

From the beginning years, students should be encouraged to use their everyday language to talk about the patterns they have observed, created or produced according to rules provided by others. During the middle years they should learn to clarify and refine their descriptions, using as the criteria that another person should be able to recreate the sequence or arrangement from the pattern description alone. Thus, describing 6, 12, 24, ... as a 'doubling pattern' isn't enough, but saying 'start with six and then keep doubling' is. During the later primary years, students should also get better at writing rules for patterns. Trying to follow the rules of others will help them to identify what is needed in a rule.

Some ideas about describing patterns are provided in the Background Notes (page 258).

Students should come to understand that sometimes there is enough information to make it possible to work out for sure what the pattern must be, even if we personally find it difficult or even impossible to work out. At other times, there is not enough information to be sure what the pattern must be (e.g. we might only know the first three terms of a sequence such as 1, 2, 4, ...). However, there may be enough information to work out what the pattern could be or is likely to be (see Background Notes, page 258).

Students who have achieved the outcome at Level 1 use language such as 'over and over', 'repeat' and 'again' to describe patterns and to say what is the same about two versions of the same pattern. At Level 2, they follow and describe rules to generate straightforward adding and subtracting patterns such as in sequences, addition tables and 100 charts, but may not recognise ambiguity in their descriptions or attempt to test their own rules. Those who have achieved Level 3 produce number sequences by following rules based on addition and subtraction such as 'begin with 1, 2 and then each number is worked out by adding the previous two numbers'. They can recognise ambiguities in rules given to them by others and, with prompting, attempt to test their own rules to remove ambiguities. Thus, they understand why they need both the starting number and constant multiplier in order to generate the sequence 4, 12, 36, ...

At Level 4, they describe sequences within their repertoire sufficiently well to enable a peer to reproduce them, although their descriptions will generally be in natural language and involve describing the relationship between one term and the next. However, those at Level 5 are able to describe the relationship between a term and its position in the sequence directly, write simple general rules that describe the relationship between two quantities, and rewrite rules expressed in natural language in shortened form to make them easier to follow.

SAMPLE LEARNING ACTIVITIES

Beginning ✓

Number Scrolls

Extend 'Number Scrolls' (see Understanding Whole and Decimal Numbers, Key Understanding 4, and Calculate, Key Understanding 8). Have students use a rule to create and write a number pattern, then leave out part of the sequence and have a partner find the rule to fill in the missing part.

Variation on Number Scrolls

Have students give their partner the missing section of their number scroll for them to work out a rule and generate a sequence of numbers backwards to see if it matches. If it doesn't, both students explain their rule to each other.

What's My Rule?

Ask students to predict missing parts of a sequence by first working out the pattern, then saying what the missing part must be. For example: One student makes a pattern of four repeating units using Pattern Blocks behind a barrier and covers two of the units. They ask their partner to look at what is not covered and make the hidden part. Extend the activity by using different objects for the same number pattern.

What's Next?

Extend the previous activity by having students predict what the next object will be in their partner's sequence. Ask: Why would that be the right piece? What will the tenth piece be in the sequence? What about the 20th?

Recording

Use activities from Key Understanding 2, such as 'Necklaces', 'Lining Up' and 'Stairs' (page 214), for students to record all of the numbers in the sequence and to say what the rule is that generated the pattern. For example: *It's two one, repeated over and over.*

Story Patterns

Have students count objects illustrated in stories to see if there is a pattern, and predict how many will be on the next page. For example:

- *Ten in the Bed* (Dale, 1988). During the reading, ask: How many things do you think will be left in the bed next? Why do you think that?
- *The Hungry Caterpillar* (Carle, 2000). Ask: How many things will he eat the next day? Why do you think that? (Link to Understanding Whole and Decimal Numbers, Key Understanding 2.)

How Many?

Have students use a number pattern to plan how many objects they will need. Ask them to choose a number pattern from the class chart made previously (see page 215), say 1, 4, 2, and choose from three containers where there are twice as many shells as nuts and straws to make a pattern. Help them plan how many of each of the objects they will need if they make three repeats.

Function Box (1)

Invite students to work out a rule that is used to change one number of things into another number of things. For example: A student sits inside a box with a collection of pencils and a rule such as 'add two'. Another student feeds in three pencils through a slot. The student inside adds two, wobbles the box and feeds out five pencils. Others look at the change to the number and say what the function of the box is.

Function Box (2)

Repeat the previous activity using a note with a number on it, e.g. five. The student inside the box crosses out the five and replaces it with seven, and feeds the note out. Repeat with different numbers for others to say what the rule is. Include doubling, halving and subtraction.

SAMPLE LEARNING ACTIVITIES

Middle ✔✔

Objects

Have students create a pattern along a length of card, using their choice of materials. Ask them to record the pattern by writing the number of objects for each part of the pattern below the materials. They remove the objects and give the card to a partner to recreate the pattern using different objects. Ask: How is the second pattern similar or different from the original? How can you ensure that your partner recreates exactly the same pattern? Have students write a rule in words to describe their original pattern and pass this to their partner. Ask: Does this help to create the same pattern? Why?

Bicycles and Pedal Cars

Following the 'Tricycles' activity (page 216), have students generate similar number sequences for bicycles and pedal cars. They then write a rule to help a new factory worker decide how many of each part will be needed for any number of bicycles/pedal cars. For example: For 64 pedal cars you would need to times the number of cars by four to find the number of wheels and tyres.

Calculator Patterns 1

Have students create a number pattern on a calculator, then write a rule for the pattern. For example: Enter 1 2 + 3 then press = = = to create 12, 15, 18, 21, ... They pass their written rule to another student to read and create the number sequence described. Ask: How are the sequences the same or different? What part of the description needs to be changed to make sure everyone writes the same sequence?

Calculator Patterns 2

Extend the previous activity by asking students to predict whether a given number will appear in their sequence when they use the constant function. For example: 1 4 + 8 = = = ... 22, 30, 38, 46, 54, 62, 70 ... Ask: Will 113 be in the sequence? How do you know?

Function Box

Extend the 'Function Box' activity (page 227). Have students create a collection of rules for a student in the function box to apply to the numbers pushed through the slot. The students who wrote the rule say whether the answer is the one they expected. Ask: If not, why not? Suggest to the students that they refine and rewrite the rule so that it always gives the expected answer.

Same Answer

Have students place the rules created for the previous activity into groups that give the same answer. Ask: Why is it that 'add four take two' gives the same result as 'take three add five'?

What's My Rule?

Ask one student to think of a rule for others to guess, e.g. 'add four' or 'times two'. Have students give a number and the leader uses the rule to give the answer. After five turns of calling out a number to the leader, students decide what rule is used. Compare the suggested rules with the original. Ask: How are they the same/different? (Link to Calculate, Key Understanding 5.)

What Comes Next?

Have students write the next three numbers in sequences and write their rule for each. For example:

- 2, 9, 16, 23, ..., ..., ...
- 16, 15, 13, 10, ..., ..., ...
- 1, 2, 4, 7, 11, ..., ..., ...
- 3, 3, 6, 18, ..., ..., ...

List the different number sequences the students make for each example. Ask: What rule did you use to write the numbers? Why is it possible to think of different rules for each sequence?

Roman Numerals

Have students write numbers 1–20 using Roman numerals and decide on the patterns and rules used as its basis. Ask them to test the rules by writing bigger numbers, e.g. 328, 1054, 1998, 50 348. Ask: Does your rule work for these? If not, how can it be modified so that it does? Have students investigate the patterns and rules in other number systems and compare to our Hindu-Arabic system. (Link to Understanding Whole and Decimal Numbers, Key Understanding 5.)

Seven

Ask students to investigate how many times the number seven is used in a book with 87 pages. Ask: How many fives in the same book? How do you know? Have students write a rule to find the number of pages for a book of any size, then test the rule.

Homework Patterns

Have students use different rules to describe and extend a number sequence. Present this scenario: Sam and Mahalia were doing their homework. They had to look at the pattern and fill in the box. The pattern was 50, 62, 74, ☐, 98. They both put 86 into the box. The next instruction was to continue the sequence from 98. Mahalia wrote 110, 122, 134. Sam wrote 1010, 1112, 1214. Ask: What rule do you think Sam used? What rule do you think Mahalia used? Who do you think was correct? Why?

SAMPLE LEARNING ACTIVITIES

Later ✓✓✓

Triangle Toothpick Design

(See page 218.) Have students find a rule to describe a pattern. Ask them to make the first four shapes of this design.

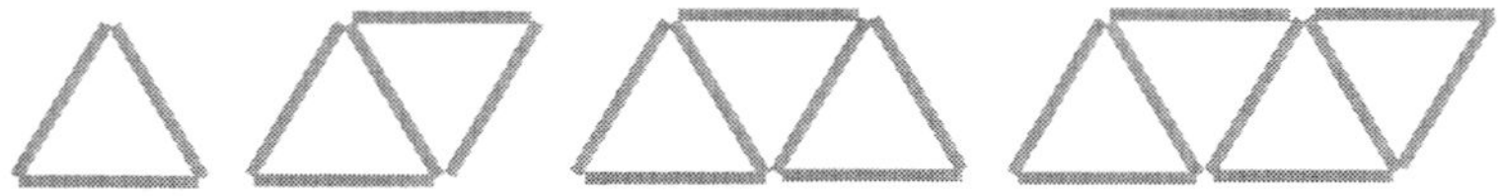

Write a rule to say how the number of toothpicks changes with each new shape. Ask students to write a rule in their own words, which connects the position number of the shape to the number of toothpicks. Have students exchange rules with their partner and use their rule to find the number of toothpicks in the next few shapes. Ask: Did the rule work? Use the toothpick pattern to explain why their rule works. Ask: Would your partner be able to predict the number of toothpicks for any shape position using your rule? Why?

Different Rule, Same Pattern

Extend the previous activity so students see that apparently different rules can produce the same pattern. Present this scenario: When Lee and Allison swapped rules for their triangle toothpick designs, they discovered that their rules sounded different. Lee said: *You can say it's three, add the number of the shape less one, times by two.* Allison said: *You times the number of the shape by two and then add one.* Ask: Has someone made an error or do both rules work for this pattern? Have students use their toothpicks or diagrams to explain their reasoning.

Hexagon Patterns

Extend the previous idea to another design. Present this scenario: Students were making a hexagon toothpick pattern.

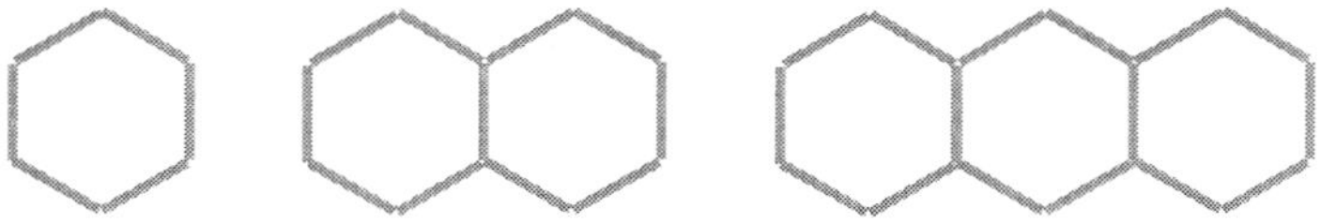

Jeremy and Sophie swapped rules and discovered that their rules sounded different. Jeremy said that the number of toothpicks was equal to five times the position number of the shape, add one, and he wrote it as $5 \times n + 1$. Sophie said that the number of toothpicks was six times the number of the shape, take away the number of the shape less one. She wrote it as $6 \times n - (n - 1)$. Ask: Do both rules work for this pattern? Use the toothpicks or diagrams to show why each rule works. Find some other rules that work.

River Crossing and Beyond

Have students find rules to describe various number patterns. See Sample Lesson 3, page 232.

Sum Patterns (1)

Invite students to find rules to make calculating easier. Ask them to examine these number sentences: 1 + 2 + 3 = 6, 2 + 3 + 4 = 9, 3 + 4 + 5 = 12, 4 + 5 + 6 = 15 and say what patterns they find. Ask: What are the next three number sentences? Repeat the activity with these number sentences: 1 + 2 + 3 + 4 + 5 = 15, 2 + 3 + 4 + 5 + 6 = 20, 3 + 4 + 5 + 6 + 7 = 25, 4 + 5 + 6 + 7 + 8 = 30. Ask students to write more for a partner to find the answer without adding the numbers.

Sum Patterns (2)

Extend the previous activity with this scenario: Gemma came up with the rule that you can times the middle number by three to get the answer. Tom said that with four consecutive numbers you times the second number by four to get the answer. Ask: Do these rules work? How do you know? Find rules that do work for adding four or five consecutive numbers.

Everyday Formulas

Have students recognise formulas used in everyday life, e.g. in money conversions. Present this scenario: Alisha sat in a cafe in Bali. The prices were in Australian dollars and Indonesian rupiah. The stir-fry cost $A4.00 or 20 000 rupiahs; soft drink was $A1.20 or 6000 rupiah; tea was $A1.30 or 6500 rupiahs. Have students organise this information to help Alisha work out an exchange rate for Australian dollars to Indonesian rupiahs. (Link to Understand Operations, Key Understandings 3 and 4.)

Magic Calculating Machine

Ask students to describe relationships between two quantities. For example: Display a diagram of a magic calculating machine. Tell students the machine will apply a certain rule to any input number to create the output number, e.g. when seven is put in, 3.5 comes out; when 4.5 goes in, 2.25 comes out; three in, 1.5 out; ten in, five out. Ask: What rule is used to calculate the output numbers? How can you be sure?

Graphs

Have students find and compare rules that connect points on a graph. For example: Plot these points on a graph—(14, 16), (0, 2), (5, 7) and (12, 14). Ask: How are the pairs of numbers linked? What could the rule be? Ask students to use their rule to plot the other numbers up to ten (horizontal axis). Ask: How do you know your rule works? Now graph this rule: Double the number on the horizontal axis, add four and divide by two. What do you notice when you compare the two graphs? How can the graph have two different rules?

SAMPLE LESSON 3

Sample Learning Activity: Later—'River Crossing and Beyond', page 231

Key Understanding 3: To describe a number pattern means to provide a precise rule that produces the pattern.

Working Towards: Levels 4 and 5

Build On Existing Knowledge

This lesson was an extension of the 'River Crossing' activity described on page 221. In particular, I wanted the students to develop their capacity to express rules in general terms that can be applied to any suitable number.

Almost all the students had decided upon 401 trips for 100 adults. I decided to return to the couple who seemed a little unsure later and to press on. I did so by offering another challenge. *I know I started out by saying I only wanted to know how many trips were needed for 100 adults, but now I am going to really challenge you. How many for 1000 adults and the same two children?*

Almost immediately their hands went up. The general consensus was 4001, which I entered in the table. I then asked Andrew if he could explain how he did it. *It was four lots of 1000 and one more,* he said confidently. *How did others do it?* I asked. Several students offered their approaches, which were essentially the same. *So what if there were 25 adults?* I said? *104!* they said.

At this point I asked students to work with a partner to write an instruction that would help someone who hadn't been through it with us to work it out for any number of adults. I then asked volunteers to record their rules on the board. Most were variations of the following:

- how many adults times by four and add one
- times four by the number of adults add one.

I then asked students to test each rule on 25, 100 and 1000. Realising that they would probably apply the rule meant rather than what had actually been written, I also 'tested' them, and for the second rule above wrote:

25 adults —> 104   100 adults —> 404   1000 adults —> 4004

We then compared the expressions and agreed that although some looked different they were all mathematically the same because they all produced the same pattern of trips. Some had forgotten about the extra trip needed at the end for the two students to complete the crossing but quickly realised where the one in the rule came from when peers pointed it out.

The students immediately pointed out that I was wrong. *But that is what the rule says,* I said, *four times by* (pause) *the number of adults plus one, so that's four times* (pause) *25 add one, which is four times 26, which is 104*. The students hastened to explain that I had to multiply first and then add one. *But it doesn't say that,* I complained. *How can we make it clear?* After a few moments, we had an alternative:

- times four by the number of adults and then add one.

I suggested that students revise their rule if they needed to and give it to another pair of students to test. *Make sure you are testing what people really wrote,* I said, *and not what you think they meant to write*. After students were happy that their rules were clear and fitted all the number pairs in the table, we refined any rules on the board that needed it.

I then asked if they could shorten their rules, prompting them by writing:

- The number of trips needed =

Students then produced a series of more simplified rules

- The number of trips needed = how many adults x 4 + 1
- The number of trips needed = (4 x the adults) + 1
- The number of trips needed = the number of adults x 4 + 1
- The number of trips needed = 4 x number + 1.

Although I knew that we would later want students to be able to reduce this further to the algebraic expression 4 x n + 1 or 4n + 1, I did not pursue it. Instead, I focused on the need to be sure that our rules fitted all the data we had and said it clearly. We then compared the rules and decided that they all said the same thing.

Linking Back

At this point, I felt that the key points about checking that rules fitted the data had come out. I then asked students to see if they could explain to each other why their rule worked. Again I prompted them to look back to their original problem.

I was happy to find that most students realised that the multiplication by four in their rules related to the 'counting by fours' pattern they'd found when they added on the number of trips taken as each adult crossed the river. I asked them to write in words what they'd found and obtained a range of expressions that we decided all matched the 'four times' number pattern.

Allow students to express their 'rules' in personal ways and try not to lead them to one 'correct' rule. They need to see that what is the same about the different general number sentences they devised is that they all produce identical number patterns, and are therefore mathematically equivalent.

Number of Adults	Number of Trips Needed
1	5
2	9
3	13
4	17
5	21
6	25
8	33
10	41
12	49
15	61
25	101
100	401
1000	4001

KEY UNDERSTANDING 4

There are strategies that help us become better at recognising common types of patterns.

This Key Understanding should develop in conjunction with Key Understandings 2 and 3. Students should come to see that pattern recognition is not simply a matter of 'look and see' or luck or ability. They should realise that they will become better at identifying patterns by the use of good pattern-finding strategies, including by recognising common types of patterns. Advice on this is provided in the Background Notes on pages 261 to 265.

Students should investigate a range of pattern types, but simply providing variety without structure is unlikely to be helpful. They are more likely to recognise pattern types with which they have had systematic experience and where their attention is focused upon:

- *The similarities between certain patterns*: students should look for what is the same and what is different between various patterns, leading to simple classifications of patterns.
- *The strategies that they found helpful in identifying patterns*: it can be difficult to recognise a pattern immediately, 'just by looking'; having some 'search strategies' is essential.

The repertoire of numbers and operations involved in pattern-searching activities should expand over the primary years, as should the complexity of the patterns. Students who have achieved Level 1 of the outcome can recognise counting patterns and repeating patterns based on whole numbers. The repertoire of those at Level 2 has expanded to include sequences involving addition and subtraction of a whole number and patterns in addition tables and a 100 chart. At Level 3, they use strategies to identify patterns involving each of the operations on whole numbers, and can describe how terms in a sequence are linked by multiplication or a more complex addition/subtraction-based rule. Those at Level 4 apply their pattern-finding strategies to sequences involving any one of the four operations on whole numbers, decimals and fractions and to relating pairs of numbers in simple 'guess my rule'-type games. At Level 5, they can also identify patterns in sequences or sets of number pairs that are based on more than one operation.

SAMPLE LEARNING ACTIVITIES

Beginning ✔

Stairs

When making a 1, 2, 3, 4, 5, 6 pattern, e.g. building a staircase (see Key Understanding 2), have students say what the change in the numbers is each time a new step is added. Ask: How many squares will be in the next step? Why do you think that? Check to see.

Identifying Patterns

Have students identify and record number patterns, e.g. dots arranged in growing patterns on the overhead projector

●	●●	●●●	●●●●	●●●●●
1	2	3	4	5

Ask: What is the difference between one and two, two and three? What is happening each time? Could the next number be seven? Why? Ask: How is this pattern the same as the 'stair' pattern?

Search Strategy

Encourage students to develop a search strategy that focuses on the difference between the first and second terms, second and third terms, and so on. For example: In the 1, 2, 3, 4, 5, 6 pattern, help students to see the constant difference is 'add one'.

Find the Rule

Use the above strategy to find the rule for a given sequence of numbers, e.g. a previously generated number scroll: 2, 4, 6, 8, 10, 12. Have students find the numbers on a number line and work out the difference between each of the numbers, then test out their conjecture using the constant function on the calculator to generate the sequence.

Practising Strategies

Have students practise using pattern-searching strategies, and make a chart for each strategy. Ask students to record the number sequences they were able to work out using that strategy. For example: By comparing adjoining numbers in the sequence 2, 4, 6, 8, students see that a pattern is generated by repeatedly adding two. They may name the strategy as 'Write What Changes From One Number to the Next'.

Beginning ✔

Make a Pattern

Use a beginning unit to generate a pattern, e.g. one shell, two leaves, one shell. Students may come up with different rules. They may see the unit as 1, 2 and repeat that, or they may repeat the 1, 2, 1 unit. Others may add one to each new unit: 1, 2, 1, 2, 3, 2, 3, 4, 3. Use this beginning unit several times for students to focus on using different rules to make different patterns.

Monkey Matters

Use story contexts for students to link pairs of numbers in an organised way. For example: Read *Five Little Monkeys* (Hanzl and Gardner, 1998). Have five monkey templates for students to move. Begin with one monkey in a small tree and four in a large one. Write a number sentence. Ask: If there are two monkeys in the small tree, how many in the large one? Continue rearranging the two groups. Draw attention to the numbers going up one side and down the other. Focus students on working out the rule. Ask: What is happening each time? Look at the change between 1 + 4 and 2 + 3. Have students say what happens in each. (Link to Understanding Whole and Decimal Numbers, Key Understanding 2; Understand Operations, Key Understanding 2; and Calculate, Key Understanding 2.)

Fairytale Steps

Have students use a rule to generate different number patterns. For example: Draw a stepping stone number line for students to say what their rule is and then move storybook characters along—the giant uses an 'add five' pattern, Jack uses 'add two'. Ask students to record the number sequence made by each rule.

SAMPLE LEARNING ACTIVITIES

Middle ✓✓✓

Farmyard

Ask students to use ten blocks to create a yard for some plastic horses, cows or chickens. Ask: How many blocks will be needed for a yard one layer high, two layers high, three layers high? Have students create a number sequence to describe the sequence of layers. Change the fence so that it has 12 blocks for the first layer and then write a number sequence to show how many blocks are needed for two layers, three layers, etc. Ask: How is this number sequence the same as the last sequence? How is it different? (Link to Key Understanding 2.)

Constant Function

Have students use the constant function on the calculator to generate other doubling patterns, e.g. 3, 6, 12, 24, ... Ask them to compare their patterns with others and say how they used the calculator to generate the sequence. Ask: How does the size of the numbers help you to know if a sequence you are given is a doubling pattern? What is the difference between the consecutive numbers in the sequence?

Halving

Invite students to investigate halving sequences using paper tape. Ask them to choose a length of paper between 30 and 40 cm. They fold the strip, measure and record the length of half, fold it in half and record, fold again and record. Have students compare sequences. Ask: What is happening to the numbers in each? How could you generate the same sequence using a calculator? What is the difference between the consecutive numbers in the sequence? How is this different from a subtraction sequence?

Three

Have students choose their own starting number and generate a sequence using the constant function on the calculator to + 3 each time. Start with the same number and generate another sequence using – 3, then another using x 3 and another for ÷ 3. Ask: What is the difference in the sequences? Which one increases quickly? Which increases slowly? Which decreases? Why? Does this happen for all +, –, x and ÷ sequences? Try starting with 24 and using x 0.5 to generate a sequence. Ask: Why did this sequence get smaller?

Create a Sequence

Following the previous activity, have students start with the same number (e.g. 12), choose one sign and use this with a set number (e.g. 4) to generate their own sequence. Ask them to give their partner the sequence and see if they can say which sign was used and how they know.

Middle ✓✓✓

Doubling

Have students investigate a doubling pattern by folding a rectangular sheet of paper. For one fold you get 2 rectangles, two folds give 4 rectangles, three folds give 8 rectangles. Have students tabulate the results. Ask: What happens to the number of rectangles as the number of folds increases? From this, predict the number of rectangles for five, six and seven folds. Ask: Is there a limit to the number of folds that can be made? (Link to Understand Operations, Key Understanding 3.)

Triangular Numbers

Ask students to investigate the sequence of triangular numbers after creating them in various ways (see 'Triangular Numbers', page 217). Ask: What is the difference between one term and the next in the sequence? How can you use this information to say if the following is a sequence of triangular numbers: 45, 55, 66, 78?

Dot Patterns

Have students create number sequences for a series of dot patterns and then say how the sequences are the same. For example:

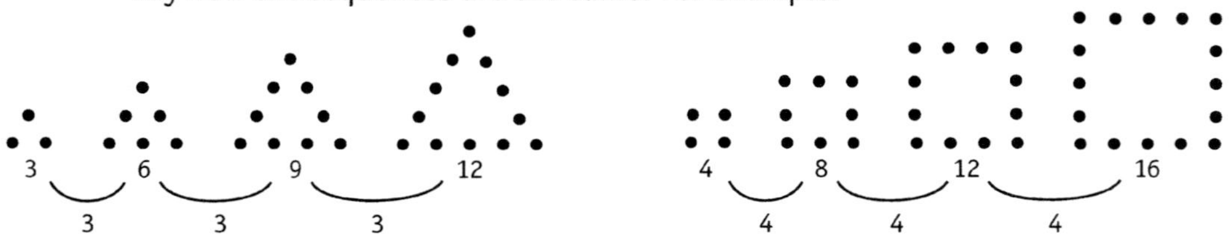

Ask: What is the difference between the numbers in each sequence? How is the difference related to the shape? What would be the difference between the terms in the sequence for hexagons? (Note: These are not the triangular numbers, nor the square numbers.)

Function Box

During a 'Function Box' activity (see page 228), have students work out what the rule is by writing a list of the 'in' and 'out' numbers and then organise this into a table. After finding a few rules in this way, students compare the tables of numbers and look for similarities in the differences between the 'in' and 'out' numbers. Ask: How will we know if the person has used addition/subtraction in their rule?

Puppies

Extend the 'Puppies' activity (see page 217), so that students work out the changes in the dogs' weight each month and use this to predict their weight at ten months. Ask: Was the difference in the dogs' weight the same for each? How are the two patterns the same? How are these patterns different from other addition patterns, such as the dot patterns above?

SAMPLE LEARNING ACTIVITIES

Later ✓✓✓

Pattern Pairs

Have students identify patterns linking pairs of numbers in grids and tables. For example: You are making home-made icy poles and need to make up a price list. Fill in the missing prices. Ask: How does the price change? Can you think of a rule to help work out how much any number of icy poles would cost?

Number of icy poles	1	2	3	4	5	6	7
Cost			45c	60c			

Extending Patterns

Ask students to find the difference between terms in order to extend the pattern, e.g. 'River Crossing' Sample Lesson 2, page 221. Ask students to use a table to record the trips needed for one adult, two adults and three adults. Ask: Can you see a pattern? What do you think the next number in the sequence will be? How do you know?

Times Tables

Have students find patterns in the 13 times table in order to continue the table without a calculator. Ask: What strategies did you use to extend the pattern? Repeat this with other difficult times tables.

Sticky Instructions

Ask students to write instructions for the continuation of number sequences. Write a range of number sequences on strips of paper. For example:

24, 21, 18, 15	2, 3, 5, 8, 12
1, 4, 7, 10, 13	10, 15, 19, 22
1, 4, 9, 16, 25	1, 1, 2, 3, 5, 8
6.4, 3.2, 1.6, 0.8	1, 3, 7, 15, 31
1, 3, 6, 10, 15	$\frac{1}{3}, \frac{1}{6}, \frac{1}{12}, \frac{1}{24}$

Ask students to attach sticky labels to the strips with instructions for continuing the sequence. Have students use others' instructions to continue the sequences.

Later ✔✔✔

Classifying

Have students examine and classify number sequences such as those in the previous activity, according to the type of differences between the terms. Ask: Are the differences all the same? Where the differences are not the same, students can find out what happens when you find the difference of the differences. How could this group be re-sorted?

Graphs

Extend the previous activity by having students draw graphs of a range of number sequences. Ask: Are there graphs that seem to have a similar appearance? Have students sort and classify the graphs according to how they seem to grow.

Constant addition

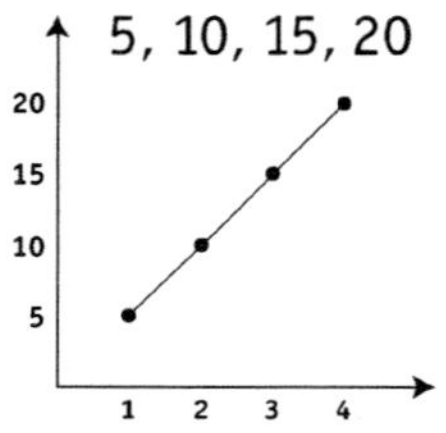

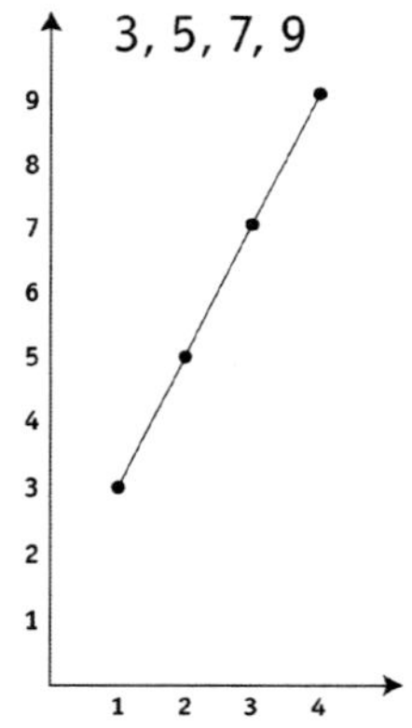

Adding a increasing amount

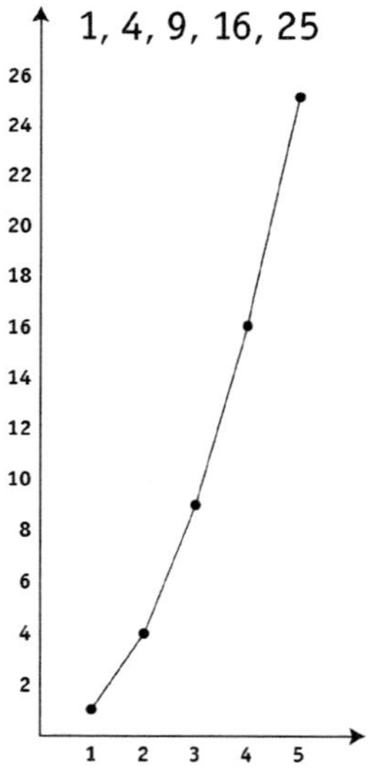

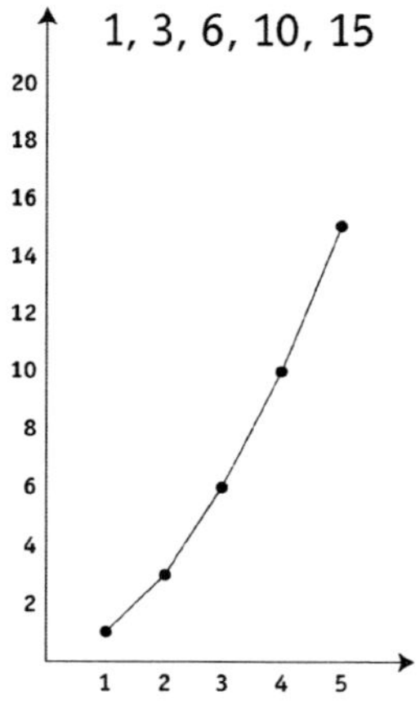

Problem Situations

Have students classify common number patterns that represent problem situations. Over time, have students record and display problems, along with the number patterns used to solve them. Ask: What kind of problems have sequences that go up by a constant amount? Which problems have number sequences that grow rapidly? Are there other different kinds of number sequences? (See Key Understanding 2.)

Sum Patterns

Revisit 'Sum Patterns' (page 231) Ask: How did you organise the information to make pattern-finding easier? What strategies did you use?

Relationships

Ask students to work out the relationship between terms in a pattern. For example: Ask students to experiment with a calculator to work out the rule used to produce the following patterns:

60, 600, 6000, 60 000, ...

60, 70, 80, 90, ...

60, 6, 0.6, 0.06, ...

60, 50, 40, 30, ...

Ask students to sort the patterns according to those in which you are constantly adding/subtracting and those in which you are constantly multiplying/dividing. (Link to Understanding Whole and Decimal Numbers, Key Understanding 8.)

Triangle Toothpick Design

(See 'Triangle Toothpick Design', page 230.) Have students organise the number of toothpicks needed for the first four shapes in a table. Ask: How does the number of toothpicks change each time? Does multiplying each term by two work as a rule? Do you need to add or subtract as well, to make it work? (One rule may be to multiply by two and add one.) Explain why your rule works using the toothpick design. What will the 20th term be? (For explanation of 'term', see Background Notes, page 260.)

Picture Frames

(See 'Picture Frames', page 218.) Have students represent the first four frames and then find patterns that enable them to answer questions such as: How many border squares are in the 20th frame? How many squares are there in the tenth frame? Have students find rules so they could answer the different questions for any frame number. Ask: What was it about the number sequences that helped you decide on the rule?

Pascal's Triangle

Invite students to research Blaise Pascal, the famous mathematician, to find out what Pascal's Triangle is. Present them with a diagram of the first six rows of the triangle. Ask them to continue the different number sequences in the triangle, say what the pattern is and what they did to find out. Ask: What did you do to continue the sequence 1, 4, 10, 20?

1

1 1

1 2 1

1 3 3 1

1 4 6 4 1

1 5 10 10 5 1

KEY UNDERSTANDING 5

Our numeration system has a lot of specially built-in patterns that make working with numbers easier.

Patterns are the basic building blocks for students' understanding of our numeration system (i.e. the way we write and say numbers) and consequently, for their capacity to count with large and small numbers, understand the order and relative magnitude of numbers, and calculate. For example, it is recognition of the patterns in the way we say and write numbers that enables students to count backwards and forwards from any number in tens—an essential skill in mental arithmetic. Also, it is the patterns in the way we write numbers that enable us to know immediately what the result is of multiplying (or dividing) by ten, and that 187 cannot be a multiple of five. As such, numeration patterns are a major focus of many of the activities in Understand Whole and Decimal Numbers, Understand Fractional Numbers and in Calculate, and students should spend considerable time observing, describing, explaining and using patterns on number lines, on the 100 chart, and in addition and multiplication tables.

However, the essence of this particular Key Understanding is on students:

- working out *why* numeration patterns occur
- realising how such patterns can help them do other things.

Firstly, students are more likely to develop an understanding of our numeration system if they try to explain why certain patterns occur. For example, if we shade the numbers on a 100 chart by starting with any number and repeatedly adding 11, we get a diagonal. Students may notice and even find this 'pattern' interesting but think of it simply as a surprise, a piece of magic or a party trick, and learn nothing from it about how place value works. It is when they attempt to explain to themselves and others *why* we must get a diagonal, that such an activity has the potential to extend their understanding and use of place value.

Secondly, students are more likely to appreciate the significance of patterns in number, and to be prepared to look for them in future, if there is some real and immediate 'pay-off' for them in terms of things they can do more easily. For example, using patterns in the multiplication table for nines can make it easier to remember multiplication facts and also make mental arithmetic with nines easier.

Thus, while this Key Understanding will largely be developed though activities that are also used elsewhere, the suggestions here complement and extend those activities by making explicit the need for active reflection by students on the nature and role of pattern. As students progress through the primary years, they should show an increasing:

- capacity to explain (rather than simply notice or describe) the numeration patterns they observe
- appreciation of how seeing these patterns can help to make working with numbers both easier and more interesting.

SAMPLE LEARNING ACTIVITIES

Beginning ✔✔

Teens

Have students chant and sing counting rhymes involving one to nine. Extend to the teens. Record the numbers in order and draw out that the digits zero to nine are repeated in the same order (except that we don't write the first zero). (Link to Understanding Whole and Decimal Numbers, Key Understanding 4.)

Decades

Record the counting sequence as students count aloud up, over and through the decades. Draw out that the digits (zero to nine) repeat within each decade and that the decades (tens) also repeat the digits in order (except that we don't write the first zero). (Link to Understanding Whole and Decimal Numbers, Key Understanding 4.)

Number Sequence

Have ten sets of ten different coloured squares for students to make a number sequence from one to 100 to display around the room. They write one number per square, keeping the sequence of colours the same for every set of ten. Display the first ten and ask questions that encourage students to work out which number comes next, which colour comes next, which numbers used that colour before. (See Understanding Whole and Decimal Numbers, Key Understanding 4.)

Hundreds

Using a calculator as a counting machine, have students count together and record the sequence from 95 (enter 9 5 + 1 = = = = etc). Stop at 109 and ask: What will the next number be? How do you know? Continue counting and stop at 119. Ask: What will the next number be? Why? Continue up to and over 200. (See 'Did You Know?', Understanding Whole and Decimal Numbers, Key Understanding 1, and link to Key Understanding 4.)

Constantly Adding Tens

Have students record the numbers from the calculator display on their own 100 grid. Ask students to shade a specified number between one and ten, say six. They then add ten and shade again, and repeat until the numbers 'run out' at 96. Students read the numbers 6, 16, 26, 36, ... and say what they notice about them. Ask students to then choose another number, say five, and predict which numbers will be in this list if they constantly add ten and shade the numbers. Ask: Why does every number in the list end in five? Why does it make a straight line up and down on this chart? Have students count the squares between the shaded squares to find the pattern. (Link to Key Understanding 3.)

Make the Number

Have students use bundling material (e.g. MAB blocks or straws bundled into ones, tens and hundreds) to show what is happening each time ten is added to, say 99, 109, 199. Ask: How does the material and the way the number is written match? (Link to Understanding Whole and Decimal Numbers, Key Understanding 5, and Calculate, Key Understanding 4.)

Number Scrolls

(See Understanding Whole and Decimal Numbers, Key Understanding 4.)
As students generate lists of numbers by:

- repeatedly adding one. Ask: Why do the numbers after nine have two digits? Why do the numbers between 19 and 29 start with a two? What do the numbers after 29 start with? How many start with three? Why?
- skip counting in twos. Ask: What do you notice about the list of numbers in the ones column? What is the highest number in this column? Why? Look at 20. How many times did the calculator add two before it changed to 30? What about between 30 and 40? Is it the same between 50 and 60, 90 and 100? Why?

(Link to Understanding Whole and Decimal Numbers, Key Understanding 1, and Understand Operations, Key Understanding 5.)

SAMPLE LEARNING ACTIVITIES

Middle ✔✔✔

Page Numbers

Show students a book with at least 100 pages. Ask: How many times do you think seven is used in the page numbers? Why do you believe it will be that many? Check to see. Ask: Have we missed any? Are you sure? Can we explain why it is that number? Provide a 100 chart and encourage students to use it to explain why there are that many sevens. Ask: How many sixes will there be? Fives? Zeroes (the tricky one!)?

Hide the Numbers

1	2	3	4	5	6	7	8	9	10
10	12	13	14		16	17	18	19	20
21	22	23	24				28	29	30
31	32	33	34	35		37	38	39	40
41	42	43	44	45	46	47	48	49	50
51	52	53	54	55	56	57	58	59	60

Provide various pentominoes (each made of five squares of the same size as those on the 100 chart). Have students work in pairs and use a pentomino to cover parts of the chart and say what numbers are hidden, explaining to their partner why they think that.

Move to other parts of the chart and repeat. Turn the pentomino and repeat. Draw students together and ask: How did you decide? What patterns did you use? How did the way our numbers are written help? (Link to Understanding Whole and Decimal Numbers, Key Understanding 5.)

Constantly Adding Tens

Repeat this activity from page 245. Ask students to explain to their partner why when they begin with a number and constantly add ten, the resulting numbers are all in a column. Discuss as whole class. Choose a larger number, say 57. Ask: What happens if you constantly subtract tens? Why? (Link to Calculate, Key Understanding 4.)

Constantly Adding Nines

Have students choose a number between one and nine, and shade squares on their 100 grid as they constantly add nine (without a calculator). They then compare their result with others. Ask: What is the same? What is different? Some students may correct their shading at this stage. If so, draw out that the pattern enabled them to notice their mistake. Ask students to work with their partner/group to explain why they always get that same arrangement of shaded squares when they add nines. Ask: Why does it 'go down and back one' each time? Does it link to what happens when constantly adding ten? Link to nine being one less than ten. (Link to Understanding Whole and Decimal Numbers, Key Understanding 5, and Calculate, Key Understanding 4.)

More Nines

Have students begin with any number less than 50 and shade squares as they constantly add nine. Ask: Can you predict the shaded squares before you actually add the nine? (See Key Understanding 1.) What do you expect to happen if you subtract nines? Test. Help students explain why it happens, relating to nine being 10 – 1. After drawing out the pattern in adding nines, challenge students' mental arithmetic skills by asking: What is 37 + 9? (Down to 47 and back to 46.) Do several of these immediately and reinforce over following days and weeks. (Link to Calculate, Key Understanding 4.)

Adding and Subtracting

Extend the previous activity to adding and/or subtracting any number between one and nine, e.g. start at 34 and add seven repeatedly. Ask: Does thinking of seven as 10 – 3 help explain the arrangement of the squares? Does it help with mental arithmetic? (86 + 7 is three less than 96.) (Link to Calculate, Key Understanding 5.)

Answer Patterns

Have students investigate the answer patterns in related sets of additions or subtractions, e.g. 15 – 8, 25 – 8, 35 – 8, 45 – 8. Ask them to explain why it happens, and use this to predict related calculations, e.g. 95 – 8.

100 Grid

Ask students to make a rectangular grid, arranging the numbers one to 100 in whatever number of rows and columns they wish. For example:

1	2	3	4	5	6
7	8	9	10	11	12
13	14	15	16	17	18

Ask them to use their grid to look for patterns in the numbers. Then ask them to quickly find, say, 67 or 42. Place a 10 x 10 grid for all to see and ask: What changes from one row to the next? Why? What changes in the other grids? Why? In which grids is it easiest to find particular numbers? Why? Have all students make a 10 x 10 grid for their personal use. (Link to Understanding Whole and Decimal Numbers, Key Understanding 5, and, Calculate, Key Understanding 4.)

Division Patterns

Encourage students to investigate division patterns. For example:

1 ÷ 2,	10 ÷ 2,	100 ÷ 2
2 ÷ 2,	20 ÷ 2,	200 ÷ 2
3 ÷ 2,	30 ÷ 2,	300 ÷ 2

through to 900 ÷ 2. Ask: Why do the answers have either a five or a zero at the end? How does the change in the size of the numbers in the questions affect the size of the numbers in the answers? (Link to Understanding Whole and Decimal Numbers, Key Understandings 5 and 7.)

SAMPLE LEARNING ACTIVITIES

Later ✓✓✓

Hide the Numbers

Repeat this activity from page 246. This time, use various hexominoes (each made of six squares of the same size as those on a 1000 chart constructed in rows of ten).

Multiples of Nine

Ask students to shade in multiples of nine on a 100 chart. Ask them to investigate patterns in the resulting display. Prompt where appropriate: Is there a pattern in the ones place of the multiples of nine? What do you notice? What is happening in the tens place?

Finger Patterns

Have students hold up their ten fingers and drop the first finger on the left. How many fingers can you see? (nine) Lift that finger and drop the second finger from the left. How many fingers to the left of the dropped finger are there? (one) How many to the right? (eight) So the second dropped finger makes one, eight. Drop the third finger (makes two, seven). Ask: Can you link what you see with your fingers with nine times table?

Ask: What do you notice? Why does this happen? How can it help you remember the nine times table? (Link to Understanding Whole and Decimal Numbers, Key Understanding 5.)

Number Race

Display ten different three- or four-digit numbers to the class, e.g. 357, 985. Allocate the numbers 2, 3, 4, 5, 6, 7, 8 to different groups of students in the classroom. Have a race to see which group can be first to work out if their number is a factor of each of the numbers displayed. Ask: Was that a fair race? Why? What is it that makes that an easy question for some groups and not others? (Link to Understanding Whole and Decimal Numbers, Key Understanding 5, and Calculate, Key Understanding 5.)

Working to Rule

Have students use the 100 chart to explain why rules work. Ask students to draw a 3 x 3 square anywhere on a 100 square, and to add the corner numbers of their small square. For example: The corner numbers might be 38, 40, 58 and 60 and you get 196 when you add them. Divide the total by four.

What do you get? Repeat this process with other 3 x 3 squares. What do you notice happens each time? What rule can you use to easily calculate the sum of the corner numbers? Why do you think the total of the four corner numbers is the same as four times the middle number? (Link to Understanding Whole and Decimal Numbers, Key Understanding 5.)

Multiples of Tens and Tenths

Invite students to use a calculator to set up tables showing the number sentences and results of multiplying and dividing the same number by 10, 100, 1000 and so on, and by 0.1, 0.01, 0.001 and so on. Ask: Can you use the information to derive rules for multiplying and dividing by very large and very small numbers?

Relationships

Have students arrange materials to match the relationship between places in our numeration system. For example: Put out a small MAB block, then the large 1000 cube. Ask: How many times bigger is the second cube than the first? What do you think the next-sized cube would look like? Do you have enough large cubes in the school to build the next-sized cube? How do you know? Do you have enough to build just the frame of the cube? Ask students to write the numbers for each of the cubes, and imagine what the fourth cube would look like. Ask: How do you say that number? (Link to Understanding Whole and Decimal Numbers, Key Understanding 8.)

Calculator Experiment

Ask students to experiment with a calculator to work out the rule used on the calculator to produce patterns such as the following:

60, 600, 6000, 60 000, ...

60, 6, 0.6, 0.06, ...

60, 70, 80, 90, ...

60, 50, 40, 30, ...

Sort the patterns according to those in which you are constantly adding or subtracting and those in which you are constantly multiplying or dividing. Ask: How are they related to the way our number system is organised?(Link to Understanding Whole and Decimal Numbers, Key Understandings 4 and 5.)

Grid Paper

Have students use 1 mm grid paper to show the relationship between places in our number system. (Link to Sample Lesson 4, Understanding Whole and Decimal Numbers.) In the top left-hand corner, students draw around a 1 mm square. Next, include the drawn square but draw around a square that is 100 times larger. Draw the third square 100 times larger than the second square. Record the numbers in each square. Estimate how much space you will need to make the fourth square. What number would that be? How do you know? (Link to Understanding Whole and Decimal Numbers, Key Understanding 8.)

KEY UNDERSTANDING 6

Some numbers have interesting or useful properties. Investigating the patterns in these special numbers can help us to understand them better.

Students should investigate properties of numbers, and patterns associated with those properties. This should at least include odd and even, prime and composite, and square and cubic numbers.

When we partition collections and represent the result as a multiplication, we think of both the number of groups and the number in each group as factors of the original number. Thus, partitioning underpins the concept of 'factor' and the classification of numbers into odd and even and composite and prime.

Students should develop the following understandings:

- Some collections can be shared into two equal groups (those with **even** numbers of items) and some can't (those with **odd** numbers of items).
- If a collection can be shared into equal collections, then we say that the number of equal collections and the number in the equal collections are each **factors** of the number in the original collection. For example: 14 items can be shared into 14 collections of 1 item and 1 collection of 14 items, and into 7 collections of 2 items and 2 collections of 7 items. So we say that 14, 7, 2 and 1 are all factors of 14. 14 cannot be shared into collections of 3, so we say 3 is not a factor of 14. (Another name for factor is **divisor**.)
- Some collections (those with a **prime number** of items) can only be shared into smaller equal collections, if the smaller collections hold 1. So there are only two factors: one and the number.
- Some collections (those with a **composite number** of items) can be shared into smaller equal collections, with the smaller collections holding more than 1. So there are more than two factors.
- The number 1 has only one factor, which is 1. So the number one is neither prime nor composite.

A closely related concept is that of **multiples**. A collection of 12 items can be thought of as a unit that is replicated to produce 12 items, 24 items, 36 items, 48 items, and so on. The numbers 12, 24, 36, 48, ... are then called the multiples of 12. Because of the inverse relationship between multiplication and division, we can, in turn, say that 12 is a factor of each of the numbers 12, 24, 36, 48 and so on.

Students should represent numbers in a wide variety of ways that bring out their properties. Thus, in the beginning primary years students might investigate the occurrence of odd and even numbers and note that every second one is even and every second one is odd. In the middle primary years they might note the pattern of digits in the units place for odd and even numbers, and use it to decide what side of the street houses will be on, or whether a particular number could be the solution to a problem. For example: Can 127 be one of the numbers in the sequence 4, 8, 12, 16, ...? In the later primary years they might use patterns to make a generalisation about the effect of multiplying any number by an even number.

As an interesting variation on the idea that patterns are useful because they enable us to predict, students should also learn the reason that prime numbers are useful for cryptography (i.e. for making secret codes) is because there is *no* pattern in the sequence of the prime numbers. Therefore, we cannot predict what will come next or later.

Older students should begin to learn about the more common irrational numbers, in particular π (pi), and the idea of non-repeating decimals. Thus, they should be introduced to the idea that when you express π (pi) as a decimal, the sequence of digits after the decimal point goes on forever with no repetition or pattern (that is, it does not recur). This means we *cannot* write π (pi) exactly as a common fraction, although $\frac{22}{7}$ is a reasonable approximation. They can also use their calculator as a tool for investigating terminating and recurring decimals, to find that both *can* always be written exactly as a common fraction. For example: $3.125 = 3\frac{1}{8}$ and $3.125125125125 \ldots = 3\frac{125}{999}$.

KU 6

SAMPLE LEARNING ACTIVITIES

Beginning ✓

Game Plans

Have students set out materials to represent players or use pairs of small name cards to plan rosters for using equipment or games that involve partners. Focus on the use of odd and even numbers of students who want to play. Ask students what to do when there is an odd number of players.

Handfuls

Ask students to identify odd and even numbers by playing 'Handfuls'. Working with a partner, one student grabs a handful of straws or bottle-tops, then passes it to their partner. If the partner can share it out between the two people, they get a point. If not, the point goes to the other person. Ask students to record the numbers as they go. What do you notice about the numbers you can share?(See Understand Operations, Key Understanding 5.)

Function Box

(See Key Understanding 3, page 227.) Extend this activity by having a student write a number on a piece of paper and enter it into the box. Tell the students that the box is programmed to multiply by two. Ask: What numbers could come out? Will the number coming out be odd or even? How do you know? (Link to Understand Operations, Key Understanding 5.)

Finding Groups

Have students use materials to work out which numbers from one to 12 can be made into equal groups. Ask them to make a chart showing the different groups for each number and refer to this when deciding on a number when equal groups are needed. (See Calculate, Key Understanding 5.)

Doubling

Invite students to investigate the built-in pattern when odd numbers are doubled. Ask them to create a card with ten spots, squares or stars on it. They cover some and say how many are left. They predict how many would be there if the spots were doubled and use a mirror to check. Ask: What has happened to the six dots? What will happen if you double five dots? When an odd number is doubled, do you get another odd number? Could you ever get an odd number when an even number is doubled? (Link to Key Understanding 5.)

Odds and Evens

Have students describe numbers of things that occur naturally in odd and even groupings. For example: When making collage pictures or constructions of animals, insects or vehicles, each student selects their materials before beginning the picture or structure, and uses 'odd' and 'even' to describe the size of their collections. Ask: Have you got an even number of ears? Is that number of legs an odd or even number? Is one an odd or even number? How do you know which numbers are odd (or even)? (See Understanding Whole and Decimal Numbers, Key Understanding 2.)

Diagrams

Following the previous activity, have students recall which numbers were odd and even and use diagrams to represent them.

Hands

Extend the 'Hands Up' activity (see Understand Whole and Decimal Numbers, Key Understanding 2) by having students record whether the results are odd or even each time. (Link to Calculate Key Understanding 4.)

Halving

Ask students to look for patterns when halving. Start with a collection of, say, 12 jelly beans and halve and then halve again. Record this as a sequence of numbers: 12, 6, 3. Start again with 24 jelly beans. Ask: Why do the same numbers appear?

SAMPLE LEARNING ACTIVITIES

Middle ✓✓

What's My Number?

Have each student make a set of 20 small blocks that are numbered from one to 20. Choose a number and give the students clues. For example: It is an even number. The students remove the numbered blocks that it couldn't be. Continue with clues such as: You say it when you count by 5s; When you write it, it has two places; It won't make three equal groups. Talk about the clues with the students after the game and ask: Which were the most helpful clues? Why? What did you need to know to answer the ... clue? Eventually, have a student help give clues, then move on to a student leading the game.

Constant Function

Ask students to use the constant function on the calculator to generate multiples of numbers up to ten. Using a 100 chart, cover the numbers with different coloured counters and discuss the pattern each number makes. Have students look for overlap in patterns. For example: The fours pattern only uses numbers from the twos pattern. Ask: Why is this so? Look at the chart to see if any numbers are still exposed. Discuss why these numbers have not been covered (are they prime?).

Prime Numbers

Extend the 'Handfuls' game (page 252) to get two points if the objects can be made into a 2 x ☐ rectangle, three points for a 3 x ☐ rectangle, and so on. Have students say which collections won't give them any points and why.

Twenty-seven

Have students investigate whether 27 can be found by: adding two odd numbers, two even numbers, or an even and an odd number. Ask them to investigate other numbers and say if there is a pattern in the results. Extend to other operations. (Link to Calculate, Key Understanding 10.)

Odd and Even Patterns

Ask students to investigate patterns associated with odd and even numbers. For example: Start with 19 and add six each time—what number sequence is created? Start with 89 and subtract 11 each time—what sequence is created? Have students predict whether the next number will be odd or even and test their predictions with the calculator. (Link to Calculate, Key Understanding 5.)

Pyramids

Have students use blocks to build a pyramid. A pyramid one layer high uses 1 block, two layers high uses 4 blocks, three layers high uses 9 blocks. Students predict how many blocks are needed for the fifth, sixth and tenth layers.

Investigating Primes

Invite students to investigate prime numbers by using blocks to design crates that will hold different numbers of bottles. The crates must be rectangular (including square), at least two bottles wide and hold up to 24. Ask students to record the crates made and the number of bottles they will hold. Ask: Can you make a crate to hold only seven bottles? Why not? Have the class identify the numbers that cannot be made into crates. These are prime numbers. (Link to Understand Operations, Key Understanding 5.)

Times Tables Patterns

Have students investigate odd and even number patterns in the times tables. Ask: Are the answers to the two times table all even, all odd, or a combination of even and odd? Is there a pattern of odd and even numbers in the answers? Is there a pattern of even and odd numbers being multiplied? Look at all the other tables and work out a rule to say what happens when two even numbers are multiplied, two odd numbers are multiplied and an even and odd number are multiplied. Ask students to test out their rule: If you add an odd number to a multiple of nine, the result will be—sometimes odd, always odd, always even, never odd?

Shapes

Ask students to use shapes to investigate factors. For example: They take a 'good' handful of straws, and decide how many triangles they can make. How many rectangles? Pentagons? Ask them to record the results using pictures and number sentences. Draw out the idea of factors, asking: Why is it that you get straws left over for some shapes and not for others? (See Calculate, Key Understanding 3.)

Multiples of Three

Have students build up multiples using the inverse of the previous activity. For example: Make one triangle using three straws, two using six straws, etc. Ask students to write the list of multiples of three next to their diagrams of the triangles to show how many straws were used altogether. (See Calculate, Key Understanding 3.)

Factors

Encourage students to use factors to solve problems. For example: We have 24 lamingtons to put into trays. How could we arrange them into rectangle shapes? How do you know you have found all possible shapes? How can you work out factors of numbers without using materials? (See Calculate, Key Understanding 3.)

Is It a Multiple?

Have students use the constant function on the calculator to find multiples of a number and predict whether a given number will be a multiple. For example: Will 51 be a multiple of four? This can become a game by taking turns to predict the next number before pressing the = key. (See Calculate, Key Understanding 3.)

SAMPLE LEARNING ACTIVITIES

Later ✔✔

Equal Groups

Have students make different equal groups from the same quantity and record with a multiplication number sentence. For example: Make arrays with 36 squares. Ask: Can you make an array with seven in a row? Can you make an array with five rows? Why? How do you know if you have made all the arrays?

Venn Diagram

Ask students to construct a Venn diagram using three circles. Label these 'divisible by 2', 'divisible by 3' and 'divisible by 5'. Have students choose a two-digit number and decide in which section of the Venn diagram it belongs. They examine and describe the patterns formed in each section. Ask them to use the pattern to predict where a larger number belongs.

Factor Trees

Have students investigate factors and products by making different factor trees for the same number, e.g. for 36:

Ask students to compare the factor trees. Ask: How do the numbers in the last row show that there are no more factors? (See Calculate, Key Understanding 5.)

Investigate Factors

Invite different groups of students to carry out the following factor investigations:

- Classify the counting numbers according to the number of factors.
- On a 100 chart, put counters of one colour on all the multiples of two, a different colour on multiples of three, four, five and so on up to ten. What do you notice about the height of the stacks of the counters?
- Select a number of square tiles. Record how many different rectangles you can make using all the tiles. Repeat for other numbers of tiles. How many different rectangles can you make with the squares? Do it for some more numbers. Put your findings together with others in your group and then organise the information.

At the completion of the three tasks, have students look for overall patterns in their classifications. Ask: What is the same about them? What is different? (Link Understand Operations, Key Understanding 5.)

Square Numbers

Have students use an activity like 'Pyramids' (page 254) to generate consecutive square numbers. Ask: What pattern can you see in the differences? How can you use this pattern to work out the square numbers that come after 121 and 144?

Areas of Squares

Extend the previous activity by presenting this scenario: When finding the areas of different sized squares, Miles recorded the areas along with the square numbers 1^2 ,2^2 , 3^2 and so on. He then noticed that the difference between the square numbers 2^2 and 3^2 was the same as 2 + 3, and the difference between 3^2 and 4^2 was the same as 3 + 4. Ask: Does this pattern work for larger consecutive square numbers? Is there a similar pattern in the differences between alternate square numbers? Why?

Square and Triangular Numbers

Investigate how square numbers are related to triangular numbers. Have students generate triangular numbers. (See 'Triangular Numbers' page 217.) For example: Build a set of steps with one block for the first step, three blocks for the second step, six blocks for the third step and so on.

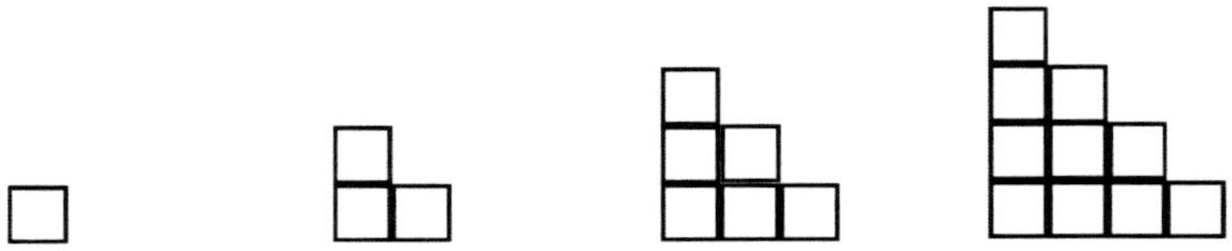

List the first six triangular numbers, then add consecutive numbers. Ask: How can you prove and show that each square number is the sum of two triangular numbers? Is there a way of predicting which square number will result from the eighth and ninth triangles?

Fraction Patterns

Ask students to use a calculator to investigate patterns that occur when changing common fractions to decimal fractions. For example, enter **1** **÷** **7** **=** to change $\frac{1}{7}$ to a decimal fraction. Then change $\frac{2}{7}$ and $\frac{3}{7}$. Ask: What do you notice about the numbers? Can you predict the decimal fraction for $\frac{4}{7}$, $\frac{5}{7}$ and $\frac{6}{7}$? Explore the patterns in decimal fractions for other common fractions.

Terminating Decimals

Have students predict which unit fractions will have a decimal that terminates and which ones will have a decimal that doesn't terminate. Ask them to use a calculator to classify the denominator from 2 to 20 according to whether or not they are factors of either 10, 100, 1000 and so on. Ask: If the denominator is a factor of a tens number, what kind of decimal do you get? If the denominator is not a factor of a tens number, what kind of decimal do you get?(Link to Understanding Whole and Decimal Numbers, Key Understanding 8.)

BACKGROUND NOTES

Finding the Rule For a Pattern

Students' work with patterns during the primary years should lay a foundation for their understanding of why we try to find patterns in things and how we go about it. They should investigate patterns in the familiar occurrences of their everyday lives, in their natural and made environment, and the more mathematically structured situations of the classroom.

Often, we have sufficient information to be able to decide what a pattern is exactly and make very reliable predictions from it. For example, we can work out exactly how much paper it takes to produce the A series of paper (e.g. A1, A2, A3, A4). However, at other times, we have incomplete information from which we have to or want to make inferences. For example, we may have some information about whale numbers but not complete information. We nevertheless try to find a pattern or relationship that fits the data we have and use that pattern or relationship to make predictions about the future. Another way of saying this is that we generalise about the situation and apply the generalisation to new instances.

Young students are usually not reluctant to generalise and suggest a rule that describes a pattern. The problem more often is that they generalise too quickly and do not test their rules against all the information. For example, given a sequence beginning 1, 2, 4, 7, ... they might see a doubling pattern for the first three terms and not check that it keeps working. This is not helped, of course, by textbooks and tests that expect students to continue sequences such as: 1, 2, 4, ... and accept only one possible extension. While we can hypothesise about what a pattern might be, given only the first three terms of a sequence, there is not enough information to say what it *must* be.

Sometimes more than one pattern will fit the information we have

Given no other information, the same short sequence of numbers could be the result of many patterns. For example, for a sequence beginning 1, 2, 3 to continue with 4, 5, 6 appears obvious, and it might well be that a person beginning 1, 2, 3 might have the sequence of counting numbers in mind, but there are other possibilities. Thus the rule might be:

- begin with 1 and add one each time (that is, 'count') — 1, 2, 3, 4, 5, 6, 7, 8 ...
- begin with 1, 2, then repeatedly add the previous two numbers — 1, 2, 3, 5, 8, 13, 21, 34 ...
- begin with 1, 2, 3 and repeat — 1, 2, 3, 1, 2, 3, 1, 2, ...
- begin with 1, 2, 3, 7 and repeat — 1, 2, 3, 7, 1, 2, 3, 7, ...

Each rule fits the information we have; each is correct in that it fits the existing data. Thus, depending upon the rule, the next number could be 4, 5, 1, 7 or any other number! However, if we have additional information about the pattern, it may become clear that only one of the possible rules can be right. Suppose students were asked to use toothpicks to build a row of squares by adding on just enough toothpicks each time to add one square to the row:

At the first stage there is just one square and it takes four toothpicks; at the second stage there are two squares and it takes seven toothpicks; at the third stage there are three squares and it takes ten toothpicks. The sequence for the number of toothpicks required at each stage begins 4, 7, 10, and students could conjecture that the rule connecting successive terms is 'add three' and that the next number should be 13, and the next 16. In this case, they can check that their pattern rule works and even test it for the 100th diagram should they wish! We would probably not choose to check, since the diagrams explain *why* the pattern occurs and hence convince us that it is correct even for parts of the sequence we have not built.

The important point here is that, given ONLY the numbers 4, 7, 10, ... the best we can do is to find rules that fit the sequence and these rules might lead to any number of ways to continue. Any rule that fits the available information is correct and we cannot decide upon one of them for sure.

However, given more information about where the numbers 4, 7 and 10 came from and what the underlying principle was, we can decide for sure. That is, since we know how the toothpick sequence continues, we can work out how the number sequence must continue.

A pattern rule is right when it fits all the information we have and describes the pattern precisely

Where there is enough information to be able to work out for sure what the pattern must be, we say a rule is correct if it **must** work in every possible case. Where there is not enough information, we can still conjecture about what the rule is likely to be. Then we say a rule is correct if it fits all the information we have. In these cases, more than one pattern may fit the information we have.

Either way it is important that the rule we provide is precise. A rule that simply says 'each number is double the one before' is not precise because it does not tell you where to start. Learning to describe a pattern precisely is not always easy, but there are some conventional mathematical ways to describe patterns which students should begin to use during the primary years.

For example, in the toothpick pattern described on page 259, *physically* making a square with toothpicks, and then adding just enough toothpicks to make another square in the row, and then another could lead students to conclude: *You start by making a square with four toothpicks and then each time you add three toothpicks to make an extra joined-on square.* Such a description is quite precise and quite correct and it makes it fairly easy to get from one element in the sequence to the next (this is often called a 'term').

However, using this description to continue the pattern to larger numbers is a little harder. While students may be able to suggest how many toothpicks it would take to make the tenth arrangement (the 10th term) or even the 100th, they would need to be careful to add on the right number of threes—a tricky business. This difficulty leads us to try to describe the relationship in a general way, by thinking of the 1st, 2nd, 3rd and 4th term in the sequence as having a position number (1, 2, 3, 4, ...) and linking the position number to the number of toothpicks needed:

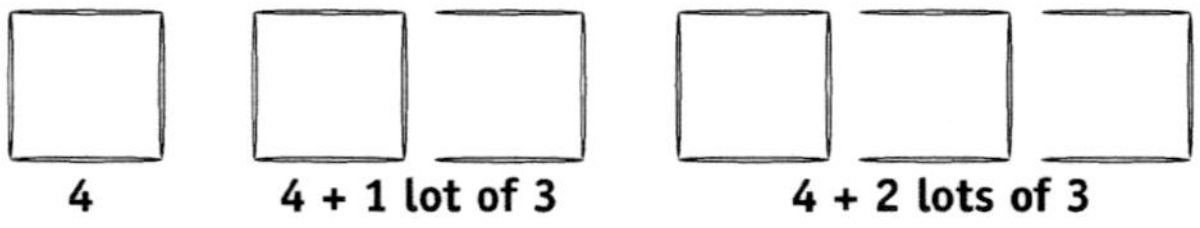

Position 2 has one lot of three extra toothpicks, position 3 has two lots of three extra toothpicks. So the number of toothpicks needed is four added to (one less than the position number) lots of three. So:

Number of toothpicks = 4 + (position no – 1) x 3

From this it is easy to see that the 100th term will be
4 + 99 x 3 = 4 + 297 = 301!

Students should also learn to describe relationships that link pairs of quantities. For example, after playing 'guess my rule'-type games, they should be able to state the rule clearly (e.g. *Whatever number we said, you halved it*). They should also learn to recognise the formulas that are used in daily life as examples of pattern rules. Thus the formula for the area of a square, or for converting from Australian dollars to Indonesian rupiah, or for adding the right amount of water to the plant food are rules that link two quantities that 'vary together'.

Two rules that sound/look different but produce exactly the same pattern are called equivalent (or equal)

Often when two people observe the same pattern, they will think about it differently. For example, two students each described this as a 'doubling' pattern: 1, 2, 4, 8, ... However, one student suggested that you get each term by starting at one and then doubling the term before. The other student had looked at the differences between successive terms (also 1, 2, 4) and said, *You start at one, add one and after that the differences doubled each time*. These two rules sound different but they are mathematically equivalent or equal because they describe exactly the same pattern. After a discussion, these students could see why they were the same.

Sometimes thinking of a pattern in a different way helps us to write an equivalent rule that is easier to use. With the toothpick sequence on page 260, it is possible to 'see' the arrangement of toothpicks like this:

1 + 1 lot of 3   1 + 2 lots of 3   1 + 3 lots of 3

So: *Number of toothpicks = 1 + position no x 3*
So, the 100th term will be 1 + 100 x 3 = 1 + 300 = 301.

These two rules are equivalent because they must produce exactly the same sequence of numbers.

Recognising Common Types of Patterns

Students will get better at identifying patterns if they have sufficient and appropriate experiences in recognising, producing and describing patterns. This experience needs to be as carefully planned as any other part of the mathematics curriculum to ensure that students experience a range of pattern types, learn to recognise common pattern types, and develop some of the strategies that are helpful for finding patterns. As students explore various patterns in number, their attention should be drawn to:

- the strategies that they found helpful in identifying patterns
- the similarities between certain patterns.

Helpful strategies

It can be difficult to recognise a pattern immediately just by looking, and having some search strategies is essential. With sequences it often helps to test for common types. For example, in the middle and later primary years, students could test a sequence of numbers by finding the difference between successive terms and ask themselves: Is the difference constant? If not, is there a pattern in the differences?

Sequence	3		6		10		15 ...
Difference		3		4		5	

Other search strategies for finding the pattern in a sequence of numbers include:

- Is there a constant ratio (or multiplier) between the successive terms? For example: 3, 6, 12, 24, ...
- Does doubling or halving work? For example: 36, 18, 9, 4.5, ...
- Is it the square numbers? Is it 'almost' the square numbers? For example: 2, 5, 10, 17, 26, ...
- If there are fractions, what is happening to the denominators? Or to the numerators? Would using a common denominator help? For example: $\frac{1}{8}, \frac{1}{4}, \frac{3}{8}, \frac{1}{2}$ is the same as $\frac{1}{8}, \frac{2}{8}, \frac{3}{8}, \frac{4}{8}, \ldots$

0 + 20
1 + 19
2 + 18
3 + 17

Similar sorts of strategies can be used in looking for patterns linking pairs of numbers. In this case, organising information systematically will often help. For example, a student might find numbers that add to 20 by trial and error, and record them as they find them. Organising the pairs vertically so that the first addend is increasing (see left) highlights the relationship between successive pairs. This should help the student see the pattern. Students should be assisted to organise their data in tables in ways that assist pattern-searching:

Position number	1	2	3	4	5
Number of blocks	1	3	6	10	15

breadth	**height**
24	1
12	2
8	3
6	4
4	6
3	8
2	12
1	24

They need to learn not to focus only on the columns (or rows) of numbers but to look at the pairs themselves. Thus, in the table at left, focusing on the columns and looking for a pattern in the changes is not helpful. It is helpful to look at how the number pairs are related (in this case, the product is always 24, that is, breadth x height = 24).

Similarities Between Patterns

Students should also look for what is the same and what is different between various patterns, leading to simple classifications of patterns. During the primary years, formal approaches to patterns are unnecessary, but they should put together sequences that involve constant addition/subtraction (e.g. 'add three') and compare them with those that involve addition/subtraction by an increasing or decreasing amount (e.g. 'first add three and then add one more than you did last time'). They could then comment on how the terms 'grow' in each case. In the first example the numbers get bigger at a steady rate, but in the second example the numbers get bigger at an increasing rate as you go along. In the later primary years, students could graph examples of each and compare the shape of the graphs. They may also learn to write general rules in progressively shortened forms and some may be ready to use letters to stand for variable quantities, although this should not be pushed.

Constant Addition or Subtraction

Sequence	Rule to link terms	Table	General rule	Graph
5, 10, 15, 20, ...	start with 5 and add 5 each time	Position | Term 1 | 5 | + 5 2 | 10 | + 5 3 | 15 | + 5 4 | 20	the term is five times the number of its position = 5 x position no = 5 x n (Note that 5 is the constant difference between the terms and it 'shows up' in the rule multiplied by the positive number)	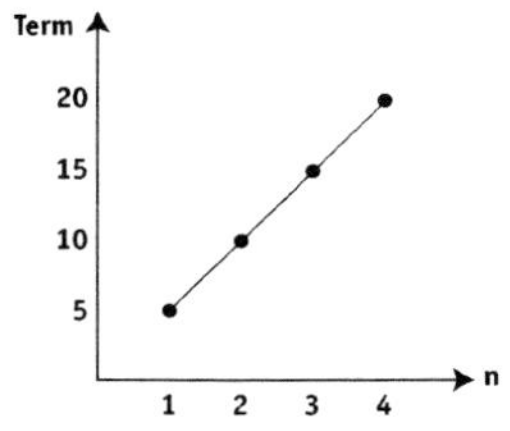
3, 5, 7, 9, ...	start with 3 and add 2 each time	Position | Term 1 | 3 | + 2 2 | 5 | + 2 3 | 7 | + 2 4 | 9	the term is two times the number of its position then add 1 = (2 x position no) + 1 = (2 x n) + 1 OR the term is 3 added to two times one less than the position number = 3 + 2 x (position no – 1) = 3 + 2 x (n – 1)	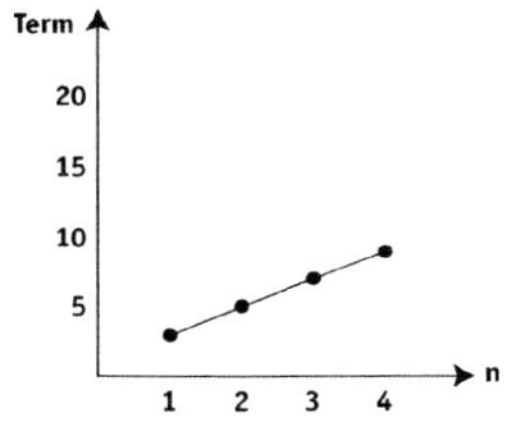
70, 60, 50, 40, ...	start with 70 and subtract 10 each time	Position | Term 1 | 70 | – 10 2 | 60 | – 10 3 | 50 | – 10 4 | 40	the term is 70 subtract 10 times one less than the position number = 70 – 10 x (position no – 1) = 70 – 10 x (n – 1) OR the term is 80 subtract 10 times the position number = 80 – 10 x position no = 80 – (10 x n)	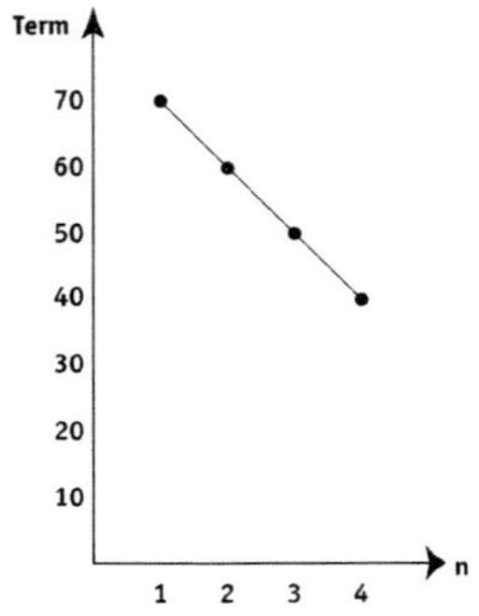
1, 3, 5, 7, ...	start with 1 and add 2 each time	Position | Term 1 | 1 | + 2 2 | 3 | + 2 3 | 5 | + 2 4 | 7	the term is two times one less than the position number and then add 1 = 2 x (position no – 1) + 1 = 2 x (n – 1) + 1 OR the term is two times the position number and then subtract 1 = (2 x position no) – 1 = 2 x n – 1	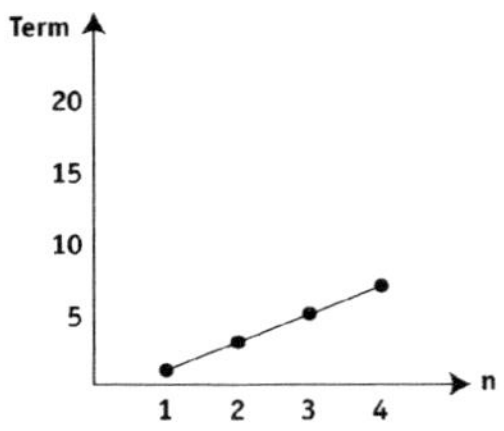

Students could draw a range of conclusions about the above patterns. For example, in the middle primary years they might conclude that the four sequences above are alike in the following ways:

- to get the next term you add or subtract a constant amount to the term before
- the difference between two terms next to each other is always the same
- the numbers go up (or down) at a steady rate.

In the later primary years, they might add to this:

- the graph is always a straight line
- the constant difference shows up in the general rule, multiplied by the position number

and they might compare the alternative general rules to convince themselves that, although they look different, they say the same thing.

Adding or Subtracting a Constantly Increasing Amount

Sequence	Rule to link terms	Table	General rule	Graph
1, 4, 9, 16, ...	start with 1 and add 3 and add 2 more than that each time *The difference between the differences is constant (2 in this case).*	Position | Term 1 | 1 + 3 2 | 4 + 5 3 | 9 + 7 4 | 16	the term is the square of the position number = n x n *These are the square numbers.*	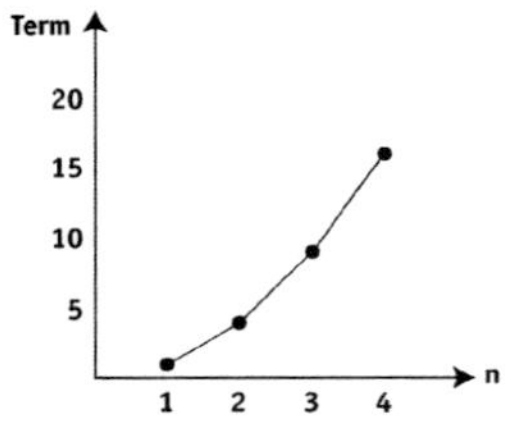
3, 6, 11, 18, ...	start with 3 and add 3 and then add 2 more than that each time *The difference between the differences is constant (again, 2).*	Position | Term 1 | 3 + 3 2 | 6 + 5 3 | 11 + 7 4 | 18	the term is the square of the position number add 2 = n x n + 2	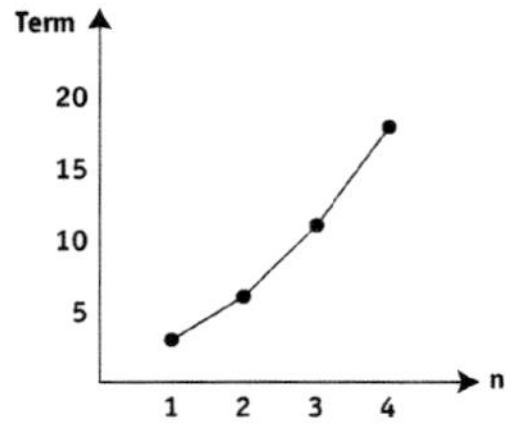
1, 3, 6, 10, ...	start with 1 and add 2 and add 1 more than that each time *The difference between the differences is constant (1).*	Position | Term 1 | 1 + 2 2 | 3 + 3 3 | 6 + 4 4 | 10	the term is the position number times one more than the position number, divided by 2 $= \frac{n \times (n + 1)}{2}$ *These are the triangular numbers.*	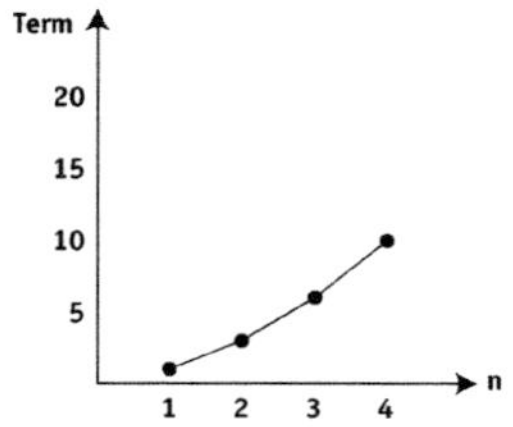

In the middle primary years students might conclude that the three sequences above are alike in the following ways:

- to get the next term you add or subtract an amount that changes each time, but the change is fixed
- the numbers go up (or down) more quickly (or slowly) as you go along.

In the later primary years, they might add to this:

- the graph is always a curve that increases or decreases at an increasing or decreasing rate
- the general rule always has a n x n in it (while the square numbers themselves will be accessible to primary-aged students, the more complex rules involving squares may be too challenging to express symbolically).

Similar approaches to other types of patterns can also be taken. Pattern types should at least include those involving:

- multiplication or division by a constant amount (3, 6, 12, 24, ...)
- reciprocals ($\frac{2}{1}, \frac{2}{2}, \frac{2}{3}, \frac{2}{4}, \frac{2}{5}, \frac{2}{6}$ ...)
- cycles or repeats (2, 4, 6, 8, 2, 4, 6, 8, ...).

Classroom Plan for Week ___, Term ___ Year Level: ___

Outcome/Key Understanding	Mathematical Focus	Activities	Focus Questions	Observations/Anecdotes

Bibliography

Carle, E. 2000, *The Very Hungry Caterpillar.* Hamilton, London.

Carpenter, T. P. 1985, 'Learning to add and subtract: An exercise in problem solving' in Silver, E. (ed) *Teaching and Learning Mathematical Problem Solving: Multiple Research Perspectives,* Lawrence Erlbaum Associates, Hillsdale, New Jersey.

Clement, R. 1990, *Counting on Frank.* Collins/Angus & Robertson, North Ryde, NSW.

Dale, P. 1988, *Ten in the Bed.* Walker, London.

Edwards, P. and Parkin, G. 1987, *Fifteen Pigs on a Pirate Ship (A 'What Do You Think?' Story).* Cheshire, Melbourne.

Hanzl, A. and Gardner, M. 1986, *Five Little Monkeys: A Popular Rhyme,* Martin Educational, Sydney.

Haylock, D. W. 1984, A mathematical think board, *Mathematics Teaching,* 108, 4–5.

Hiebert, J. and Wearne, D. 'Place Value and Addition and Subtraction in Arithmetic', *Teacher,* Vol 4, 5, January 1994, page 272–274.

Hutchins, P. 1987, *The Doorbell Rang.* Scholastic, New York.

Knowles, S. and Clement, R. 1989, *Edward the Emu.* Collins, Sydney.

Lohse, W. and Sands, J. 1993, *Is it True, Grandfather?* Ashton Scholastic, Sydney.

San Souci, R. D. and Kennedy, D. 2000, *Six Foolish Fishermen.* Hyperion, New York.

Swan, M. 1990, 'Becoming numerate: developing conceptual structures', in *Being Numerate: What Counts?,* Sue Willis (ed), ACER, Hawthorn, Victoria.

Verschaffel, L. & De Corte E. 1996, Number and arithmetic, in A. Bishop, et al (eds) *International Handbook of Mathematics Education,* Kluwer Academic Publishers, Netherlands, 99–137.